Evolutionary Economics and Path Dependence

Evolutionary Economics and Path Dependence

Edited by Lars Magnusson and Jan Ottosson

Department of Economic History, Uppsala University

Edward Elgar
Cheltenham, UK Brookfield, US

Published by
Edward Elgar Publishing Limited
8 Lansdown Place
Cheltenham
Glos GL50 2HU
UK

Edward Elgar Publishing Company
Old Post Road
Brookfield
Vermont 05036
US

A catalogue record for this book is available from the British Library

Library of Congress Cataloguing-in-Publication Data

Evolutionary economics and path dependence / edited by Lars Magnusson
  and Jan Ottosson.
        Includes bibliographical references and index.
        1. Evolutionary economics. I. Magnusson, Lars, 1952–
II. Ottosson, Jan 1958–
HB97.3.E954 1997   1001196672   96-38309
330—dc20   CIP

ISBN 1 85898 213 8

Printed and bound in Great Britain by Hartnolls Limited, Bodmin, Cornwall

Contents

List of Contributors   *vi*
Acknowledgements   *viii*
1. Introduction   1
   Lars Magnusson and Jan Ottosson
2. Mechanisms of Evolutionary Change in Economic Governance:
   Interaction, Interpretation and Bricolage   10
   John L. Campbell
3. Theory of the Firm Revisited: New and Neo-institutional
   Perspectives   33
   John Groenewegen and Jack Vromen
4. Path Dependence of Knowledge: Implications for the Theory of the
   Firm   57
   Bart Nooteboom
5. Strategic Lock-in as a Human Issue: The Role of Professional
   Orientation   79
   Michael Dietrich
6. The Microfoundations of Path Dependency   98
   Salvatore Rizzello
7. Paths in Time and Space – Path Dependence in Industrial
   Networks   119
   Håkan Håkansson and Anders Lundgren
8. The Making of National Telephone Networks in Scandinavia.
   The State and the Emergence of National Regulatory Patterns
   1880-1920   138
   Lena Andersson-Skog
9. Institutions as Determinants of Institutional Change – Case Studies
   in the Field of EEC Transport Policy   155
   Juan Bergdahl and Jan L. Östlund
10. Institutional Change and European Air Transport, 1910-1985   168
    Peter J. Lyth
11. Path Dependence and Institutional Evolution – The Case of the
    Nationalisation of Private Railroads in Interwar Sweden   186
    Jan Ottosson
References   *197*
Index   *223*

List of Contributors

Dr Lena Andersson-Skog, Department of Economic History, Umeå University, Sweden.

M.Sc. Juan Bergdahl, Department of Economic History, Uppsala University, Sweden.

Associate Professor John L. Campbell, Department of Sociology, Harvard University, USA.

Dr Michael Dietrich, Management School, University of Sheffield, England.

Associate Professor John Groenewegen, Department of Economics, Erasmus University, The Netherlands.

Professor Håkan Håkansson, Department of Business Administration, Uppsala University, Sweden.

Associate Professor Anders Lundgren, Stockholm School of Economics, Sweden.

Dr Peter Lyth, London School of Economics and Political Science, Business History Unit, England.

Professor Lars Magnusson, Department of Economic History, Uppsala University, Sweden.

Professor Bart Nooteboom, School of Management and Organisation, Groningen University, The Netherlands.

Dr Jan Ottosson, Department of Economic History, Uppsala University, Sweden.

Dr Salvatore Rizzello, Department of Economics, University of Turin, Italy.

Contributors

Dr Jack Vromen, Department of Economics, Erasmus University and Department of Philosophy, University of Amsterdam, The Netherlands.

M.Sc. Jan L. Östlund, Department of Economic History, Uppsala University, Sweden.

Acknowledgements

The contributions in this volume originate from a conference held in Stockholm, Sweden, May 1995. The generous financial support from the Swedish Communications and Transports Research Board is greatly acknowledged in making this conference possible. The editors thanks the doctoral candidates Jan Östlund, Eva Liljegren, Magnus Carlsson and Juan Bergdahl, for help on practical matters. Marion Cutting helped us improve the language in the introduction.

Uppsala, 1996

Lars Magnusson and Jan Ottosson

1. Introduction

Lars Magnusson and Jan Ottosson

Attempts to challenge the neo-classical paradigm have been increasingly common during recent years. The new institutional economics has argued against the narrow, 'institution-free', formalistic way of analysing economic life that dominates most neo-classical theorising. In the same manner evolutionary-oriented economists have argued against the static analysis of equilibrium phases, pleading for a more process-oriented view of the economy (Landesmann and Pagano 1994, p. 199).

Although these challenges have provided many new insights and broadened the scope of economics as a social science, some critique has been sweeping, tending to neglect the substantial progress made in modern neo-classical theory which has provided new research opportunities for handling complex economic phenomena. Such important new strands have been able to incorporate and build upon notions such as Simon's bounded rationality and positive feedback, which have been applied and extended in the fields of evolutionary game theory, contractual theory and network externalities, to mention a few. These modern applications of neo-classical economics have indeed much to offer in certain analytical respects, but in some instances they still do not offer sufficient tools for explanation of complex economic phenomena, such as the processes of growth and change. This argument can also be made against the still neo-classically based New Institutional Economics for focusing too heavily on comparative static and not giving enough attention to processes of change (Williamson 1985, 1991).

Austrian and other evolutionary economics in particular has turned its interest towards the process of change. Common elements in this theoretical tradition are the emphasis upon different forms of uncertainty and how they affect the behaviour of agents as well as the introduction of concepts such as 'routines' to replace the neo-classical notion of maximisation (Langlois and Everett 1994, p. 11–12; Nelson and Winter 1982; Vromen 1995). Thus, in two key respects evolutionary economics depicts a different human agent than neo-classical theory does. On the one hand it introduces behavioural assumptions such as bounded rationality and 'satisficing' in place of rationality and maximisation. On the other hand it introduces an individual who at least in the Austrian tradition of Menger and Von Mises can not merely be reduced to being a passive price taker (Vanberg 1994).

In recent years the concept of 'path dependency' has been used in order to criticise the neo-classical paradigm in a more radical fashion. While transaction cost economics emphasises for example the variation of governance structures as optimal responses to co-ordination problems, the notion of path dependency suggests that lock-in effects and sub-optimal behaviour may persist and that history matters in explaining these deficiencies (Arthur 1989; David 1994). Such arguments, that are by now well-known, suggest that minor historical events may affect development into a particular path, featuring not necessarily the most optimal solution (Arthur 1989; David 1985, 1988, 1994; North 1990). Path dependency occurs in institutions and organisations for three main reasons, according to David (1994); since institutions solve co-ordination games, several multiple expectations are possible, all being sensible and dependent on the initial event/conditions. The second argument concerns the irreversibility of investments in codes of communication within organisations. The final argument for the occurrence of path dependence, especially in organisations, emphasises the interrelatedness of tasks and functions which an organisation might want to apply and develop. Since such new functions are added sequentially, they tend to develop within the path chosen. In a broad sense the notion of path dependency challenges the neo-classical paradigm through its recognition of the importance of institutions and the role of history (North 1990; David 1985, 1994). Hence, because of information problems and the costs experienced by firms or human agents of organising economic activities – something we might call 'path dependency' occurs.

Certainly, most standard neo-classical economics does not include any costs of information or cost for organising economic activity (Landesmann and Pagano 1994, p. 199; Coase 1937; Denzau and North 1994). This does not suggest that neo-classical economics – at least not post Arrow – in theory is able to handle a number of such 'exceptions' to the general (Marshallian) rule. In this context Liebowitz and Margolis (1995) have suggested that the instance of path dependency can be, and is best, handled within traditional (neo-classical) economic analysis. In order to do this they introduce three degrees of path dependency, according to different levels of available information. In the first two instances the situation of path dependency (first and second degree of path dependence) is easily solved within a neo-classical framework. In the first instance a choice may well be the rational and optimal one, although it is only a second-rate choice, since the agents fully acknowledge that abandoning a previously chosen path is not

2

likely to occur without costs. With regard to the second degree of path dependence, the reason for following a certain path might be the incomplete information occurring at the time of the decision. Because of this an agent might later find out that the initial choice was apparently not the ultimate one. According to Leibowitz and Margolis this can not 'in a meaningful way' be defined as an inefficient solution since the information was not at hand when the decision was taken. Last, the third degree of path dependence depicts a situation when the actor may be aware of better alternatives, but still rejects them, and instead chooses the path-dependant outcome. Hence, the main argument of the authors is that the first two degrees of path dependency are consistent with neo-classical rational behaviour leading to predictable, efficient solutions, and only the third degree of path dependence is left as being not compatible with a neo-classical framework of interpretation. Hopefully enough, as they argue, the third degree of path dependency only occurs in rare circumstances and therefore we need not concentrate on it. Unfortunately, the authors do not let us know how true their wishful suggestion is. Many economists or other social scientists dealing with applied matters could most certainly list an endless number of instances where path dependency also in the third sense might be evidenced.

However, Leibowitz and Margolis are certainly right in that if 'path dependency' is to serve as anything more than a catchword for sweeping criticism of neo-classical economics, it is important that we try to be more specific regarding its theoretical status. Hence, it seems clear that path dependency in its 'strongest' sense, making it totally impossible to handle within the neo-classical approach, can be defined in a similar way to Liebowitz and Margolis: namely, as a situation where an agent is aware of a 'better' solution but avoids it. However, contrary to these two authors we believe that their first and second degree of path dependency is difficult to handle within a neo-classical approach, especially if the costs of abandoning the path *ex ante* are not known, or in a situation where radical or 'parametric' — to use Langlois' (1984) phrase — uncertainty occurs. Even more importantly, Leibowitz and Margolis does not acknowledge the very plausible hypothesis that the process of selection information (for example regarding 'best solutions') is path dependent and socially bounded. It seems to us that it is necessary also for economists to pay some attention to the arguments concerning 'the social construction of reality' which has been put forward in most social theorizing during last years. Hence, a specific choice might be taken because the already chosen path make us believe that it is the best. In the latter case path dependency can be identified as 'genuine rule following' (Rutherford 1994, p. 54 quoting Vanberg 1988, p. 3, emphasis in original); 'By contrast, *genuine* rule following involves 'a disposition to abide by the rules *relatively independently* of the specifics of the particular situational constraints'.'

Hence, if the notion of path dependency is to become a real challenge to the neo-classical paradigm, the concept of path dependency must be able to aid our understanding of how economic agents make their choices. Obviously, three opposing principles are at hand in a choice situation: the first is rational choice, the other is choice dependent upon path dependent selection of information and thirdly rule following, or path dependency. Moreover, the notion that 'rule following behaviour exists is ... widely accepted' (Rutherford 1994, p. 54). The crucial question is instead when and for what reasons rule following is adapted by agents, firms and organisations. With reference to Nelson and Winter's discussion of routines, we must furthermore acknowledge that such rule following mechanisms can be long-lasting (Nelson and Winter 1982). Moreover they are most certainly introduced when actors make their choices facing a high degree of uncertainty and imperfect information (Heiner 1983; North 1990, p. 95; Denzau and North 1994). It might also be helpful to argue in line with North that choices become path dependent only in a situation characterised by increasing returns and imperfect markets (North 1990, p. 95).

While there is much to be gained by introducing path dependency/rule following into the theory of choice there are certainly also some problems which should not be taken lightly. Hence it might be easy to think of path dependent situations in a world of uncertainty and when information is socialy selected; but how then does change occur? When is the path abandoned, and for what reasons?

Several scholars have recently argued that one way to start might be to acknowledge the existence of punctuated equilibrium situations (Gersick 1991, Andersen 1994, Nelson 1994, Romanelli and Tushman 1994). However, a problem with this approach is its focus on merely external factors (chocks) in starting the rapid process of change (Thelen and Steinmo 1992). Perhaps a more fruitful approach is to introduce some kind of adaptive rationality model, as for example suggested by Rutherford (1994, p. 80; Heiner 1983).

According to such lines of thinking, adaptation and learning occurs over time. Adaptive behaviour and learning will in turn ensure change, and even lead to the abandonment of a certain path. An advantage of this approach is that it stresses small and gradual changes over time – and not merely external shocks. The role of adaptation of learning has of course been discussed intensively during recent years and is inherent in much evolutionary theory

4

– including the Nelson and Winter approach. The crucial question, as Groenewegen and Vromen argue in their contribution to this volume, is whether and to what extent adaptive learning, with reference to Simon, can be seen as a parallel to a Darwinian selection mechanism. They argue that even though the role of history and the feedback mechanism itself might prevent the search for better rules, and adapt old rules too slowly to a changing environment, there still might be a tendency for the adaptive agent to readily recognise a better solution. However, the agent is indeed only viewed upon as *reacting*, through the mechanism of second-order rules.

Another way of dealing with the problem of path dependency and change originates in the discussion within general social science during recent years regarding the relation between structure and agency. Within this discussion – which includes names such as Giddens, Macintyre and Bhaskar – an attempt has been made to replace structuralism by a more praxis-oriented view of the interrelationship between structure and agent. Political institutionalists have also in recent years moderated the discussion by emphasising interaction processes between actors and structures, and discussing the role of internal and external factors as well as gradual and abrupt patterns of change related to processes of historical evolution (Thelen and Steinmo 1992). Thus, the notion of path dependence and related concepts has indeed been a matter of debate among social sciences, but discussion across disciplinary borderlines has been rather limited. It is true that some economists have lately recognised that institutions may somehow matter, but there is indeed a need for economists to approach other social sciences without viewing them as inferior.

A key goal of this volume is to introduce and bring together recent discussions regarding different aspects of economic change, choice and path dependency. The contributions in this volume represent new strands within the traditions of evolutionary economics and institutional economics. Both the theoretically oriented papers and the empirical ones deal with path dependencies, learning processes and institutional change. The empirical parts are focused on one specific area; institutional change in the communications and transport sector of the economy. One important reason for choosing this sector is that it is an especially interesting case of path dependency. For one thing investments in infrastructure are often very expensive and have a long-time impact. Most certainly the choice of technology within this sector at one point will have a tendency to lead to path dependent behaviour in the long run (Hughes 1983). Moreover, path dependencies are also likely to impact institutional choices since there are few other sectors in the economy which interact so heavily with the state and in so many ways, either through regulations or nationalisation. Of course, the rules and institutions upheld by the state will effect the initial choice of path as well as its prevalence (Dobbin 1994a, Dunlavy 1994).

Within the tradition of economic sociology, John Campbell discusses the important notion of bricolage in relation to the discussion of path dependence. By distinguishing between on the one hand institutional theories based upon the notion of constraints, and on the other, theories concerned with the enabling effects of institutions, Campbell conclusively shows that neo-institutional theories based upon rational choice can not explain how actors actually form their preferences. Indeed, by introducing the agent more properly, institutions may also enable actors' preferences as well as courses of action. In this respect, in Campbell's words, some of the 'black boxes of rational choice theory', may be opened. The forming of these preferences can be interpreted in a continuum, varying from stability to dramatic changes, depending on the nature of change in interaction processes among actors. This process will have impact on the redefinition process of the preferences. This has important implications for evolutionary theories since it focuses on the process *preceding* selection. Of course, rules and routines are important parts of such an explanation, but Campbell also suggests that institutions themselves may actually enable actors to recombine existing institutional settings, i.e., the process of bricolage.

Groenewegen and Vromen argue that despite the obvious differences between the new institutionalists (Williamson) and neo-institutionalists, there may be hidden intuitions in Williamson's analysis, indicating a more unified institutional theory, which to some degree takes into account the role of history in terms of path dependencies and lock-in effects. One of the basic questions in this respect is of course the relation between those who Groenewegen and Vromen call the 'new institutionalists' and the 'neo-institutionalists' of old institutional economics with regard to the notion of evolutionary processes. In the former tradition, the prevailing governance structures are considered the most efficient ones, since they already exist. This circular argument is confronted with the neo-institutionalist discussion, where existing structures do not necessarily reflect the most efficient solution. Arthur's (1991) discussion concerning learning algorithms and the possibilities of extending the choice of technologies into the field of economics and learning processes, is related to Nelson and Winter's and Williamson's work, especially regarding the notion of bounded rationality. Although actors may have tried better alternatives, they continue along other lines of action. Groenewegen and Vromen argues further, in line with

Nelson and Winter, and Arthur, that adaptive learning by itself may lead to non-efficient outcomes of evolutionary processes in the economy. In the final portion, they discuss more specifically how different types of path dependencies relate to differences found between neo-institutional economics and the new institutional economics, arguing that path dependence resembling the third degree, when actors reject superior lines of action, may be hard to incorporate into the paradigm of the new institutionalists.

Bart Nooteboom further interprets the question of knowledge in relation to path dependence and the theory of the firm. By seeing the brain as a neural network he uses this as a metaphor of learning processes on the level of the firm. In a number of predictions related to the theory of the firm, Nooteboom argues that several kinds of learning processes might be present. Also, he continues, path dependence will be at hand in these complex cognitive processes, where units send and receive signals through pathways.

Michael Dietrich discusses the nature of lock-in effects, not only in the field of technological choice, but also the implications of extending the concept by relating it to professional organisations on the intra-firm level. Dietrich also suggests that the initial choice may not only reflect random conditions, but this choice is indeed influenced by strategic leaders. The dominance of particular professional groups may therefore have a significant effect on an organisation's performance and functioning. Dietrich shows conclusively the analytical power of applying arguments concerning lock-in effects into other areas, and points out the need for further research on the conditions concerning choice.

With roots in the Austrian evolutionary tradition, Salvatore Rizzello discusses the micro-foundations of path dependency. He argues that changes in rule following and routines can best be interpreted from the level of the individual actor and the subjective processes of generating new routines. Starting with the neo-classical criticism found in Hayek and Simon, Rizzello continues by introducing cognitive psychology and its influence upon viewing economic processes of change as well as path dependency. Further, building the analysis of path dependence on an individualistic approach, he recognises the importance of Hayek, emphasising the spontaneous order and the subjectivism in this tradition.

Håkan Håkansson and Anders Lundgren penetrate the issue of 'how the past reflects changes in industrial networks'. Industrial networks consist of multi-layered relationships, bearing the role of history. These linkages are important when analysing change, and so the authors adapt a view focusing upon the importance of relationships, a view which resembles Campbell's, but they discuss it within the 'market as network' tradition. By dividing

7

path dependencies into two parts, paths as structures and paths as processes, they distinguish two features of path dependence, which both have important implications in explaining change and the abandoning of paths.

In the four empirically oriented contributions, the common theme is how path dependency occurs and develops through various types of lock-in effects within institutions. The role of policy and the uprising of various 'national styles' in this respect are crucial in understanding processes of path dependencies as well as processes of change. Also, this suggests that the interaction between actors and institutions might be better understood when focusing upon processes of policy changes and new political power relations. Instead of discussing arbitrarily choice situations, these contributions show conclusively how choice mechanisms might be influenced and disturbed by ideology. The role of second-order rules is applied and discussed with regard to the necessary conditions furthering institutional change in Juan Bergdahl and Jan L. Östlund's contribution. They examine a political decision process within the European Community regarding the goals and outcomes of a common European transport policy, and the mechanisms of changing a nearly three-decade long parliamentary locked-in situation. The authors suggest that the requirement of a unanimous vote was one of the most important hindrances to an integrated single European transport policy. This policy was revealed through the passing of the single European Act, enabling majority rule, which is considered necessary to stop the blocking tactics of individual countries in their attempt to defending self-interests. By recognising this impact of institutions governing other institutions, they contribute to the discussion concerning the process of institutional change and the importance of distinguishing between various levels of institutions. Jan Ottosson discusses the process of railway nationalisation in Sweden against the background of nationalisation experiences in other European countries. Showing that both new and old institutional economics seems somewhat reluctant towards policy issues, he recognises the importance of further interpreting the policy-making process, especially the change in policy making which emphasises the new political institutionalists. In the discussion of the interaction between the market and policy, Ottosson emphasises the role of purposeful actors in policy making. These actors offered new arguments for railroad nationalisation and changed the institutional settings regarding nationalisation of the private railroad sector in Sweden. Lena Andersson-Skog compares the growth of the telecommunications sector in the Scandinavian countries and finds various institutional settings unimportant in explaining the growth patterns in the short run. This may at first glance be an argument readily at hand for neo-classical economists claiming the non-importance of institutions. However, as Andersson-Skog points out, broadening the time perspective shows conclusively that the initial variations in institutional settings did play an important role in the ensuing development of this sector. She concludes that the differing developments in regulatory regimes in the Nordic countries was indeed important in the longer run. Peter Lyth points out the crucial role of the state in governing the first regulatory systems of the airline industry in Europe. By using the airline industry as an example of an emerging industry with no former regulations at hand, he shows how new regulatory orders are created when a new technology takes off. In this respect, the early impact of the First World War becomes crucial in understanding the position of the states which sought to protect the national identity of their aviation industry. The Second World War is also important in this respect, since it provides further explanation and extends the analysis of initial institutional settings and positive feedback in a new industry with the central role of the national state.

The contributions to this volume suggest that we must continue the most important discussion of the nature of evolutionary processes as well as the role of history. The notion of path dependency has already been implemented into areas other than the traditional case of technological change discussion; this must certainly continue. However, if the concept is to be of any use in the future – especially if it claims to challenge the neo-classical theory of rational choice – it must be theoretically developed. We hope that this collection will stimulate further thinking and writing along the existing path, which we believe is fruitful to follow.

2. Mechanisms of Evolutionary Change in Economic Governance: Interaction, Interpretation and Bricolage

John L. Campbell

INTRODUCTION

There is increasing agreement among economists, political scientists and sociologists that we need to understand better how economic institutions change in evolutionary and path-dependent ways.[1] Beyond that, however, there is much debate about the mechanisms that cause institutional change to assume an evolutionary character. For instance, those following rational choice theory argue that self-interested actors will make decisions and create institutions, often in response to exogenous changes in prices or preferences, that they believe are most likely to reduce their economic costs relative to the benefits gained. Previously existing institutions, that is, formal laws and regulations, informal norms and ideologies, and their attendant mechanisms of enforcement and compliance, *constrain* the range of institutional alternatives from which actors choose thereby limiting the extent to which new institutions differ from old ones and mitigating against more radical and abrupt institutional change. Incremental or evolutionary change is the result (North 1990; Ostrom 1990; 1991). Conversely, those subscribing to social constructionist views hold that actors suffer from extremely limited information and high levels of uncertainty and thus are driven more by concerns for doing what is institutionally acceptable and culturally appropriate than by some kind of cost-benefit analysis (DiMaggio and Powell 1991, pp. 15–19). Hence, actors construct new institutions by extending already existing institutional principles, conventions and concepts to new realms of activity (Friedland and Alford 1991, p. 254). In this sense institutions provide actors with social scripts that *enable* (or empower) them in ways that contribute to the evolutionary nature of institutional change

10

(March and Olsen 1984; 1993; Jepperson 1991, p. 146).[2]

Some scholars have recognized that institutions are simultaneously constraining and enabling and have called for a theoretical synthesis in this regard (e.g., Jepperson 1991, p. 157; Rutherford 1994, ch. 7). However, only limited progress has been made with respect to models of evolutionary economic change. For instance, Douglass North (1990), who deduced a theory of economic change from the rational choice principles of the new institutional economics, acknowledged that in addition to constraining behavior informal cultural institutions affected how actors interpreted their world and provided important elements of continuity that help account for the incremental nature of change. Nevertheless, North admitted that he was unable to incorporate a theory of culture and ideology into his model and thus failed to explore how this interpretive process, which he called 'procedural rationality,' actually operated (North 1990, pp. 42–4). Leon Lindberg and I developed a heuristic model of evolutionary change that blended five theories of economic transformation (Campbell and Lindberg 1991). Our model was based on an inductive analysis of changes in the institutional governance of eight sectors of the US economy and was different from North's in many respects. However, our model was consistent with his insofar as we argued that the evolutionary character of institutional change stemmed primarily from the fact that historically given political, economic and cultural institutions constrained subsequent institutional transformations. We also neglected the manner in which institutions are enabling. That is, although we assumed that actors are motivated by their interpretations of their institutional situations and experiences (Campbell and Lindberg 1991, p. 330; Lindberg *et al.* 1991, p. 6), like North, we did not explore the process of interpretation itself and, as a result, our claims about interpretive action were not substantiated empirically or theoretically.

This paper revisits the constraint-oriented model of evolutionary economic change that Lindberg and I developed by taking into account recent theoretical and empirical advances in the study of institutions by organisational sociologists and political scientists (e.g. Powell and DiMaggio 1991; Scott 1994; Thelen and Steinmo 1992). It explores the enabling effects of institutions and argues that institutions provide interpretive frames and patterns of interaction that influence how actors define their problems, interests and solutions in ways that facilitate evolutionary change - something that most evolutionary theories neglect due to their preoccupation with constraints. In other words, the processes through which actors define means and ends constitute important institutional mechanisms of evolutionary change that should not be taken for granted by analysts even if they are

11

by the actors themselves. The article begins by reviewing our earlier model of governance transformation and elaborating its weaknesses in this regard. The next two sections of the paper discuss how institutions enable actors, first, to define their problems and interests, and second, to devise solutions and courses of action in view of these definitions, and how in both cases this contributes to the evolutionary nature of institutional change. This discussion draws on a wide range of examples of economic and political change. Finally, some theoretical implications of the analysis are discussed. The result is not so much a fully specified theory as it is an orienting framework indicating mechanisms that have been largely neglected in studies of evolutionary economic change and that may be incorporated into more constraint-based perspectives.

AN EVOLUTIONARY MODEL OF GOVERNANCE TRANSFORMATION

In our initial model Lindberg and I sought to explain how economic and political actors create and modify the institutions through which economic activity is governed, that is, organized, conducted and regulated. The focus was on the transformation of interorganisational relationships involving firms, associations, various sorts of informal networks and the state rather than on the governance of activity within a particular organisation. The unit of analysis was the industrial sector as a constellation of interacting organisations rather than isolated organisations per se.

We argued that organisational actors respond to various *pressures for change*, such as new economic conditions, new technological developments, shifts in state policies or laws, and attempts by actors to alter the balance of power within the sector. They do so by engaging in a complex process whereby they seek collectively to select new interorganisational arrangements, which we called governance regimes, in order to better deal with these pressures. We maintained that this *selection process* can involve trial and error experimentation, negotiation and bargaining, and the use of political and economic coercion. However, the model focused largely on how this selection process is constrained by a variety of factors and how these constraints infuse institutional change with an evolutionary quality. Specifically, we argued that already existing interorganisational relations embody a degree of rigidity out of which it is difficult for actors to break. Furthermore, the existing balance of power limits the ability of less powerful actors to pursue institutional changes that would increase their power.

12

State actions, such as upholding or striking down existing property rights, sustains or alters the relative power of different actors and constrains the types of interactions that occur and institutions that may be created. Cultural factors including norms of fairness, competition and cooperation constrain the range of actions and institutional outcomes that actors may pursue. Thus, the new institutional arrangements that evolve through this process of constrained selection reflect to a large degree the pre-existing institutional arrangements, power relations, state actions, and cultural traditions from which they were born.

Two things were missing from the argument. First, we did not provide an analysis of those aspects of the selection process where groups of actors defined their problems, i.e., pressures for change, and in turn their interests. Second, we did not theorize how actors developed ideas about possible alternative institutional arrangements after they had determined their problems and interests. That is, we argued that actors experimented, bargained and struggled over possible institutional solutions, but we never discussed how these possibilities were constructed initially. In short, although defining problems, identifying interests, and developing ideas for solutions are integral parts of institutional change these processes remained analytic black boxes waiting to be opened and explored. More important, to the extent that these boxes may have concealed important mechanisms of evolutionary change, our model was incomplete. The reason for these omissions was straightforward. The industry case studies from which we constructed our model provided little data about these processes.[3]

In more general terms, the problem was that we lacked an analysis of agency and interpretation to complement our analysis of constraint. Such an analysis involves explaining how actors define their goals and how they believe they should achieve them. In this regard, we shared common ground with rational choice theories of institutional change. These theories *assume* that actors seek to reduce their costs relative to benefits as best they can (e.g., Williamson 1985, ch. 2). By making such assumptions they avoid explaining how actors form these preferences and how actors identify possible institutional changes that might best serve their preferences (Friedland and Alford 1991, pp. 233–4; Piore 1995, p. 100).[4] As a result, regardless of whether theorists assume that actors maximize, optimize, or act opportunistically, these behavioral assumptions *substitute* for an analysis of the *processes* through which actors define means and ends. These processes are generally exogenous to their models. North is clear on this point when he admits that rational choice theorists like himself 'know very little about the sources of changing preferences or tastes...[and that] improved understanding of institutional change requires greater understanding than we now possess of just what makes ideas and ideologies catch hold' (North 1990, pp. 84–6). In sum, although we did not share the same behavioral assumptions, the black boxes of rational choice theory are very similar to those in our model of governance transformation. The task at hand is to open these boxes, explore their contents and identify their effects on institutional evolution.

DEFINING PROBLEMS AND INTERESTS: INTERACTION AND INTERPRETATION

The process of problem definition and interest formation is largely one in which actors subjectively interpret their objective situations (Scott 1994, pp. 57–59). Of course, this does not occur in a vacuum but in light of historically given interpretive frames and meaning systems that enable actors to view the world from certain points of view (e.g., Hattam 1993). This is an important reason why different actors may interpret similar situations in remarkably different ways. For example, during the early twentieth century politicians, managers, and organized labor in Germany interpreted their country's industrial backwardness as resulting from waste, disorder, lack of discipline within the work place and managerial greed, among other things. This view was based on an interpretive frame steeped in Protestant asceticism and reinforced by images and themes of modernism, standardization and efficiency that were very popular during the period in German music, art, architecture, literature, media and popular culture. Given its emphasis on efficiency and discipline, scientific management was widely embraced as the institutional solution to the backwardness problem. In Spain, however, the problem of backwardness was interpreted from within a Catholic humanist tradition and thus was defined as stemming from monotonous work, low morale, absenteeism, high labour turnover and other factors that undermined initiative and productivity. As a result, the solution to backwardness in Spain was not scientific management but institutional arrangements based on human relations theory, which stressed the importance of job enrichment, teamwork, and the like (Guillén 1994a). Although this is not the whole story the point is that different interpretive frames facilitated different understandings of the problems and interests of economic backwardness.[5]

Interpretive frames such as these lend much stability to the definition of problems and interests over time. For instance, Frank Dobbin (1994a)

14

argued that the problem of developing transportation systems was interpreted by industrialists and politicians in France throughout the nineteenth century from within an interpretive frame where the state was assumed to be the best guardian of the public interest and social order. As a result, actors generally agreed that the problem was to develop private transportation systems without allowing private interests to disrupt the coherence and efficiency of the sector. Hence, roadway development, then canal building, and finally the organisation of railroads were centrally planned, organized, regulated and financed by the French state. Because a different interpretive frame prevailed in the United States, which assumed that the source of order lay in the sovereignty of the local community and market competition rather than the national state, the problem of transportation development was interpreted differently. Actors believed that the problem was to create transportation systems within a competitive market context. In turn, the sector developed a much different institutional structure as roadways, then canals and eventually railroads assumed a much more fragmented and competitive institutional structure.

I am not suggesting that we reduce our accounts of institutional change to interpretive frameworks or that institutional constraints and power struggles are unimportant. Indeed, even when actors define their problems in ways that are consistent with well-established interpretive frameworks other institutions may constrain their ability to act on these definitions. For instance, there was also a long tradition of government financial and regulatory support for transportation development in Prussia and, in keeping with that tradition, the crown wanted to build a national railroad system during the mid-1800s. However, it faced severe fiscal and political constraints that forced it to rely on private development with only minimal state regulation. In particular, the crown needed to convene parliament in order to authorize fund raising, an option it refused to exercise for fear that this would precipitate a significant and permanent erosion of its power (Dunlavy 1992). Despite these caveats the point remains that once interpretive frames have become institutionalized, interpreting problems and interests tends to become a rather scripted, ritualistic and predictable exercise in which certain types of definitions are taken for granted and appear to be quite natural (Dobbin 1994b, p. 133). This scripting of interpretation is an important source of institutional stability.

Nonetheless, sometimes interpretive frames change dramatically. Charles Sabel (1993) notes that in response to persistent economic decline in the industrial heartland of Pennsylvania labor unions and business firms in several industries struggled against each other during the 1970s and 1980s,

15

as they had throughout much of the twentieth century, to act on what they perceived to be their individual self-interests. The unions tried to defend their wages, benefits, and jobs while businesses sought to extract a wide variety of concessions from them in an increasingly hostile and competitive atmosphere and with only limited success in terms of reversing the decline. In short, through repeated and highly conflictual interactions based on labor market exchange both parties defined their problems and interests vis-à-vis each other in zero-sum terms. However, in the late 1980s through a variety of incentives, such as the provision of joint research and development grants, consulting services, and financial support for cooperative brain storming, the state of Pennsylvania encouraged these groups in conjunction with trade associations, educational institutions and municipal governments to discuss their situations together at the local level in an effort to see whether their problems could be reevaluated and more effective solutions might be devised. The foundry industry near Pittsburgh, plastics firms near Lake Erie, apparel companies in the Lehigh Valley, and various tool-and-die firms scattered around the state were targeted. In each case the idea was that by studying their industry together actors might find new ways to revitalize it.

Gradually, participants in these efforts began to rethink their situations and develop an increasing awareness of the organisational basis for their industries' problems, particularly in light of the success of foreign competitors in Germany, Sweden, Italy and other West European countries. As a result, they redefined their problems in non-zero-sum terms, began to forge new collective interests and developed a sense of trust upon which new cooperative industrial strategies could be based. Among other things, they discovered that better training was crucial in order to begin solving other problems and that workers needed new skills in order to reorganize the work place along more flexible lines. They also discovered that collective service, marketing and manufacturing projects could be started. Overall, the situation was redefined from one where for many years actors assumed that their problems and interests were naturally given in individualistic and antagonistic terms to one where this taken-for-granted understanding was drawn into question, actors recognized their mutual dependence, and problems and interests were recast in collective terms (Sabel 1993, p. 121).

The ability to alter interpretive frames and redefine problems and interests is not limited to industrial societies. For example, rice farmers in Sri Lanka who depended on communal irrigation systems to sustain their crops had been unable for decades to devise effective institutions for rationing water when it was scarce, largely because farmers defined their problems

16

and interests in individualistic terms and so it made sense to take as much water as possible for their own paddies with little regard for the effects that this would have on neighboring farmers or the irrigation system as a whole. Thus, upstream irrigators benefitted systematically over downstream irrigators and the overall level of agricultural production suffered accordingly. However, in the early 1980s the state sent community organizers into the villages to encourage local farmers to discuss their irrigation needs among themselves. This gradually enabled farmers to redefine their interests in more collective terms, develop a sense of trust toward each other and devise new institutional arrangements for more effectively managing the irrigation system (Ostrom 1990, ch. 5).

The important lesson of the Pennsylvania and Sri Lanka cases is that alterations in patterns of interaction caused actors to gain new perspectives on their situations by enabling them to recognize, reexamine and ultimately reinterpret their previously taken-for-granted assumptions about problems and interests. Hence, changes in *interaction* may precipitate changes in *interpretation*. Indeed, variation in interaction helps to explain why actors whose objective economic situations are the same may hold much different views of their political and economic interests. For example, after controlling for sales, profits, capital intensity and other economic factors, Cathy Martin (1994) found that US corporations during the early 1990s that had been consulting regularly with each other and policy makers in various formal and informal networks were significantly more supportive of health care reform than corporations that did not participate in these networks. She concluded that different patterns of interaction led to different interpretations of the US health care crisis and therefore different definitions of corporate interests regarding health care reform. In sum, the process of problem definition and interest formation is an interactive one where groups of actors interpret their situations, either through cooperation or conflict, and gradually construct shared understandings of their problems and interests (Allen 1994; Piore 1995, ch. 5; Scott 1994, p. 59). As a result, interests are not pre-given or natural (Dobbin 1994b; Hirschman 1977). But what is it about the interactive process of problem and interest interpretation that contributes to *evolutionary* change?

If changes in interaction precipitate changes in interpretation, then it follows that the more radical the change in interaction the more likely it is that fundamental redefinitions will occur and institutional changes will diverge sharply from those of the past. Conversely, the more limited the change in interaction the more likely it is that new definitions of problems and interests will not deviate sharply from old ones and the institutional changes that

17

result, if any, will follow a more evolutionary or incremental trajectory. This also suggests that we can specify a *continuum* of change ranging from stability to evolutionary change to more radical or revolutionary change that breaks dramatically with the past (see also Campbell and Pedersen 1995; Hall 1993).

The recent history of US tax policy illustrates the point. After the Second World War changes in federal income tax policy were incremental (Witte 1985) and average effective corporate income tax rates declined gradually due in part to the slow erosion in political strength of organized labor and the liberal coalition within the Democratic Party as well as the steadily growing influence of business lobbyists (Campbell and Allen 1994; Edsall 1984, p. 65). In other words, certain groups were slowly excluded from the policy-making interactions that defined the problems toward which tax policy was directed while other groups gained an increasing presence in these interactions. The result was an evolution in the definition of economic problems in an increasingly conservative direction and declining corporate tax rates were the result. However, the nature of these interactions shifted abruptly in 1986 and Congress overhauled the tax code by closing loopholes and implementing a revenue system that treated corporations in a much more neutral manner. Political leaders who were determined to reform the tax code recognized that members of Congress generally find it difficult to resist pressure from powerful corporate lobbyists who are opposed to tax reform. As a result, for the first time in decades the legislative process was conducted behind closed doors that effectively excluded lobbyists from the policy-making process (Birnbaum and Murray 1987; Conlan *et al.* 1990). In turn, Congress, the Treasury Department, and the administration were able to construct and sustain a new definition of the nation's economic problems that rejected the prevailing albeit increasingly conservative Fordist capital-intensive growth paradigm of the past, upon which much previous tax policy had been based, and deployed instead a new post-Fordist definition that favored tax neutrality (Martin 1991, ch. 7).

Of course, other scholars have recognized that interaction affects interpretation but few have used this insight to theorize the *evolutionary* nature of political or economic change (e.g., Friedland and Alford 1991; Piore 1995; Scott 1994).[6] For instance, Peter Hall (1993) draws a distinction between incremental and more radical changes in policy making. Following Kuhn, he argues that revolutionary reinterpretations of situations, which he calls 'paradigm shifts,' are triggered by highly anomalous events that cast doubt on the prevailing definitions, assumptions and causal models of policy makers (see also Dobbin 1993). In seeking to understand these anomalies changes in the locus of policy-making authority and the range of participants interacting in the policy process occurs. Specifically, a more public discussion of policy issues transpires that includes a larger number of public and private actors. In his view more modest evolutionary changes in interpretation apparently do not involve changes in interaction. My point is that they do and that this is an important but much neglected mechanism through which interpretive frames and thus institutional arrangements *evolve* over time.

A necessary step toward further substantiating this argument empirically involves thinking more carefully about those aspects of interaction which when changed affect interpretation. Although a thorough classification of different types of interaction patterns and their effects on different types of interpretations is well beyond the scope of this paper, the Pennsylvania and Sri Lanka cases suggest two factors that are important. First, as the *composition* of the interaction changes so does the interpretive frame. After all, in both examples when a broader range of community members were drawn together to discuss the economic situation individualistic, zero-sum interpretations gave way to collective, non-zero-sum interpretations. Hence, more inclusive interactions may yield more collectively oriented interpretations.

Cross-national comparisons corroborate this point. For example, in Denmark much policy making and institution building is the result of a highly negotiated process at the national level that is very inclusive. Briefly, Danish public policy making and institution building are the product of sustained politically mandated, financed, and sanctioned, negotiations among business associations, state actors, labor unions and other centrally organized groups. Through these negotiations actors define socioeconomic problems and recommend solutions for them, campaign for their different points of view among policy makers and each other, specify more precisely and examine scientifically the relative advantages and disadvantages of the alternative solutions that have been proposed, select final solutions in light of this evidence and establish frameworks for implementation, and enforce agreements once they are made. This process typically leads to the construction of a *shared* view of what is good for society overall that cannot be reduced to the self-interested preferences of individual actors. In other words, these negotiations are complex forms of institutionalized interaction and discourse that are organized in such a way as to systematically yield *collective* definitions of problems, interests and courses of action. Because the institutional basis for this sort of negotiated economy has been in effect for so long it has become largely taken for granted by all participants, as has the notion that political and economic problems *ought* to be defined in collective ways, that is, within a shared socioeconomic frame of meaning that apparently seems quite natural to most Danes (Nielsen and Pedersen 1991; Pedersen 1990).[7] For complex historical reasons this sort of interaction is much less common in the United States (Salisbury 1979; Wilson 1982). This is an important reason why policy making and institution building is often such a conflictual process there and why it is so difficult for actors to define problems, interests, and solutions in collective terms (Lindberg and Campbell 1991, pp. 392–95).[8] As a result, because there is much less interorganisational negotiation over problems and interests it is not surprising that many Americans subscribe to an interpretive framework that grants pride of place to individualism and particularistic self-interested action (e.g., Bellah *et al.* 1985, ch. 6; Gans 1988; Piore 1995).

Second, as the *focus* of interaction changes, so does the interpretive frame. In addition to changing the composition of the interaction in Pennsylvania, state government provided grants and other incentives to deliberately encourage business, labor and other local community members to shift their attention from issues of exchange, such as struggles over wages and benefits, to a broader discussion about the structural competitiveness of industry and regional economic revitalization in general. Indeed, one of the primary criteria that political leaders used to determine who would receive government assistance was the ability of the applicant to demonstrate a commitment to adopting this sort of focus (Sabel 1993, p. 127). Of course, the problem for future research is to think more clearly about how we might differentiate or measure the degree to which a change in focus occurs and what the range of foci might be toward which interaction is directed. The distinction between focusing on exchange and non-exchange problems is one way to think about this but more refined approaches are surely conceivable. For obvious reasons this is less of a problem with respect to the composition of interaction at least insofar as we can imagine a simple continuum ranging from bilateral to increasingly more multilateral interactions (e.g., Lindberg *et al.* 1991). Whether shifts toward more inclusive and less exchange-based forms of interaction systematically yield more collective and cooperative interpretive frames as these examples suggest requires further research.

In any case, the essential hypothesis is that as changes in the composition and/or focus of interaction occur changes in the interpretation of problems and interests will follow. Relatively minor changes in interaction and interpretation will likely precipitate institutional change that is more evolutionary in nature. Relatively fundamental changes in interaction and interpretation will likely lead to more radical and abrupt changes in institutions. Of course, as new frameworks of interpretation and their underlying interactive structures are locked in or institutionalized through repetition they become more or less taken for granted and provide the apparently 'natural' scripts that enable actors to define their problems and interests in broadly similar ways over time. It is this institutionalized interaction and scripting that is responsible in part for constituting the unique institutional logics that characterize different national political economies and guide their trajectories of economic growth (Zysman 1993).[9]

DEVELOPING SOLUTIONS THROUGH BRICOLAGE

The process through which solutions are developed after problems and interests have been defined involves additional mechanisms that foster evolutionary change. Of course, trying to specify the innovation process is the raison d'être for a significant body of evolutionary theory in economics. Much of this literature contends that institutional (and technological) change stems from both intentional and unintentional effects (Rutherford 1994, ch. 5). To begin with, actors deliberately design new institutional forms that they perceive will help them resolve their organisational problems, generate more profits, capture greater market share, and so on. However, the evolutionary character of change stems from the fact that once designs and innovations are deployed some are selected to survive more or less unintentionally over others either by the invisible hand of various processes, such as market competition, first mover advantages, and the like, or by political and other institutional constraints that determine which innovations are acceptable and survive (Brunner 1994; Nelson 1994). Thus, the evolutionary character of institutional and technological change is attributed largely to the environmental selection constraints that limit the probability that innovations will endure.[10]

Despite the many important insights of this literature, focusing on how evolutionary change is the product of selection constraints ignores how the design process that *precedes* selection may exert considerable evolutionary effects in its own right. Sometimes evolutionary theorists examine this process and attribute its evolutionary effects to the search routines and decision rules that specify when and how actors within organisations try to innovate. These rules, it is suggested, limit the probabilities that some innovations will be developed rather than others (Nelson and Winter 1982, pp. 246–62). Although this is an improvement, the focus is still on how institutions constrain innovation. However, the institutions within which actors innovate are also *enabling* to the extent that they provide a *repertoire* of already existing institutional principles (e.g., models, analogies, conventions, concepts) that actors use to create new solutions in ways that lead to evolutionary change. Actors gradually craft new institutional solutions by recombining these principles through an innovative process of *bricolage* whereby new institutions differ from but resemble old ones (Douglas 1986, pp. 66–7).[11] Ironically, a small handful of evolutionary economists have described this sort of innovative process in passing but without articulating its evolutionary implications (e.g., Nelson and Winter 1982, pp. 128–34).

The concept of bricolage is also helpful for other reasons. First, by recognizing how actors identify the means with which they construct solutions to their problems it provides a corrective to much rational choice theory that neglects to explain this process. Notably, neoclassical economic theory assumes that individuals optimize and in so doing make clear distinctions between means and ends. However, neoclassical economics does not explain how either means or ends are identified in the first place (Piore 1995, p. 100). Second, although some scholars have characterized the evolution of policies and institutions as a process of social learning whereby institutional and policy legacies inherited from the past provide models and resources that are adapted to serve new purposes (e.g., Hall 1993; Heclo 1974; Weir and Skocpol 1985), the concept of bricolage emphasizes more forcefully the innovative and creative side of institution building by drawing our attention to the fact that bits and pieces of *several* legacies (or principles) are creatively combined in a variety of new ways that contribute to evolutionary change. In this regard, the concept of bricolage captures how institution building is a process of *dynamic innovation* whereas the concept of institution building with historical legacies alludes more to a process of *mechanical imitation*, although the two are not necessarily incompatible.[12] Thus, bricolage also puts greater emphasis on agency.

Nonetheless, those who discuss the process of bricolage generally do not specify systematically the different types of institutional principles whose recombination yields evolutionary effects (e.g. Douglas 1986; Friedland and Alford 1991, pp. 254–6; Scott 1994, p. 75; but see Pierson 1993).[13] Insofar as institutions consist of technical and symbolic principles (March and Olsen 1989) we can conceive of three types of bricolage.

Much institutional change is undertaken in order to achieve various technical goals. Insofar as economic institutions are concerned these goals include such things as reducing transaction costs, increasing market share, managing labor relations problems, improving product quality, and so on.

Technical bricolage involves the recombination of already existing institutional principles in order to address these sorts of problems and thus follows a logic of instrumentality. For instance, Taiwanese entrepreneurs built massive hierarchically organized conglomerates after the Second World War by combining the institutional principles of large multi-divisional business firms that had already started to develop in Taiwan with the institutional principles of family honor that had persisted in Taiwan for centuries. As principal owners of fledgling private firms began to recognize during the 1950s that survival and growth depended on building larger and more far flung corporations they also realized that managing these conglomerates would become increasingly difficult, in particular due to principal-agent monitoring problems. They branched out into new and unrelated lines of business by extending the multi-divisional form but they placed close family members (i.e., siblings, sons, daughters and in-laws) in top divisional posts in order to ensure that the operations were run by people whom they could trust (Lin 1995). In short, two well established institutional principles were combined in order to solve a critical managerial dilemma.

However, institutional change also involves the recombination of symbolic principles through a process of *symbolic bricolage*. In this sense bricolage may also follow a logic of appropriateness. This is particularly important insofar as the solutions actors devise must be acceptable and legitimate within the broad social environment. Social scientists have recognized that in order for new institutions to take hold they must be framed with combinations of existing cultural symbols. The utilization of symbolic language, rhetorical devices, lofty and culturally accepted principles, and analogies to what is believed to be the natural world are central to the framing exercise (e.g. Campbell 1995; Douglas 1986; Snow *et al.* 1986; Swidler 1986). To the extent that actors frame institutional solutions by drawing upon these already existing cultural artifacts, their innovations are less likely to represent total breaks with the symbolic past thereby leading to evolutionary rather than radical institutional change at the symbolic level. In the Pennsylvania case, for instance, the idea that the state should provide limited consulting services, small grants, and the like to encourage local actors to reassess their situations collectively was pursued by policy makers in part because it could be framed in acceptable ways. On the one hand, it appealed to conservatives because it was framed as a marginal state intervention that would make more consequential state interventions unnecessary later. On the other hand, it attracted liberals because it was a way to reshape markets through politics (Sabel 1993). Thus, at the symbolic level the innovation was developed by imaginatively combining already existing principles of local political culture.

Economists tend to forget that institutional innovations require symbolic framing (Douglas 1986, p. 46; Hodgson 1988, p. 156). However, this is an integral part of the process even when creating the most basic economic institutions, including markets. For example, when the European Commission set out to build a single market in the European Community (EC) in response to the stagflation of the 1970s and 1980s it realized that unless it could produce ideas that could be framed in ways that were appealing to the nation states and the industrial interests involved it would be unable to forge the coalitions required for success. Hence, the Commission's market creation strategy focused on devising rules of exchange rather than rules that would alter the property rights of business or rules that would undermine governance within sovereign countries. Creating and framing solutions in ways that resonated favorably with concerns for maintaining nation-state sovereignty and the sanctity of private ownership and control of the means of production - two very important and well-established principles in the prevailing EC culture - assuaged the doubts of national political and business elites and thus facilitated ratification and implementation of the Single Unitary Market Project (Fligstein and Mara-Drita 1996).

In fact, institutional development often involves the combination of both technical and symbolic principles and follows the twin logics of instrumentality and appropriateness (e.g., Offe 1995). The emergence of total quality management (TQM) systems in Japan during the 1980s and 1990s provides an illustration of this *hybrid bricolage*. In an effort to improve productivity and product quality, reduce employee absenteeism and turnover, alleviate bureaucratic paralysis and resolve a variety of other technical problems, Japanese managers combined elements of three quite different organisational models with which they were familiar. First, employees and managers were taught production management, statistical control and other techniques from scientific management to improve efficiency and quality in product design, manufacturing, distribution and sales. Second, drawing on the human relations model, attitude surveys, teamwork, quality control circles and the like were adopted to improve worker motivation, cooperation and responsiveness. Finally, from structural analysis models firms learned to reduce the levels of bureaucracy, form federations of companies and increase divisional autonomy to eliminate bureaucratic rigidity. Moreover, all of this was framed within the ideology, symbolism and rhetoric of the human relations approach, which emphasized personal improvement and job satisfaction. Thus, TQM evolved from the recombination of both the technical and symbolic elements of older organisational models. The result was a new form of corporate organisation but one that shared a strong albeit eclectic resemblance to its predecessors (Guillén 1994b).

All of this suggests that institutional changes may actually be far more evolutionary than we might otherwise expect. Nowhere is this more evident than in postcommunist Europe (Campbell and Pedersen 1995). For instance, after the collapse of communism and the creation of formal private property rights in Hungary several large state-owned enterprises each established limited liability and joint stock companies in which they were the major shareholder along with various smaller private owners. In each case, this resulted in a network of semi-autonomous mixed-ownership companies sur-rounding a large public enterprise. In many cases the new postcommunist corporate satellites were the direct organisational successors to earlier inter-nal subcontracting partnerships that had been established informally between workers and managers during the 1980s within these same state-owned enterprises. Through internal subcontracting employees had earned extra money by working over time and on the weekends, using enterprise assets, and producing goods and services for the enterprise that were diffi-cult for managers to obtain externally through normal channels. In short, old internal subcontracting principles were combined with a new set of property rights and thus transformed into external interfirm networks (Stark 1996). Remarkably, what might appear at first glance to be an obvious example of radical institutional change is actually the result of a far more evolutionary process (see also Ostrom 1990, p. 140). In this regard, Schumpeter (1934, pp. 65–7) was wrong when he argued that the creation of 'new combina-tions of productive means,' which he viewed as the key to economic devel-opment, was a process that led to discontinuous rather than evolutionary or incremental change.

None of this contradicts the fact that actors also operate under routines, decision rules and other institutional constraints as they devise solutions to their problems or that these constraints have evolutionary consequences. Nor is this argument incompatible with the idea that institutional constraints help to determine whether a solution, once devised, will eventually be implemented or not. Indeed, in the Prussian case the crown abandoned its initial approach to railroad development once it recognized the stiff political constraints that were involved. The point is that without an analysis of how already institutionalized principles and concepts enable actors to engage creatively in bricolage it is difficult to see how actors envision solutions to their problems and construct the means with which they strive to realize their interests in the first place (Dobbin 1993, p. 3).

25

Finally, it is worth mentioning that because bricolage is a process that is guided by a logic of appropriateness as well as a logic of instrumentality the argument presented here does not imply that actors devise solutions that are necessarily more efficient over time. This is a major departure from some theorists who assume that more efficient institutional outcomes eventually evolve as a result of the selection process of market competition (e.g., Chandler 1977). Indeed, given the possibility that certain relatively inefficient practices may become institutionalized inadvertently (David 1985) and insofar as these institutions then provide the technical and symbolic means with which actors construct new solutions later, efficient solutions may be rather elusive in some cases.

DISCUSSION

To summarize briefly, evolutionary change is a process that is based to an important degree on interaction, interpretation and bricolage - three mechanisms that reveal the enabling, as opposed to the constraining, effects of institutions. This perspective improves upon the constraint-based models that characterize much evolutionary economic theory by specifying the processes through which actors define their problems and interests and through which they devise the means for dealing with them. As a result, the analysis presented here shows how actors are *subjects* shaping their institutional world rather than simply *objects* being constrained by it. The concept of bricolage is especially important in this regard insofar as it captures most clearly this duality. On the one hand, actors creatively recombine and extend the institutional principles at their disposal to devise institutional solutions to their problems. In this sense, already existing institutions are *enabling* because they provide the technical and symbolic means with which actors build new institutions as active subjects. On the other hand, the relative availability of different principles also *constrains* in a probabilistic sense the range of solutions that actors are likely to envision. In other words, if certain principles are unavailable, then certain solutions that might otherwise be quite obvious will be difficult to imagine. For example, fifteenth century artisans could envision building an array of structures ranging in size from small huts to massive cathedrals by combining in different ways the wood, nails and stone that were available to them. But because wood, nails and stone rather than steel and cement were the resources at hand, then they surely had great difficulty imagining how they might construct an edifice as tall as a skyscraper. All of this has several implications.

To begin with, this analysis bears directly on recent neo-Schumpeterian theories of economic development. Economists and economic historians within this tradition maintain that the production of value and comparative advantage turns largely on the ability of firms to develop new ways to design or produce new products and that this requires entrepreneurs to obtain privileged access to human and physical resources and devise organisational structures to coordinate the use of these resources. The ability to create organisational structures that facilitate collaborative decision making is essential to this innovative process and is facilitated in part by state policies that support research and development, education, interfirm cooperation, and the like (e.g., Best 1990, ch. 4; Lazonick 1991, pp. 70–91). My argument complements this perspective, first, by depicting the innovation process as a process of bricolage, a notion that resembles Schumpeter's earlier idea of combination but that emphasizes the importance of combining institutional and organisational principles more than simply the material resources and productive means that Schumpeter stressed (e.g., Schumpeter 1934, pp. 65–74). Second, although this literature argues that collaboration is an important part of the innovation process it is not always clear why. The answer is that collaborative decision making, depending on its composition and focus, tends to create a wider range of interpretive frames and solutions than is likely to occur if entrepreneurs operate in isolation, particularly because it creates greater possibilities for bricolage. Finally, as is true for economists in general, neo-Schumpeterians tend to neglect the importance of symbolic resources. Yet the fact that they recognize the critical role that the state plays in facilitating or inhibiting innovation implies that issues of legitimacy loom large and that the viability and success of innovative bricolage probably depends in part on the symbolic principles that are involved. Indeed, organisational analysts have demonstrated that the symbolic acceptability and legitimacy of different institutional forms is at least as important as their efficiency in determining which forms emerge and survive (March and Olsen 1989; Tolbert and Zucker 1983).

Insofar as some, but certainly not all, neo-Schumpeterians seek to specify the organisational and institutional conditions that facilitate or inhibit innovation it is ironic that they pay relatively little attention to how these organisations and institutions arise in the first place. Michael Best's (1990) otherwise excellent analysis of the organisational basis of competitive advantage in the United States, Britain, Japan and Italy is an example. The result is an exercise in *comparative statics* rather than *historical dynamics*. Recent scholarship in political science has stressed the importance of developing the latter approach in order to better understand how institutions, such as those that Best describes, develop (e.g., Thelen and Steinmo 1992). However, the approach taken by these historical institutionalists is to think about significant institutional changes as constituting 'paradigm shifts' (Hall 1993) or 'punctuated equilibria' (Krasner 1984). The problem is that they often neglect how institutional principles often carry over from one institutional period to the next via bricolage. Metaphors such as these convey the impression that fundamental institutional change is a discontinuous process when, as noted earlier, even ostensibly revolutionary institutional changes often embody significant evolutionary qualities.

To the extent that rational choice theories systematically neglect how ends and means are identified (Friedland and Alford 1991, pp. 233–4; Piore 1995, p. 100) the arguments presented here are also useful as a corrective to theories of evolutionary change that are based on rational choice principles (e.g., North 1990). Scholars have had difficulty reconciling rational choice assumptions about individualistic, self-interested action with the sort of interpretive analysis advanced in this paper (e.g., Blauwhof 1994). Indeed, rational choice scholars who have tried to integrate an interpretive analysis into their models of institutional change still assume that action is motivated fundamentally by self-interest and argue that interpretation only affects how individuals weigh the relative costs and benefits of different optimizing strategies that ultimately determine institutional outcomes (e.g., Ostrom 1990). In short, interpretation remains partitioned conceptually from the self-interest rationality and merely determines *how* actors optimize, not *whether* they do so in the first place. The implication of my argument is that such self-interested action cannot be assumed to be a universal condition and should not be reified as such (Hirschman 1977). Indeed, like other interpretive frameworks, a rationality of self-interest is socially constructed and thus may be more or less institutionalized in different historical periods and social contexts depending on the prevailing patterns of interaction (Meyer *et al.* 1987; Meyer 1994). Arguably, given the different patterns of political and economic interaction that obtain cross-nationally, the belief that one's problems, interests and courses of action are (or should be) defined from within a framework that grants pride of place to individual self-interest is quite variable, as the Danish-US comparison illustrates. The point is that an analysis of interaction and interpretation is not incompatible with rational choice theory if it is recognized that self-interest is one among several possible rationalities that may obtain, depending on local historical and institutional conditions.[14]

Specifying the conditions under which individual self-interest rather than another interpretive frame of political and economic means and ends obtains also has policy-making implications. There has been much discussion since the late 1970s about how nations can improve their structural competitiveness in the increasingly competitive global economy. Insofar as the United States is concerned many observers have advocated that more decentralized, flexible, and networked institutional arrangements should replace the centralized, rigid, hierarchically organized institutions that dominated the economic landscape during much of the twentieth century and that are believed to be too inflexible to permit firms from competing effectively in the current environment (Piore and Sabel 1984). A first step toward initiating this sort of institutional evolution, it is argued, is to recognize, as neo-Schumpeterians and others do, that we need to begin thinking about economic competitiveness in more collective and cooperative terms that puts community interests above individual interests and, in turn, organizes economic activity in collaborative ways (Best 1990; Block 1990; Piore 1995). In short, many scholars are calling for the development of a new interpretive framework including an overhaul of the neoclassical economic models that guide much public and private policy making and that base their analysis of competitiveness on assumptions about individual optimization (Lazonick 1991). To the extent that such a shift in interpretive framework requires new patterns of interaction and not just the development of new economic models and theories (Piore 1995) the question is how these new interactions can be devised.

A full exegesis on how patterns of interaction are changed and institutionalized is well beyond the scope of this paper. Nonetheless, it is worth remembering that in several cases mentioned earlier it was the state that played the critical role in establishing the prevailing interaction framework and thus the manner in which actors defined problems, interests and institutional solutions. First, the state may impose constraints that force certain types of interaction and prohibit others. Insofar as these facilitate more inclusive interactions that are focused on broader and long-term economic issues they constitute what Wolfgang Streeck (1993) called 'beneficial constraints.' For instance, he argued that if employers are free to operate unilaterally they tend to focus on short-term competitive performance and see their success as depending on the ability to extract wage concessions from labor and maintain easy access to external labor markets. This is often typical in the United States. However, if they are forced to cooperate with labor they may define their interests in the long-term and realize that they could benefit from paying higher wages, enhancing job security, and incorporating workers into corporate decision making in order to reduce labor turn-over, improve the performance of workers and facilitate more flexible production strategies. This is what happens in Germany where the state requires co-determination and a degree of industrial democracy. Second, as the Pennsylvania and Sri Lanka cases suggest, the state can encourage certain patterns of interaction and frameworks of interpretation through the deployment of various incentives, such as grants and subsidies, or the provision of personnel whose job it is to encourage actors to change their interaction patterns. Hence, the transformation of economic institutions often begins with the exercise of political power (Campbell and Lindberg 1990; Polanyi 1944).

One caveat is in order. Where significant differences in power exist, such as between employers and employees, the constraining effects of institutions may be necessary in order to get actors to interact collaboratively. Labor-management cooperation in Germany may have been unlikely in the absence of strong political constraints, such as co-determination legislation, that forced the interaction. In contrast, the collective management of common resources in Sri Lanka and elsewhere occurred in situations where the users were more or less equals in terms of status, power and most resources (Ostrom 1990). Therefore, it may be that when power differentials are substantial, cooperation and the collective definition of problems and interests will require the imposition of institutional constraints whereas when power differentials are less extreme, institutional inducements may suffice. Of course, the Pennsylvania case suggests that even when power differentials are great, such as between business and labor, if a situation is so severe that it threatens everyone involved then actors may be more apt to be induced to experiment with new forms of interaction and interpretation anyway and, as a result, the state can encourage such experimentation with little coercion.

In any case, all of this suggests that the evolution of economic institutions is an exceedingly complex process that is not easily reduced to parsimonious theorizing. Indeed, evolutionary theorists have often found it necessary to modify the simple behavioral assumptions of neoclassical theory and to incorporate insights from a variety of other disciplines, such as organisational analysis (e.g., Nelson and Winter 1982; North 1990). This paper complicates things further by arguing that an analysis of interaction, interpretation and bricolage needs to be incorporated into more conventional constraint-based models of evolutionary economic change. Nevertheless, as Albert Hirschman (1992, ch. 6) has suggested, parsimony needs to be sacrificed occasionally in order to gain a more accurate understanding of economic reality.

NOTES

* Several of the ideas in this paper were stimulated by conversations with or suggestions from Frank Dobbin, Marshall Ganz, Peter Kjaer, Leon Lindberg, Lars Magnusson, Klaus Nielsen, Jan Ottosson, Ove K. Pedersen and Yasemin Soysal.

1 Evolutionary change generally refers to change that depends heavily on the structure of already existing institutional arrangements and rationalities. Hence, the choices that actors make today bear heavily on future choices and change occurs incrementally in a path-dependent way.

2 For a comparison of these two views as applied to the evolution of economic institutions, see Blauwhof (1994). Debates over these and related issues are more than just interdisciplinary turf wars where sociologists, for example, argue against economists and vice versa. Indeed, these paradigmatic differences have also created profound divisions *within* economics (Rutherford 1994), political science (March and Olsen 1989), sociology (Swedberg and Granovetter 1992) and anthropology (Granovetter 1993).

3 This lack of data stemmed largely from the fact that everyone who was involved with the project operated from a theoretical perspective in comparative institutional analysis that tends to neglect the processes through which problems, interests and possible solutions are generated (e.g., Katzenstein 1978; Streeck and Schmitter 1985). This perspective, recently labelled historical institutionalism (Thelen and Steinmo 1992), has undergone considerable change since then and some of its proponents have started to pay more attention to these processes (e.g., Katzenstein 1994; Streeck 1993).

4 Such assumptions are particularly dangerous for the analysis of institutional changes that occurred long ago. Scholars need to take great care when studying such changes to pay attention to how the actors under investigation defined the problems for which they crafted institutional solutions. Otherwise, researchers may unwittingly substitute their own assumptions about the interests and interpretations of these actors for those that actually motivated action. For further discussion of these methodological issues, see Campbell (1995) and Hattam (1993, p. 29).

5 A number of additional factors also influenced why different countries adopted different managerial strategies to facilitate industrial development, including the international political and economic position of the country, the impact of professional groups, such as engineers and academics, the political and organisational strength of labor, and state policies (Guillén 1994a).

6 Ironically, some theorists who are closely associated with this theoretical tradition and who recognize that changes in interpretive frames yield institutional changes now deny that interaction is a necessary condition for a transformation of interpretive frames. For them it may be enough that actors identify rather than actually interact with each other for interpretive frames to change (e.g., Strang and Meyer 1993).

7 A similar situation seems to obtain in Sweden (Lundqvist 1980). See Richard Samuels (1987) for an extremely detailed discussion about how policy is negotiated through another kind of institutionalized interaction process in Japan that he calls the 'politics of reciprocal consent'. Samuels' point is that the form of interaction that typically transpires among businesses and the state in Japan has produced an interpretive framework wherein actors generally agree that policy ought to be geared to benefit both public and private interests simultaneously.

8 However, this does not mean that the negotiation of problems and interests does not occur in the United States. It does, but primarily *within* rather than between organisations. Indeed, this is precisely the sort of 'dialogical' process that Offe and Wiesenthal (1980) attributed to labor unions as being essential in order for workers to define what their problems and interests are and that other scholars have argued also tends to occur within the business community through employer and business associations (Streeck 1991).

9 The idea that the frequent repetition of interaction patterns is the basis for the institutionalization of interpretive frameworks is not the same thing as saying that stable interpretive frameworks are simply the result of socialization. To focus on socialization leads to an 'oversocialized' view of the individual that ignores human agency (Granovetter 1985). To focus on repeated interaction grants human agency a prominent place in the analysis and holds open the possibility that prevailing interpretive frameworks may be deinstitutionalized if patterns of interaction change.

31

10 Similarly, scholars who see evolutionary change as the result of path-dependent processes where a particular organisational form or technology, perhaps selected initially for idiosyncratic reasons, is more or less locked in as a result of large initial set-up costs, learning effects, coordination effects and the like are making an argument about how future choices are constrained by the institutionalization of past decisions (e.g., Arthur 1988a; David 1985; McGuire *et al.* 1993; North 1990, pp. 98–9).

11 The notion of bricolage is much like the processes of 'crossing and grafting' and metaphorical extension of institutional principles that Veblen described (Rutherford 1994, p. 95).

12 Similarly, bricolage is different from diffusion, which involves the rather straightforward percolation of a practice with little modification through a population of actors who use it for the same purpose for which it was originally intended (David and Foray 1994; Strang and Meyer 1993). The process of bricolage is one where institutional principles are modified and adapted by actors to situations for which they were not originally intended. Again, it is a more creative process than the copying upon which diffusion is based. The fact that institutional principles created through bricolage do not always diffuse easily, at least cross-nationally (Guillén 1994b, p. 84), highlights the difference between bricolage and diffusion.

13 The concept of bricolage directs our attention to the construction of solutions by actors within a particular institutional context or economic sector. Of course, solutions can also be imported from external sources, such as through outside experts or consultants (e.g., Guillén 1994a). Nevertheless, to the extent that externally imposed situations are often adopted in combination with local institutional principles, bricolage is operating and evolutionary change is implied (e.g., Campbell 1993; Campbell and Pedersen 1995).

14 Indeed, not all rational choice theory ignores how interaction and interpretation affect outcomes. Notably, game theory recognizes that definitions of strategies and interests, that is, means and ends, vary according to whether exchange will be repeated or not. But this sort of insight remains rather limited insofar as it theorizes interactions with a narrowly defined *focus* and *composition*. After all, game theory generally examines only exchange-based interactions with a very small number of participants. Thus, game theory addresses only a small subset of a much broader set of interaction, interpretation and outcome possibilities.

3. Theory of the Firm Revisited: New and Neo-institutional Perspectives

John Groenewegen and Jack Vromen

INTRODUCTION

In economics institutions seem to matter more and more, but economist differ about the extent institutions should be part of economic analysis. Following Putterman (1986, p. 21) we distinguish the following positions: institutions matter, but in a free society institutions respond optimally to environmental requirements; institutions matter and they respond over time to requirements; institutions matter, but there is no reason to assume optimality. In this paper we discuss several theories of the firm with respect to the question of optimality: in developments over time what do the different theories tell us about efficiency and path dependencies? New institutionalists assume that the operation of selection mechanisms result in efficient governance structures, whereas the neo-institutionalists hold that no reasons for optimality exist, and that path dependent development can easily result in inefficient institutional structures.

After having resolved some terminological issues (section 1), we give a rough and ready characterisation of new and neo-institutionalism (section 2). Next the differences between new and neo-institutionalism will be outlined in more detail (section 3) in a comparison between Oliver Williamson's TCE theory of the firm and new theories of the firm that draw their inspiration from old institutionalism. We argue that in contradistinction to Williamson's comparative static analysis, new neo-institutionalist theories of the firm try to develop a truly dynamic theory in which path dependencies, lock-in effects, cultural embeddedness and power relations figure prominently. In section 4, however, it will be pointed out that underneath Williamson's comparative static analysis crude but definite intuitions are hidden concerning evolutionary mechanisms that are supposed to govern processes of economic change. We shall argue that if these intuitions are taken seriously, then path dependencies and lock-in effects (and in general: history) should matter to new institutionalist theories of the firm also.

TERMINOLOGY

Two concepts need clarification: what is meant by 'institution' and what do we mean when we use the labels new and neo-institutionalists?

Institution

All definitions of 'institution' refer to a framework of behaviour: institutions reduce uncertainty and guide behaviour of actors in society. For instance: collective actions in control of individual action are regarded as institutions, and so are the highly standardised social customs and prescribed patterns of correlated behaviour. A useful distinction can be made between the 'institutional environment' (the fundamental political, social and legal ground rules that govern elections, contracting and the like) on the one hand and the 'institutional arrangements' (the arrangements between economic actors that govern the ways the actors cooperate and/or compete) on the other. The firm and other 'governance structures' are institutional arrangements; norms, routines, legal rules etc. are part of the institutional environment. The distinction is important, because the new institutional theories of the firm focus on the institutional arrangement as the variable to be explained (explanandum), while the other category of neo institutional theories focus on the institutional environment.

We define 'institution' in the broad sense including the institutional environment as well as the institutional arrangement as: norms, rules and structures that guide, constrain and facilitate behaviour of human actors.

New and Neo-institutionalists

Institutional economics has its roots in American economists like Thorstein Veblen, John R. Commons and John Mitchell. These economists are called old or classical institutionalists. Oliver Williamson introduced the label 'new institutionalists' in his *Markets and Hierarchies* (1975). He wanted to distance himself both from received orthodoxy and from old institutionalism. Contrary to received orthodoxy, Williamson takes the firm to be an institutional arrangement that is to be explained, while his analytical framework is different from the old institutionalists. Meanwhile Marc Tool and Allan Gruchy had called the followers of Veblen, Commons and Mitchell (like John K. Galbraith and Gunnar Myrdal) the neo-institutionalists. These economists clearly worked in the traditions of American institutionalism, but differed in accent and variables included into the analysis (see below). It all became very confusing with the publication of Eggertson

(1990), who discussed the broad group of economists that retain in the explanation of institutions the hard core of neo-classical economics. That is to say social scientists who follow the hard core of neo-classical economics and use rational choice models are labelled by Eggertson as neo-institutional economists.[1] In order to avoid further misunderstanding we suggest making a distinction between new institutionalism and neo-institutionalism.

We follow Latsis (1976) in defining the 'hard core' of neo-classical economics as the proposition that individual agents always find themselves in single-exit situations.[2] Single-exit situations are situations in which choices of individual agents are uniquely determined by situational circumstances, that is by situational constraints and obstacles and by the preferences of the agents involved. Neo-classical economists typically assume that agents choose options that serve their interests best. To foreclose possible misunderstanding, we want to stress here that what is central to this identification of the hard core of neo-classical economics is *not* that individual agents are engaged in conscious deliberations. What is central is that their overt, observable behaviour is the behaviour a fully rational, perfectly informed individual agent would choose (given her preferences and the prevailing situational constraints and obstacles). Thus conceived, neo-classical economics does not (necessarily) entail a claim about the processes (deliberative or otherwise) that individual agents go through before making their choices. In Latsis's words, 'the notion of single-exit situations enables neo-classical economists to ignore the '... decision-maker's inner 'environment' (p. 17). As we will see later on, this interpretation of the hard core of neo-classical economics allows for the possibility that neo-classical economists believe individual agents display optimal behaviour *because* they have gone through some evolutionary process (see note 9 in Latsis 1976, p. 5 on Pareto).

On this reading, neo institutionalists do not assume *a priori* that individual agents are always involved in single-exit situations. Information about the preferences of individual agents and their situational circumstances (in the limited neo-classical sense of prices, budgets and the like) falls short of predicting what the agents will do. We need to know more both about the agents and about the institutional settings in which they operate in order to give a plausible account of the behaviour of the agents. It cannot be ruled out in advance that agents sometimes behave in the way that is predicted by neo-classical economics. But, *pace* neo-classical economics, it cannot be taken for granted either that they will always do so. Only further detailed analysis can tell whether or not individual agents can be expected to behave optimally.

To sum up we distinguish two lines of reasoning. One springs from American institutionalism and is called old, or classical institutionalism and refers to Veblen, Commons and Mitchell. The followers of this line of thought are called neo-institutionalists and include economists like Galbraith, Myrdal, Tool, Bush, Samuels, Munkirs and the like.[3] The other line of thought has its roots in neo-classical economics and retains the core of neo-classical economics in explaining institutional arrangements. New institutionalism as developed by Oliver Williamson certainly has strong neo-classical elements, but on the other hand also ideas of old institutionalists like Commons can be found in his work. Below we will discuss the position of new institutionalism in more detail.[4]

NEW AND OLD INSTITUTIONALISM CHARACTERISED

The focus, or *explanandum*, in new institutional economics (NIE) is the governance structure to be defined as the institutional matrix within which transactions are negotiated, co-ordinated and executed. The firm, labour unions and contracts are examples of governance structures. The *explanantia* in NIE are economising actors operating in well-defined institutional environments. The characteristics of the individualistic cost minimising actors, bounded rationality and opportunism, explain the governance structures depending on the characteristics of the transaction (frequency, uncertainty and asset specificity). Hypotheses are formulated in terms of a match of governance structure and type of transaction. The methodology of the NIE can be consistently characterised in terms of methodological individualism, deductivism and confirmation oriented testing.

Old institutional economics (OIE) has a different focus: the explanandum is institutional change: why do norms, rules and structures such as firms change over time? A broad range of explanantia can be found in the works of the Old Institutionalists: technology (Veblen), collective action based on conflict and power as well as efficiency (Commons) and complex interdependencies between private and public actors (Galbraith). The methodology of the OIE is to be characterised as multi-disciplinary, holistic and systematic (but see Rutherford 1994 for a more fine-grained discussion). Open–ended pattern modelling in which specific historical conditions play a crucial role is a way to characterise the methodology (Wilber and Harrison 1978).

The differences between neo- and new institutionalism can be illustrated by comparing their view on markets and firms. In neo-classical economics markets are assumed to be efficient. Competition is conceived of as a selection process: the fittest (or fitter) will survive. When a large number of individual firms compete, given the technology and the preferences of consumers, they are forced to select and produce the most efficient combination of capital and labour (static technical and allocative efficiency). In neo-classical economics firms are production functions, which react to changes in their environment according specific rules of behaviour. Actors are not supposed to organise markets and when they do so it is considered a market imperfection, which should be eliminated by the government applying competition policies.

In new institutional approaches to markets, firms do organise competition in order to reduce production and transaction costs. But this does not mean that they can escape the type of market pressure that neo-classical economics takes to be omnipresent. Because of competitive pressures firms are forced to select the most efficient governance structures available which, due to bounded rationality, are not the 'fittest' but only the 'fitter'. Therefore, that such private ordering should not be interfered with strong government intervention based on competition law is repudiated.

In neo-institutional approaches markets are not neutral selectors. Selection processes are taken to involve more than just the elimination of inefficient ('unfit') market participants: selection processes filter the interest of specific groups and individuals involved in markets. It cannot be assumed that markets are efficient, it all depends on the type of technology, the stage of the product life cycle, the power and interests of the actors involved and the like. In general, firms organise markets in order to influence processes and performances. By means of organisation uncertainty can be reduced; on the one hand through the production and diffusion of information and on the other hand through attempts to control processes by means of agreements with competitors and customers. Private ordering can increase efficiency for all parties involved, for example when R&D investments are stimulated resulting in innovations. However, private ordering can easily transgress into collusion and serve only the specific interests of the parties involved. When efficient private ordering fails or results in collusion, then public ordering can be efficient. Public institutions can order the market in many ways: provide and diffuse information, regulate the rules of the game, act as brokers to bring private parties together in co-operative arrangements, reduce uncertainty by guaranteeing public markets or organise networks in the framework of industrial and technology policies. In neo-institutional economics it is explained that the evaluation of private and public ordering of markets is difficult and demands detailed and careful case studies in which the complex interactions between the governance structure, the institutional environment and the individual behaviour are explicitly taken into account. The differences between new and old institutionalism is illustrated in Figure 3.1.

Figure 3.1. A Layer scheme

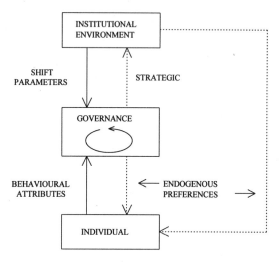

Source: Williamson (1996)

In analysing individual behaviour Williamson takes bounded rationality and opportunism to be crucial concepts. Neo-institutionalists point out that the use of these concepts raises questions. With respect to bounded rationality Williamson nowadays seems to prefer the concept of farsightedness. Individuals are not capable to calculate fully ex ante the transaction costs of different governance structures, but they look into the future far enough to anticipate opportunistic behaviour of others, to create safeguards, to adapt the price or select another technology.[5] Neo-institutionalists then point out that this implies the introduction of perceptions, of learning and demands the endogenization of preferences (the dotted arrow in Figure 3.1). The same holds for opportunism. The conditions under which trust and opportunism occur differ and are subject to strategies of actors involved and path dependent developments. The 'homo economicus' should be replaced by a

38

'homo socialis', whose behaviour can only be properly understood in relation to his environment. Opportunism can or cannot be relevant depending on the conditions and thus not only the degree of asset specificity is important, but a number of conditions like attitudinal orientation, bases of power (coercive or legitimate) and type of bureaucratic organisation (see John 1984) also play a role in understanding opportunism. Other conditions are important for understanding trust (see Noorderhaven 1996) like consistency, discreteness, loyalty, openness and receptivity. In short, neo-institutionalists believe that extensions are necessary to understand better the relation between the (social) individual and the governance structure.

With respect to the institutional environment Williamson takes the position that the environment can best be considered a shift parameter. Changes in the rules of the game (norms, legal rules and structures) change the comparative costs of governance structures. Neo-institutionalists argue that such a recognition is not sufficient. A detailed understanding of the institutional environment should always be the starting point of research of economic organisation: an analysis of, for instance, the subcontracting relations of a firm should start with a detailed study of the institutional environment, that is,. the legal rules (contract law, competition law), the political pressures (ministries stimulating network relations), the social attitude towards co-operative business relations, the cultural-historical development and the like. When these environmental conditions are clear it is possible to understand why firms in for instance Japan chose subcontracting as an efficient governance structure and why firms in the US opted more for vertical integration.

By noting that governance structures have a life of their own Williamson recognises such effects. He makes the point that 'such effects demonstrate the need for deep knowledge about organisations, but it does not imply that the economic approach to organisation (which easily misses such effects) is fatally flawed' (Williamson 1994, p. 11–12). Neo-institutionalist strongly underwrite the need of a 'deep knowledge about organisations'. They point out that corporate cultures can be so specific that governance structures that should exist according to new institutional hypothesis are not selected, simply because such transaction cost minimising governance structures are not part of the feasible alternatives for the corporation at hand (see Denzau and North 1994 on 'mental maps').

To sum up: neo-institutional economics pleads for extensions of the new institutional framework with respect to the nature and role of individual actors, the attention to be paid to the institutional environment (especially the strategy of actors towards changing and controlling the environment) and the need for an in-depth analysis of the 'life the organisation has of its own'.

THEORIES OF THE FIRM; A CONCISE OVERVIEW

Many conflicting theories of the firm exist. Most of them can be traced back to the different approaches towards institutions discussed in the introduction. In the following we will first discuss theories in which the institutional environment is given and the firm is considered to be a production function, then theories in which the firm as an institution is endogenous are considered but in which the approach is still straightforwardly neo-classical (firm as a nexus of contracts). Next we enter the new institutional world of transaction costs economics. In that world the firm has an identity of its own (firm as its own court of ultimate appeal). Fundamentally different approaches are discussed when we allow strategy to become part of the analysis. After the behavioural theories (such as Cyert and March 1963) which are basically short run, attention is focused on the more recent developments in which long-run strategies are considered to be the crucial characteristic of the firm. Learning, path dependencies, competence and routines are the key concepts here. In section 4 we will dig deeper into the underlying selection and path dependent ideas behind a selected number of the theories mentioned in this overview.

The Firm as a Production Function

Oliver Williamson has characterised mainstream micro economics as orthodoxy or received micro theory expressing the fact that firms are not endogenous. The neo-classical 'theory of the firm' is not really about firms as organisations, but about production functions in which a specific relation between inputs and outputs is presented. These 'firms' are profit-maximising entities operating in well-known given environments of market structures and technology. In fact only the minimum efficient scale determines the size of the firm. The models are perfect examples of situational determinism (Latsis 1976).

Nexus of Contracts

The firm became an explicit object of analysis in agency theory (AT) of which the work of Alchian and Demsetz on teams has been pathbreaking. The idea that a firm is a 'nexus of contracts' has been elaborated upon by

Jensen and Meckling (1976) among others. Individual agents make contracts in order to deal with 'post-contractual opportunism'. In a world of utility-maximising actors the property rights are traded in such a way that Pareto efficiencies result. Firms have no special identity: they are just bundles of contracts.

Governance Structure

In Oliver Williamson's approach contracts also play an important role, but intrafirm contracts are distinct from the contract with the 'grocer', because 'fiat' and authority are involved. The firm is 'a court of ultimate appeal', different from public courts. No doubt cost-minimising behaviour, farsightedness, remediableness and the like are concepts which closely resemble the neo-classical approach. But in terms of the explanatory factors in Figure 3.1 TCE is a fundamental step away from traditional neo-classical economics. Important questions concerning selection and efficiency remain, however (see section 4).

Dynamic Strategic Collectivity

Criticism of the neo-classical theory of the firm also came from the so-called behaviouralists (Simon, Cyert and March). Here the firm is considered to be a coalition of groups with different interests. Crucial is the idea about goals of the firm: instead of profit maximisation of one actor now the objectives of the collectivity arise from the bargaining between conflicting groups inside the firm. The goals change as aspiration levels adjust to actual achievements. The world of optimising is replaced by a world with behavioural norms and standard procedures in which the concept of 'satisficing' is central. A sequential solving of problems is introduced in which the first alternative which looks 'satisfactory' (aspiration levels) is chosen.

The managerial discretionary behaviour is extended to strategic issues in recent contributions to the theory of the firm. Then not only firms as governance structures are endogenous, but also (parts of) the institutional environment as well as the attributes of the individuals.

The differences between the new theory of the firm which is based on the heritage of the old institutionalists and the theory of the firm based on the ideas of the new institutionalists, can be explained in terms of a static and dynamic view of the firm.

TCE is a comparative static analysis. Gregory Dow (1987) made clear that such an analysis demands an independence of transaction and governance structure. In other words: the transaction should be specified independently of the governance structure. The transaction of for instance labour in the internal labour market has to be exactly the same as the transaction in the external market; only then can one conclude that governance inside the hierarchy is chosen because transaction costs were lower than outside. Now internal labour markets also have benefits in terms of the development of idiosyncratic skills. Because of the use of internal allocation labourers develop skills and over time the actors and their transactions change due to the governance structure selected. This has to be excluded in TCE by assuming that the skills remain exactly the same (which can be subsumed under an unspecified *ceteris paribus* clause, for example). Dynamics, in the sense that over time characteristics of actors and the transactions change, cannot be part of TCE.

Likewise, strategic issues in which firms purposefully invest and develop capabilities cannot be implemented in TCE. If strategies with respect to market position and the development of future capabilities are considered the crucial characteristic of the firm, however, then TCE should be complemented with theoretical concepts that capture the more strategic and dynamic issues. From recent contributions it has become clear that concepts of competence and power become crucial then (Dietrich 1994; Hodgson 1995). In the context of short-run operational decisions the input combination and the technical efficiencies are a function of the organisational characteristics. In a long-run perspective, however, the organisation and the market structure are endogenous. The idea then is that the governance structure is not to be derived from the characteristics of the transaction, or the market situation (comparative static analysis), but is to be considered to be subject to strategic decision making. It is an important insight that governance structures are purposefully selected and developed because these have a benefit in strategic terms. For instance vertical integration can contribute to the development of specific skills and/or a stronger market position. Now in such a dynamic strategic perspective concepts of power, embeddedness, routines, path dependency and culture are crucial.

With respect to power, the theory of the firm should include concepts to operationalize the power relations inside as well as outside the firm. This is poorly done so far. Efficiency then becomes 'contextual', that is to say that the lower-level (in)efficiency of the firm as a collectivity has to be distinguished from the higher-level social (in)efficiency of the sector, region or nation. It also requires reconsideration of the whole idea of 'survival of the fitter (let alone fittest)', because the anonymous process of selection is replaced by purposeful strategic actions.

With respect to embeddedness routines internal to the organisation as well as norms in the institutional environment become important. On the one hand the firm is constrained by the institutions, on the other hand the firm is able to influence them.[6] Routines purposefully developed can become an asset, a capability with which the firm can strengthen its position in the market. On the other hand a routine is also a lock in, a constraint.

The dynamics of the firm become path dependent and the path is partly subject to strategic decision making. Important for firms seems to be the entry to other varieties through for instance networks which open relations with different sources of knowledge. All this cannot be understood and analysed from a comparative static new institutional perspective, but demands a dynamic neo-institutional framework.

Before discussing how static and dynamic approaches could be combined we investigate in more detail the selection process and path dependencies in the theories of the firm of Oliver Williamson, Herbert Simon and Richard Nelson and Sidney Winter.

PATH DEPENDENCE AND NEW THEORIES OF THE FIRM

In this section we examine in detail whether the notion of path dependency matters, or should matter, to Williamson's TCE and Nelson and Winter's evolutionary theory.[7] Before we are able to address this issue, however, we need to have a more profound understanding of the explanatory mechanisms that feature in these theories. We start with a discussion of Simon's notion of bounded rationality, because this notion gives us the key, we shall argue, to uncover the notions of economic evolution that are at stake in Williamson's TCE and in Nelson and Winter's evolutionary theory.

Herbert Simon's Notion of Bounded Rationality

Herbert Simon's name is inextricably linked with the introduction of the notion of bounded rationality in economics. Individual agents lack the cognitive capacities, Simon argues, that are required to conduct the elaborate information gathering and processing and to display the sophisticated reasoning that they are assumed to do in standard neo-classical theory. At first Simon proposed to replace the neo-classical notion of maximising by his own notion of satisficing (Simon 1956, 1959). 'Satisficing' initially referred to a different sort of mental process of decision making than maximising. Not only were satisficers assumed not to know all options and their payoffs in advance, they were also assumed to settle on an option that yields satisfactory results (that is, that lie above some aspiration level). As a consequence, Simon argued, satisficers may well continue to choose an option (as long as it keeps yielding satisfactory results) that does not produce the maximum payoff.

Later on Simon acknowledged that the neo-classical notion of maximising does not (or at least need not) entail any claim about the deliberations agents may be going through (Simon 1976, 1978). It only entails a claim about actual, observable behaviour that may or may not be the outcome of some process(es) of deliberation.[8] Simon now coins 'substantive rationality' to denote this exclusive concern for actual, observable behaviour. By contrast, Simon introduces the notion of procedural rationality to mark his own interest in investigating processes of human decision making. In Simon's account of human decision making problem solving rules and routines play a pivotal role. When faced with recurrent problems, agents are supposed to follow rules or routine procedures that so far have done well. Only when they are confronted with new, unprecedented problems (or when their rules or routine procedures cease to work well in recurrent problems) are agents enticed to search for new behavioural rules. The search activities of agents, Simon holds, are also governed by (higher-order) search rules (see also Cyert and March 1963). Agents do not search randomly but selectively. Their search rules function as positive heuristics. It is observed by Simon himself that there is a notion of adaptive learning involved in his account of human problem solving that is strikingly similar to the notion of natural selection in Darwinian evolutionary theory (Simon 1983, 40):

> The generator-test mechanism is the direct analogue, in the behavioural theory of rationality, of the variation-selection mechanism of the Darwinian theory. Just as in biological evolution we have variation to produce new organisms, so in the behavioural theory of human rationality we have some kind of generation of alternatives – some kind of combinatorial process that can take simple beliefs and put them together in new ways. And similarly, just as in the biological theory of evolution the mechanism of natural selection weeds out poorly adapted variants, so in human thinking the testing process rejects ideas other than those that contribute to solving the problem that is being addressed.

Indeed, we believe that given this analogy between natural selection and adaptive learning, adaptive learning can be called an evolutionary mechanism just as natural selection. The general idea (which we can not elaborate upon here) is that both natural selection and adaptive learning work via negative feedback loops.[9] In each mechanism, actual results of variants are linked with the variants' subsequent possibilities for reproduction and

expansion. If variants have poor actual consequences, they will be eliminated in due time.

The phrase 'weeding out of poorly adapted variants' might suggest that
processes of adaptive learning may result precisely in the outcomes that are
predicted in neo-classical theory (based on substantive rationality): eventually only the best solutions prevail. Simon is aware of this. Indeed, he
argues that some of the neo-classical results that are derived from their
notion of substantive rationality are compatible with his own notion of
procedural rationality. But on the whole there is no general presupposition *a
priori* that adaptively learning agents will by necessity converge on the best,
most efficient solutions. Remnants from the past may prevent adaptively
learning individuals from arriving at optimal solutions. For one thing, each
time some behavioural rule leads to satisfactory results it is positively reinforced. This may prevent agents from looking after better rules. In this
sense, success can be said to be the enemy of experimentation. Furthermore,
even if agents search after better rules they will be guided by already
existing second-order routines. And it may well be that such search rules
were successful at the time they were established, but are maladapted to
govern search in a new, altered environment. Given this impact of historical
factors, Simon argues, only investigation of actual problem solving and
search processes can tell us whether adaptively learning agents arrive at the
best solutions.

There can nevertheless be said to be an 'inbuilt tendency' in Simon's
idea of adaptive learning that points in the direction of convergence on the
best solution. True, there is no guarantee in Simon's idea that adaptively
learning agents will ever hit on the best solution. But if we assume that
aspiration levels adapt to the ease with which they are exceeded, there is a
tendency in Simon's idea of adaptive learning in the direction of the best
solution. Implicit in Simon's idea seems to be the supposition that as soon
as an adaptively learning agent hits upon a superior solution, she at once
learns about its superiority. And if she adjusts her aspiration level in an
upward direction, it may well be that in the end only the superior solution is
satisfactory to her.

Economic Evolution in Williamson's TCE

As noted earlier, bounded rationality is one of the behavioural cornerstones
of TCE. Yet Williamson is reluctant to accept Simon's notion of satisficing.
Williamson seems to believe that 'satisficing' entails irrational behaviour.
According to Williamson, 'satisficing' belongs to psychology, not to eco-

nomics. One of the things that Williamson does not want to take over from Simon is that individuals may have different (and changing) aspiration levels and that they all may rest content with less-than-the-best. Williamson seems to be not only faithful to the traditional economic notion of rationality in that he assumes individuals to be after optimal (rather than satisfactory) results, but also in that they do not suffer from myopia in doing so. In Williamson's view, boundedly rational individuals intend to bring about optimal results and are capable of looking ahead in time.

In what sense then can the Williamson type of boundedly rational individuals be said to be limited in their pursuit of best results? Williamson argues that although individuals are farsighted, they cannot foresee all future contingencies that they would have to foresee if they were to draw complete, comprehensive contracts. This is one of the main reasons, if not *the* principal one, why Williamson disagrees with property rights and agency theorists. Yet Williamson also argues that individuals are farsighted enough to anticipate the relative net benefits of different governance structures so that they are able to choose the most efficient one. This raises the suspicion, we think, that the degree to which Williamson takes the rationality of individuals to be bounded is tailor-made to serve his theoretical purposes (see also Lindenberg 1995). It does not seem to rest on an independent judgement on Williamson's part of the cognitive capacities and limitations of individuals.

At any rate, even if we silence this suspicion there still are several pertinent issues to be resolved in Williamson's explanatory scheme. Williamson follows Simon in rejecting strong-form selectionism and accepting weak-form selectionism: survival-of-the-fittest is replaced by survival-of-the-fitter (Williamson 1987a). But if individuals are farsighted enough to estimate *ex ante* the net benefits of different candidate governance structures, why then cannot they be supposed to chose the most efficient (the fittest) one? Is this merely due to their lack of imagination? In other words, does this stem from the fact that the most efficient governance structure does not come to mind by any of the individuals involved?

If we look more carefully at Williamson's own explanation of the replacement of the U-form organisation by the M-form organisation (Williamson 1988), it becomes clear that there is more at stake than mere lack of imagination. Williamson starts from the plausible presumption that at first some managers were more alert in spotting the potential advantages of the M-form organisation over the U-form organisation. Only after their shift from the U-form to the M-form turned out to be a success, other managers followed. Thus the M-form organisation spread over the economy through imitation.

Williamson also assumes that the M-form organisation proved to have cost-saving advantages that the initiators were initially unaware of (see Williamson 1987a on the so-called full functionalism). This strongly suggests that though boundedly rational individuals can look ahead and form reasonable expectations on the basis of the information that is available at the time, they can never be certain in advance whether their expectations will be fulfilled. They may always be surprised by unexpected and unanticipated consequences. Each and every choice that a boundedly rational individual makes cannot be but a more or less informed guess, trial or conjecture.[10]

It seems that Williamson cannot have it both ways. Williamson needs the behavioural assumption of bounded rationality to distance himself from contractual theories of the firm in which the firm is conceived of as a nexus of contracts. But he also wants to go along with the presumption that these theories share with neo-classical theory that in the end only efficient firms survive. For some time Williamson (1987a) recognised the need for process analysis (analysing processes of cultural evolution in which adaptive learning and imitation play a pivotal role) that is implied in Simon's notion of bounded rationality. But after a while he seemed to have acknowledged that explicit process analysis might lead him in directions he did not want to go. He opened a Pandora's box, but once he realised the consequences he tried to shut it again.

Williamson seems to be left then with one possible escape: to argue that the question whether he is justified to assume that boundedly rational individuals always will end up with the most efficient governance structures is a non-issue really. And this is precisely what he seems to be arguing nowadays. He seems to treat the presumption that prevailing governance structures are efficient as some sort of a hard core proposition in the Lakatosian sense: a proposition which is immunised against empirical falsification. In this line of thought the real test for his TCE-research program is whether it yields novel facts that are subsequently borne out by the facts. New testable implications are to be derived from TCE-research program that have to be subjected to empirical tests. Critics of the TCE program are invited by Williamson to do the same: to develop their own research program, to derive testable implications from it and to subject them to tests.

But, given the foregoing discussion, it also seems to be perfectly legitimate, to say the least, and perfectly in tune with a true Simonian spirit to pursue process analysis further. How do managers learn about the relative

47

advantages of different governance structures? What goes into their search and learning processes and, in particular, does history, in any sense, play an important and irreducible role in them? After having discussed path dependencies and lock-in effects, we will return to these questions.

Economic Evolution in Nelson and Winter's Evolutionary Theory

Nelson and Winter (1982) also accept Simon's notion of bounded rationality. But unlike Williamson they follow Simon all the way. They take over Simon's contention that behaviour is for the greater part rule-governed. And they also share Simon's belief that search is failure-induced. Search is triggered only if the payoff of some existing rule falls below some threshold value (aspiration level). Furthermore, search itself is also guided by higher-order search and learning rules in Nelson and Winter's evolutionary theory. In their theory, however, the unit of analysis is not the individual agent, but the firm. Nelson and Winter seem to be quite confident that Simon's ideas on the individual problem-solver carry over to the firm. In fact, they argue that there are reasons to believe that firms are even more attached to routines in their daily behaviour than individual agents. A firm's routines are taken to serve the function of a *truce* that keeps latent and manifest intrafirm conflicts within predictable bounds. And they are also be said to serve the function of the firm's *memory*: in a firm's routines an important part of its specific tacit operational knowledge is stored.

Winter (1986) provides additional reasons for the persistence of specific routines in firms. The establishment of organisational routines, Winter argues, involves investment in physical and human capital. Frequently such investments are of a highly specific and irreversible nature (so that they bring 'sunk costs' with them). Another reason that Winter gives for the stability over time of a firm's routines is that firms are often confronted with weak rather than strong alternatives. Orthodox neo-classical theory starts from the presumption that decision makers are faced with strong alternatives: different options for action that are clearly distinguishable and that have clearly discernible consequences. In important decision situations in economic life, Winter argues, alternatives are mostly not that strong; the relative costs and benefits of the options available are difficult to estimate. Winter contends that weakness of alternatives implies a high level of inertia. All these reasons add up to the conclusion that a firm's resistance to change its routines may be understandable and even rational, even if changes in the firm's environment seem to demand changes in its routines.

The picture that emerges in Nelson and Winter's evolutionary theory is one of industries that are populated by a variety of firms, all having their own rigid, firm-specific routines. But in Nelson and Winter's theory there are also mechanisms working, both from within firms and from the outside, that account for change and dynamics. First (as we have already seen) firms are assumed to be engaged in processes of adaptive learning. Although these processes may themselves be governed by already existing higher-order rules they may bring about changes in the (first-order) standard operation procedures and routines. And, second, Nelson and Winter take firms to be subject to economic 'natural selection'. Only if firms succeed in making positive profits, Nelson and Winter argue, can they gather additional resources that they need to expand (and to increase their market share). Otherwise, if firms suffer losses, they cannot but contract.

The two evolutionary mechanisms that govern change in Nelson and Winter's evolutionary theory – adaptive learning and economic 'natural selection' – tend to drive industries into the direction of 'orthodox' efficient equilibria.[11] The 'inbuilt tendency' that we saw in Simon's adaptive learning is reinforced here by a tendency in the same direction produced by economic 'natural selection'. This is clearly illustrated in Nelson and Winter's evolutionary analysis of industry change caused by changed market conditions, in which they reproduce the theoretical results of neo-classical comparative static analysis. Nelson and Winter are at pains to argue that the operation of evolutionary mechanisms need not result in neo-classical efficient equilibria. But, given their own account of these mechanisms, they have to locate possible sources of inefficiency outside these mechanisms (in perpetual changes in the environment, for example).

Path Dependency

We are now ready to discuss path dependency and its relevance for the new theories of the firm discussed above.

Generally speaking, 'path dependency', as it is developed by authors like P. David and B. Arthur, is the idea that accidental historical 'small' events may determine the course of subsequent developments. In this sense, path dependency implies that history matters. History matters not only in the Simonian sense that remnants of the past affect present and future activities. When there is path dependency history matters in an even more profound way: small historical events may trigger a process in the direction of an inefficient equilibrium even when in the course of this process superior lines of action are tried. 'Path dependence' is opposite to the traditional idea

49

(that dominated economic thought for long) that systematic forces or mechanisms steer economic development to some unique and efficient equilibrium position. In this traditional idea economic development is not and cannot be affected by accidental historical events. No matter what initial steps are taken, the traditional story goes, systematic forces see to it that eventually the unique and efficient equilibrium will be reached.

Arthur and David do not start from the presumption that all economic processes have unique and efficient equilibria. In competition between different technologies (or different standards in technological applications), for example, there are typically multiple equilibria. 'Path dependency' is of interest especially when the initial steps taken are not the superior ones in terms of efficiency (among the set of feasible initial steps). Even though these first inferior steps would be outcompeted initially by superior ones (if they would have been tried), the first inferior steps actually taken may set a self-reinforcing, irreversible process in motion, so that after a while the superior lines of action cannot outcompete the inferior ones any more. 'Lock-in effects' may then obtain; the economy may get stuck in an inefficient equilibrium.

How do these notions of path dependence and lock-in effects fit in with Williamson's TCE and Nelson and Winter's evolutionary theory? At first sight these notions do not fit in at all. The primary reason seems to be that 'path dependence' and 'lock-in effects' presuppose the existence of *positive* feedback, whereas Williamson and Nelson and Winter follow Simon in basing their ideas on economic evolution on *negative* feedback. Let us explain. As we have seen, neither Simon nor Williamson nor Nelson and Winter presume *a priori* that the best, most efficient line of action will ever be tried. Accordingly, they reject the claim that the most efficient, the fittest, will by necessity survive. But they are all wedded to the idea that if the most efficient line of action is tried, there will be a tendency to replace lines of action that are displayed so far by this superior line of action. For there will be negative feedback then: agents will observe that the actual consequences of displaying the lines of action that are followed so far are worse than those of displaying the superior one, and, consequently, they will shift from the inferior ones to the superior one.

By contrast, Arthur and David argue that adoption of some inferior line of action may be self-reinforcing even if some superior line of action is tried. The reason for this is that there may be increasing returns to adoption: the more the inferior line of action is displayed, the higher the return of each additional adoption of this line of action. Even though the returns of the superior line of action exceed that of the inferior one initially, they cease to do so after some critical point is trespassed. From then on increasing returns to adoption (of the inferior line of action) result in positive feedback, leading to lock-in to an inefficient equilibrium.

It can be argued in addition that Arthur's and David's notions do not fit in with Williamson's TCE in particular for the following reason. Arthur (1988) lists several sources of increasing returns to adoption. All sources relate to technology. For example, the adoption of some technology sometimes offers advantages to 'going along' with other adopters of it. Then it is attractive to join a network of users who all profit from 'network externalities'.[12] Another source of increasing returns of adoption that Arthur mentions is technological interrelatedness. As a technology becomes more adopted, a number of other sub-technologies become part of its infrastructure. The technology may then be at an advantage if its technological infrastructure is relatively well developed. Now it is not difficult to imagine how these examples of increasing returns to adoption are, or at least should be, of interest to Nelson and Winter's evolutionary theory. For the focus of Nelson and Winter's theory on routines as a firm's specific and tacit 'know-how'.[13] But the examples do not seem to bear on Williamson's TCE with its focus on contractual issues. Firms that have adopted the M-form organisation form, for example, simply do not seem to profit from other firms adopting the same M-form. And neither do they seem to flourish in one sort of 'contractual infrastructure' better than in others. In short, technological interrelations seem to be quite different from, and to have quite different implications than 'contractual interrelations'.

More recent work by Arthur (1991) on learning suggests, however, that path dependency may also arise in non-technological settings. It is this work, we submit, that shows that 'path dependency' is relevant to Nelson and Winter and Williamson alike. Arthur's account of individual learning may, at least in its broad outlines, be acceptable to Williamson. For, like Williamson, Arthur embraces Simon's notion of bounded rationality without going all the way with Simon in replacing 'economic' maximising with 'psychological' satisficing behaviour. In fact, the learning algorithm that Arthur specifies is in a sense reminiscent of the type of rational learning that is compatible with the maximising paradigm: Bayesian learning. In Arthur's learning algorithm individuals are supposed to update their (prior) beliefs by taking their experience into account, just as a rational Bayesian learning individual would do. But there is an important respect in which Arthur deviates from rational Bayesian learning accounts. In Arthur's learning algorithm individuals diminish their exploration efforts when they have hit on a line of action that consistently scores well. It is for this reason that in

Arthur's account of learning individuals may not get to know what line of action is best.

In Bayesian learning exploration efforts are assumed to be independent of the previous experiences the individuals have with certain lines of action. This is why Bayesian learning individuals eventually will find out which line of action is best. By contrast, in Arthur's learning algorithm individuals tend to repeat lines of action that paid off relatively well early on (instead of exploring fresh new alternatives). This after all may look very similar to Simon's notion of satisficing. For satisficers also terminate search efforts as soon as they have found a line of action that does reasonably well (that is, the consequences of which exceed some aspiration level). But strictly speaking we can be sure of this only if the satisficers so far have not encountered the best line of action. As soon as satisficers would encounter the best alternative (without engaging in new time-consuming search efforts), they would at once notice that this alternative has better conse-quences and hence (under the supposition that they would raise their aspiration level) they would shift to this best alternative.

Not so in Arthur's learning algorithm. In Arthur's learning algorithm individuals may have tried the best alternative but may nevertheless con-tinue with another line of action. The reason for this is that the superiority of the best alternative need not show itself the first time(s) it is tried. Arthur assumes that each line of action has a distribution of rewards and that the individuals do not know of these distributions in advance. Furthermore, the actual rewards of some line of action that accrue to individuals are assumed to be drawn randomly from its distribution. The following example of Arthur (1994, p.135) nicely illustrates this point:

> [For example] one possible action – drilling for oil in a particular tract – when chosen may result in consistent payoffs clustered around $10M. An alternative – drilling in another tract – may pay zero the first ten times it is undertaken. But there may be 5 percent chance it pays $500M. There is no supposition that the agent – or any learning algorithm – knows this in advance; and it may take considerable exploration to find this out.

In an example like this, it may well be the case that the agent goes on with drilling in the tract that pays her about $10M. In Arthur's terms this means that there is a tendency then to (over)exploit this particular tract and to cease exploring the other tract. In a sense, the agent is learning too fast here. She settles too quickly on an inferior line of action that, given her first expe-riences with it, seemed more promising than the superior one. Once she continues the inferior line of action, the process may well be self-reinforcing, resulting in a lock-in to the inferior line of action.

Whether the search for more efficient governance structures is in some relevant respects similar to something like drilling for oil remains to be seen.[14] But at least the dynamics of Arthur's learning algorithm seem to accord quite well with Williamson's belief on bounded rationality. And besides that, the general idea that individuals are in the grip of processes of habituation (especially with regard to lines of action that initially do relatively well), and so resist trying other lines of action, also seems to have some independent plausibility. This is a valid reason, we think, for Williamson and others working in the transaction cost economics tradition to take path dependency more seriously than they have done so far.

As we have seen, the tension or trade-off between exploitation and exploration is crucial to Arthur's learning algorithm (see also March 1990). As long as exploration prevails, convergence on superior lines of action can be expected.[15] But when exploitation 'drives out' exploration, learning may result in lock-in to inferior lines of action. This raises the question when, under what circumstances, exploitation dominates exploration and *vice versa*. Arthur suggests that this depends on the problem(s) at hand. Exploitation tends to dominate exploration (and hence lock-in effects can be expected to obtain) if alternative lines of action and their respective payoffs are difficult to discern. If on the other hand alternatives and their payoffs are distinct and clearly different (easy to discern), then exploration tends to dominate exploitation (and hence optimal outcomes can be expected).

Arthur's distinction between easy and difficult discrimination of alternatives resembles Winter's (1986) distinction between strong and weak alternatives. As we have seen, Winter speaks of strong alternatives when the set of feasible alternatives and their payoffs (costs and benefits) are well-known to agents and of weak alternatives when those are unclear to agents. This distinction is made by Winter to make the point that agents may well stick to their existing rules and routines if they are faced with weak alternatives. Arthur arrives at a similar conclusion: if alternatives are difficult to discriminate, agents tend to be loath to explore new options for action. Agents are more likely to settle soon for lines of action that initially pay off best. And this, we have seen, can result in lock-in to inefficient lines of action. We could say, therefore, that Arthur provides Nelson and Winter with an argument to strengthen their point: economic evolution need not lead to efficient outcomes (even if we abstract from possible disturbances and counteracting forces).[16] And the sources of inefficiency need not lie outside the operation of evolutionary mechanisms. The evolutionary mechanism of adaptive learning may itself be responsible for inefficient outcomes. If this is bad news for Williamson and his collaborators in TCE, so be it.

In fact, learning processes may involve path dependencies in an even more fundamental way. Denzau and North (1994) argue that Bayesian learning presupposes that the learning agents already have the right categorisation and mental model (cf. also Binmore 1994). They argue that this presupposition is dubious in the light of contemporary theories of learning and of experimental evidence. Besides direct learning, learning within some mental model, there also is indirect learning – learning that accounts for changes of mental models. This latter, indirect type of learning need not converge in the right mental model. Thus, Denzau and North's analysis further underwrites Arthur's point that there are path dependencies in human learning, possibly leading to inefficient outcomes.

CONCLUSIONS

If we circumscribe path dependency in a very general way as the idea that historical events may prevent economic processes from converging on efficient equilibria, it is expedient, we think, to distinguish between three senses of 'path dependency'. Each of the senses corresponds to a different way in which economic processes may move in inefficient directions. First, economic processes may be interfered with by disturbing causes. For example, environmental changes may disturb processes of convergence to efficient equilibria. This first sense is non-controversial; it seems to be acknowledged by neo-classical economists, new and neo institutionalists alike.[17] Second, if we start from the assumption that individuals are boundedly rational and assume in addition that individuals are guided by antecedently established higher-order rules in their search efforts, then we have here another way in which the past may steer economic processes in an inefficient direction. For the *a priori* presumption is unwarranted that antecedently established search rules are perfectly suited to solve current problems. This second sense seems to be unacceptable only to neo-classical economists; both new and neo-institutionalists (should) have no problem in digesting it.[18] The third sense in which path dependencies may obtain, finally, is grist to the mill only to neo-institutionalists. New institutionalists such as Oliver Williamson are likely to be unwilling to take it to heart: even if we abstract from path dependencies in the first two senses, and even if the superior line of action is actually tried, there still is no guarantee that economic processes eventually settle at the superior line of action. The source of (possible) inefficiencies here lie in the evolutionary mechanisms themselves. There may be an inbuilt tendency that favours continuing inferior lines of action that initially worked out well over superior ones.

It can be concluded from our discussion that our criticism of new institutionalist theories of the firm (section 4) vindicates part of the external criticism that neo-institutionalists have formulated (section 3): history matters (or at the very least can matter) to the evolution of governance structures and routines. There is no reason to assume *a priori* that path dependence and lock-in effects pertain only to competition between different technologies in the long run. Recent developments in learning theory strongly suggest that path dependencies and lock-in effects may obtain also in short term learning processes. Yet, on the other hand it seems to be premature to declare that path dependencies and lock-in effects are ubiquitous in all processes of economic evolution. This is due mainly to the following two reasons.

First, there is a bewildering variety of different learning theories among us nowadays. This indicates that we perhaps should not rely on any of them too much. Maybe some theory will establish itself as the orthodoxy after a while. But the great number of learning theories may as well reflect the fact that learning is highly contextual (Denzau and North 1994, refer in this respect to the importance of information flows). Individuals may employ different learning rules in different situations. Our second reason is closely related to the last remark. The individuals' 'appetite' for exploring fresh alternatives may differ from the one problem situation to another (Denzau and North 1994, refer in this respect to the motivation of actors due, for instance to bad performances of their firm). And the prospects of getting close to efficient outcomes may differ accordingly. All this underwrites the need for further process analysis.

NOTES

1 Including Property Rights School, Transaction Costs Economics, the New Economic History, the New Industrial Organization, the new Comparative Economic Systems and Law and economics (Eggertson 1990, p. 6).
2 Cf. Popper's views on situational logic (or situational analysis, or situational determinism as it is also sometimes called).
3 These institutionalists can be found in associations like the Association for Evolutionary Economics (AFEE), which sponsors the Journal of Economic Issues and the European Association for Evolutionary Political Economy (EAEPE).
4 Langlois has a broad interpretation of new institutionalism; we focus on the work of Oliver Williamson.

5 See section 4. for a further discussion.

6 This approach is referred to as methodological institutional individualism. See Rutherford (1994) for a sophisticated discussion.

7 Most evolutionary economists working in the tradition of Nelson and Winter's seminal magnum opus seem to be readily prepared to embrace 'path dependency'. See, e.g., Hall (1994) who even elevates 'path dependency' to the status of a first principle in evolutionary economics. By and large, economists in the TCE tradition seem to be much more reluctant to accept 'path dependency'.

8 Simon also recognized that neoclassical economists are mainly interested in aggregate, and not in individual behaviour.

9 See Vromen (1995) for an elaboration of this point.

10 This bears some resemblance with K. Popper's view on scientific development.

11 Nelson and Winter speak of 'search effects' and 'selection effects' that are produced by the two evolutionary mechanisms respectively.

12 See e.g. also Katz and Shapiro (1985) on this.

13 Nelson (1995) now emphasizes the importance of path dependence in analyzing processes of economic evolution.

14 Silverberg, Dosi and Orsenigo (1988) argue in effect that finding out what technology is best is similar in relevant respects to Arthur's account of finding out which tract is best for drilling oil.

15 Levitt and March (1988) speak in this respect of a competence trap, due to increasing returns to experience.

16 This is gratefully acknowledged in Nelson (1995), for example. See also Dosi and Marengo (1994) in which it is argued that organizational learning about norms, competencies and corporate structures can result in multiple 'organizational trajectories', most of which are inefficient.

17 This is not to say, of course, that they all attach equal weight to these 'disturbances'. In particular, neoclassical economists tend to treat disturbances as abnormal occurrences (that are excluded theoretically in their unspecified ceteris paribus clauses). By contrast, neo institutionalists treat these 'disturbances' as essential occurrences in real economic life that any acceptable theory has come to grips with.

18 This idea is central to current evolutionary theorizing in economics. Witness, for example, the notion of technological paradigm in Dosi (1984).

4. Path Dependence of Knowledge: Implications for the Theory of the Firm

Bart Nooteboom

INTRODUCTION

There is a double meaning in the title of this paper. I will argue that knowledge, of people and organisations, is path-dependent in the usual sense that directions for future development are foreclosed or inhibited by directions taken in past development. A classic example is QWERTY: the arrangement of symbols on a keyboard (David 1985).[1] Path dependence also appears in the notion of 'technological trajectories', which Dosi (1984) associated with the maintenance of existing paradigms in 'normal science' identified by Kuhn (1962). This already provides a link with path dependence of knowledge, which we will develop further in the present paper.

I will also take up the perspective of 'neural networks', to argue that knowledge, in people and organisations, is based on paths of interaction between entities that can receive and send signals. In individual cognition those entities are, of course, neurons, and in organisational cognition they are people. I will also argue that the two issues are connected: knowledge is path-dependent in the first sense because of the way it is based on paths in the second sense.

Subsequently, I will consider some of the implications in the theory of organisations. But first I will start with a brief recapitulation of the position of economic agents and their cognition in economic theory, and the questions that need to be answered in the theory of the firm.

The present article follows an earlier, more programmatic one, which set out directions for making transaction cost theory dynamic (Nooteboom 1992). Part of that programme is executed in simulation studies of search processes by which transaction partners seek each other out and mutually contribute to each other's learning (Nooteboom 1995; Péli and Nooteboom 1995). The present article seeks to give a broader exploration of relevant questions and possible answers in the theory of the firm. The exploration is still limited: full treatment of the subject would require a book.

Of course, the brain as a metaphor, analogy or model for organisations was taken up before by others: e.g. Simon (1947), March and Simon (1958), Morgan (1986). Here, I try to expand on that work.

THE SUBJECT IN ECONOMIC THEORY

Our history of the subject in economic theory can be brief, because it is virtually non-existent even in the most subject-oriented part of economics: the Austrian school. In this summary I make use of the survey by Woo (1994).

Classical economics was preoccupied with the search for an objective basis for value in the (labour) cost of production; the subject, certainly in the form of the consumer, was not admitted on the agenda. With Marshall and Jevons, neo-classical economics started its development with an opening to the consumer in the form of marginal utility as a basis for value. But with the transition from cardinal to ordinal utility, in the work of Pareto, utility as a cause of value was replaced by a pure logic of choice, in which observed choice revealed preference, so that investigation into the formation of preference became redundant. Thus, having been admitted into the house of economics, the subject was soon evicted again in the later development of neo-classical economics of Walras, Hicks and Samuelson. This was considered to be a bonus, because it kept economics independent from the fickle science of psychology.

The Austrians (Von Mises, Hayek) are said to be subjectivists, but in fact the Austrian subject remains a black box. She was put on a pedestal, to be revered rather than studied. She is supposed to be rational, self conscious and creative. She does lack information, but 'picks it up' from the market, which is seen as a discovery process. Prices signal scarcity, and guide the entrepreneur in her search for profitable enterprise. Even in Schumpeterian economics, innovation is exogenous, as an unexplained emergence of 'novel combinations'. The formation of perception, knowledge, insight and evaluation, and the role of interaction between people, are absent from the theory. So, while in the later development of neo-classical economics the subject was ushered out, in Austrian economics she is present but empty: there is no theory of how subjects develop knowledge and form preferences. Furthermore, in Austrian economics the subject is sacrosanct, autonomous. In this, Austrian economics is as much based on methodological individualism as neo-classical economics is: no allowance is made for effects of socialisation or intersubjective interaction on the formation of knowledge and preferences.

It is absurd that economics does not contain any theory of cognition and evaluation by people and firms and in interactions between them, at a time when there is rapid and radical change in technology and markets, and firms are struggling to keep up, with an emphasis on innovation, training, learning and forms of co-operation between firms.

In the present development of 'information economics' there is recognition that economic subjects may lack information, and time and money is needed to acquire it. There is even recognition that different people may not be equal in their capacity to absorb information, and that specialists may be required to combine and analyse information (see, for example Casson 1994; Sah 1991). In his survey of fallibility in organisations, Sah (1991) identified:

1. selection bias: different people may select different parts from the 'available data'. Note that the first point assumes that there are 'available data', which suggests that those are somehow objective and equal in meaning to every person, if only she can access it. To selection bias I would add:
2. heuristic procedures in choice and decision making that violate the economists logic of choice, such as 'framing' (cf. Kahneman, Slovic and Tversky 1983);
3. distortions in communication, due to 'limited capacity for articulation and reception';
4. interpretation bias: a stimulus ('data') may generate different interpretations for different people.

Note also that Sah attributes problems in communication not to differences in understanding or meaning but only to problems of transmitting some given content of knowledge. To this I would add problems of communication due to differences in understanding. In the extreme, this may yield what Kuhn (1970) called 'incommensurability' of different 'paradigms'.

Even in the new information economics, the implicit epistemology is that of metaphysical realism, and methodological individualism is maintained. Or, in other words, the exclusion of psychology and sociology is maintained. Information, if it is acquired, is objective, concerning realities that are there to be observed. Once information is acquired it is the same for all. In particular, there is no path dependence: the meaning of information and development of cognition and evaluation are not dependent on how they developed in the past. And, connected to this, there is no variation of interpretation or meaning of information across people and contexts. Concerning preferences, on the other hand, the implicit epistemology is idealistic (cf. Woo 1994): preferences are given somehow, independently of experience. Thus we see a divorce between preference and cognition, in a peculiar mix of idealism and metaphysical realism.

With Herbert Simon as the only exception that I can think of (among well-known economists), economists have ignored the admonition to social scientists by Bridgeman (1955, p. 450, quoted by Williamson 1989, p. 135) that: 'the principal problem in understanding the actions of men is to understand how their minds work'. Williamson recognised bounded rationality in the sense that prior to a contract agents cannot be sure about the partners intentions, and there may be future contingencies that cannot be foreseen, so that contracts cannot be closed. But with Williamson also, in spite of this, there appears to be no intention to 'understand how their minds work'.

To Bridgeman's admonition we should add the need to understand how interaction between people and the institutions that they create affect how their minds work. In contrast with neo-classical and Austrian economics, neo-institutional and evolutionary economics pay attention to social dimensions; to the role of institutions. As defined by North (1989), institutions are formal and informal rules that constrain individual behaviour. However, they are short on showing how this affects the formation of knowledge and preference. Furthermore, they appear to neglect idiosyncrasy, that is differences between people with different identities, associated with different paths of development.

As Woo (1994) put it: economics as a whole is lacking in causal depth and causal breadth. Causal depth requires a psychological theory of understanding and evaluation by people, and causal breadth requires a sociology of how institutions affect such understanding and evaluation. It is only by combining the two that we can evade the causal emptiness of conduct that characterises economics, and that we can achieve a balance between the subjective and the objective. If that ends the autonomy of economics as a separate science, and ties it to a partnership with the fickle sciences of psychology and sociology, most economists may not like it, but it is the price that has to be paid. And if economists refuse, organisation scientists will do it for them. The development of neo-classical economics and its apparent inability to take cognition and institutions seriously is itself an example of path-dependence in knowledge (Eggertsson 1993). In terms of Lakatos' theory of science, the neo-classical (or neo-Walrasian, cf.

Weintraub 1988) 'research programme' has developed such a strong 'positive and negative heuristic' around a 'core' that contains methodological individualism, that the causal depth and breadth requested by Woo appears unattainable in that programme (cf. Nooteboom 1986, 1993a). On the other hand, institutional and evolutionary economics require some unifying, underlying theoretical framework to provide some coherence (to avoid what Eggertsson called the 'open field syndrome'). I propose that cognitive science, united with sociology, is to be developed to yield that framework.

COGNITION, ACTION AND LANGUAGE

So, let us seek help from cognitive science. A problem (which was to be expected) is that there also, ideas diverge.[2] The journal *Cognitive Science* (1993) recently dedicated a special issue to a debate between two schools of thought: the school of systems of symbolic representation (Newell and Herbert Simon, among others), and the school of 'situated action'. With apologies for possible sinister connotations, we abbreviate the two to 'SS' and 'SA'.

According to SS cognitions can be reconstructed in terms of operations on symbols, which are in some way embodied in patterns of neural activity. This suggests a logical distinction and temporal sequencing between symbolisation and action: the first precedes and in some sense guides the latter, by triggering motor mechanisms. Concepts are formed and then applied to action. SS does, however, admit that symbolisation occurs in interaction with the environment, on the basis of action. According to SA the formation of patterns of neural activity is so much a matter of interaction with action that the logical sequence is in doubt. Every action to some extent modifies the patterns of neural activity, to such an extent that one could just as well say that action precedes neural patterning. It is meaningless to conceptualise the latter as being independent of context; as something that can be transferred, qua entity, from one context to another. Thus, any notion of action or learning as transfer to novel contexts is misleading. Learning and action go together in the construction of neural patterns of activity.

I should say that I am an adherent of the SA view, as formulated here.[3] One reason for my stance is that in SA I see a basis for integrating sociology and psychology in the context of economics. A second reason for liking SA is that it is in line with Wittgenstein's ideas of 'meaning as use'; -

meanings being 'forms of life' - cognitive connections often having the nature of 'family resemblances' rather than membership of a common class of attributes. I believe these to be important intuitions. But they require elaboration, and in this paper I attempt to contribute to that.

However, I am not convinced that SS and SA are irreconcilable. A crucial point in the debate between them is whether the crux of a symbol is that it has a reference (denotation, extension, 'Bedeutung' in Freges terminology), and what exactly that means. Next to reference, meaning is generally thought to have a second dimension: sense (connotation, intension, 'Sinn' in Freges terminology). If reference constitutes an ordering of the world into classes, or how things are 'given', Frege characterised 'Sinn' as 'the way in which they are given' ('Die Art des Gegebenseins') (Geach and Black 1977; Thiel 1965). A crucial question now is: how determinate and context-independent is reference. In the philosophical/logical/semantic/linguistic literature, the nature of denotation is highly problematic. And therefore the difference between SS and SA is problematic, since it is based on the problematic notion of denotation. A clarification of the problematic notion of denotation might reconcile SS and SA.

To elaborate on the problem of denotation, consider the work by Quine and others on the 'inscrutability of reference', and problems of logical quantification and substitution into 'intensional contexts' (believing, thinking, expecting and the like, or modal contexts of necessity (Linsky 1977; Davidson and Harman 1972)). Consider the famous example of the morning and evening star, which in fact have the same denotation in the form of the planet Venus. But suppose you do not know that, and consider them to have different reference, since you observe the one in the evening and the other in the morning (so that they have different senses, i.e. 'ways of being given': one in the evening and the other in the morning), and have no sufficient astronomical knowledge to figure out their identity. Then you cannot substitute 'salva veritate', that is while preserving truth, 'morning star' for 'evening star' in the following proposition: 'you expected the evening star to come up around this time of the evening'. Substitution is in conflict with what you in fact believe. Substitution into such belief contexts would require not only identity of reference, but also of sense. But sense depends on both the subject and the context: how reference is given is how, in what use context, and on the basis of what prior experience and knowledge you consider it.

Often there are no universal, necessary and sufficient conditions for determining reference. What are the conditions for an object to belong to the reference of the word 'chair'? Having legs, a seat and back and/or arm rests? But there are chairs without legs. But if we drop the condition of having legs: a seat for a child on a bicycle is not called a chair. Although, perhaps in some language it is. Many years ago the newspapers printed an item, with photograph, of someone who had shaped a stuffed cow into a chair: 'Watch him sitting in his cow: what a beautiful chair'. Is this proper reference? Would it have been proper reference without the story, and without the picture of someone sitting in the cow? Whether application of a term to an item is accepted or not as 'proper reference' depends on the context: the setting and the intentions involved, in other words, on the action context.

The literature on categorisation, i.e. the formation of concepts by which we order the world, also shows that categories cannot be captured in terms of sets of necessary and/or sufficient attributes for proper assignation of reference (Neisser 1987). They are 'graded structures', involving a structure of attributes, mostly in the context of action. Children do not group objects according to their material or abstract shape, but on the things one can do with them; i.e. on how they can be fitted into meaningful action sequences (scripts). For example, they are found to classify objects not as metal spoons, boxes, hammers, pans; not round objects of wood, metal, plastic, clay; but wooden spoons, metal forks, plastic plates and linen napkins.

Scripts can be represented as lines, indicating the action sequence, with nodes, which function as variables that allow for substitution by diverse items (such as tools, materials, and the like). This seems to be the appropriate manner to conceptualise reference: a fitting into scripts. Thus, in a restaurant script, payment with cash may be substituted by payment by credit card, but the latter only after a change in the money system. This implies allowance for dubious substitutions, which may, when successful, turn out to be innovations. In other words: reference is inherently vague, or incompletely determinate, and this is a good thing since without it innovation would be hard, if not impossible. If there were sharp necessary and sufficient conditions for reference, there would be no admittance of unorthodox practice as a step towards innovation. On the other hand, for a minimum of stability in practice, some obstacle to unorthodoxy must be present. This brings us back to an argument from Kuhn: some conservatism in maintaining incumbent practice is rational. This can also be reconstructed with an evolutionary argument. The formation of routines whose adequacy is not questioned has survival value, by allowing to focus attention on crises that demand attention. But too much conservatism inhibits adaptation to changed conditions. Survival requires a balance of, on the one hand, routine, habit, conservatism, continuity, and on the other hand, adaptability,

63

innovation, shift. What the right balance is depends on the volatility of the environment. Our minds and language are masters at this. How about our organisations?

One of the purposes of the above was to find a basis for reflecting on the debate between SS and SA. I find a position which seems close to SA. Concepts and categories are not simply vats of denotation to which an item, taken by itself, is or is not properly deposited, and which one can transport between contexts to properly test denotation. Concepts are pliable: they allow for different judgements of denotation, depending on the context of action. At the same time, action, in supplying new senses (connotations) generates shifts in denotation. Or more precisely:

- reference is to some extent indeterminate;
- reference is based on sense, which depends on the action context, so that, in that sense action guides reference (and hence symbolisation).

These considerations give further reason to being an adherent of SA. However, if symbols are thus allowed to be incompletely determinate in their reference, which is guided by action, SS is correct in pointing out that they do have some continuity across action contexts. If symbols are associated with scripts, then from one context to another they may remain the same scripts, although different substitutions into nodes occur, unorthodox substitutions may be tried, different sequencing of nodes, and splits of the script into different branches may occur as the action context requires it. The question then is: what is the limit of changes under which one can still talk about the same script? That, we submit, is also context dependent: it depends on the action context, which may take the form of the exercise of a wider script in which the focal script is embedded.

BRAIN

Can the foregoing be further substantiated and clarified if we descend to the level of neurons? And if we ascend again to the level of organisations? Let us attempt to summarise insights from neurological research. The brain consists of neurons that are connected, in networks, with lines along which electro-chemical signals can be sent, fired by the neurons as a function of incoming signals and thresholds of firing. A brain function, including a concept, may then be associated with a certain path or pattern of firing. The activation of a path, triggered by some stimulus, provides a stimulus for other paths, including the generation of motor activity. Renewed stimulus from action feeds back to the path. If stimuli conform to a fixed pattern, habituation occurs: attention is inhibited, and the activity becomes unattended by conscious thought.[4] As formulated by Magoun (1969, pp. 170–180; quoted in Heyting 1971, p. 31):

> With recurring presentation of the same signals, which initially provoked orientation, arousal and related changes become progressively reduced in intensity and duration, until they fail to occur at all and a stage of habituation ensues. This is not attributable to fatigue or other generalised impairment ..., for, during habituation, whenever signals regain a novelty, by some change in their parameters, full-blown orientation is again evoked.

If I understand correctly, habituation takes place by a narrowing of the scope of neurons to respond to stimuli, and with inhibition of its ability to trigger higher level paths that form the basis of conscious orientation. Note that, given boundedness of cognitive capacity, this is rational: it allows our cognitive system to focus limited capacity for attention on what is not routine. Further, success of action or the lack of it may trigger adjustments to the path. Parts of a path that go together with success are reinforced (by adjustments of thresholds), and parts that are not are weakened. In this way paths are 'etched in', and irrelevant appendages and connections are deleted. Additions to the path, as contexts of activation shift, are also possible. It appears that some trial and error is indispensable in this: additions are appended more or less at random, to be reinforced or not according to their association with success.[5] As a result, a path is to some extent robust under deviations: new connections can be included in the path without affecting its overall pattern of connections to other paths. Concepts can be mutually related in the sense that the activation of one path may be triggered or inhibited from another.

The implication is that brain functions can be both triggered and inhibited; are localised, modular, connectable and hierarchical; are subject to functional redundancy; and are subject to reconfiguration.

Not only are 'large' modules of function localised in the brain, such as vision in the visual cortex, co-ordination of movement in the cerebellum, intellectual capabilities in the prefrontal cortex, and emotion in or near the amygdala, which is situated near the brain stem. Within functions of emotion, separate functions, such as fear, appear to have separate locations. Some functions are embodied in connections between regions. Connections between the prefrontal lobe and the amygdala can inhibit fear response by rational argument. For example, it can inhibit the fear of lions in a zoo

65

where lions are behind cages. In an experiment rats were taught to fear some stimulus which was accompanied by a shock of pain. Elimination of the amygdala eliminated the fear. A person with some damage to the amygdala could no longer recognise facial expressions of emotion, while she could still recognise faces as familiar (family, friends) (*International Herald Tribune*, 8-12-1994).

In spite of the fact that some functions are localised, in case of physical removal of a corresponding part of the brain there is an ability, to some extent, to regenerate the function elsewhere. This phenomenon, plus the phenomenon of adaptability of functions by inclusion and exclusion of elements of pathways implies redundancy of function, up to a point (cf. Morgan 1986, p. 98). This means that a node in the network (neuron) can function in various configurations of connections, i.e. in various functions. Note that there is a trade-off between specialisation and functional redundancy: specialisation (assignment of functions to fixed units) is more efficient, due to habituation, but less flexible than functional redundancy (ability to perform different functions within one unit), and requires a greater overhead and more hierarchy for communication and coordination.

A particularly interesting case of function by connection between hierarchically lower levels of functioning is the evidence that language is based on connections between the pre-frontal cortex and the cerebellum, which in evolution grew together. This suggests a connection between language and co-ordination of movement (*International Herald Tribune* 10-11-1994). This is intuitively appealing: in both cases numerous elementary functions (motor activities, linguistic terms) need to be incorporated into meaningful strings (movements, sentences) that are apposite to the context, while the variation of contexts allows for an infinitude of possible combinations. In cases of William's syndrome, where there is great aptitude in language and sociability, but otherwise severe intellectual retardation, the cerebellum is relatively large. The reverse is the case in autism, where intelligence is normal or high, but there are problems with language and other social aptitudes.

This basis of language yields another indication of the linking between action and thought emphasised in SA: it is in the interaction between co-ordination of motor activities (cerebellum) and intellection (pre-frontal cortex) that the symbolisation of language emerges.

The notion of the brain as a neural network, as indicated above, suggests that there are several forms of learning:

1. path becomes more efficient as irrelevant parts and connections are eliminated and successful parts reinforced;
2. depending on the context, paths are differentiated, to contain some parts or connections in some contexts but not in others;
3. new connections between paths are established;
4. paths are broken up, and new paths are formed from parts of old ones.

Concerning the first form of learning, also consider Pribram (1969, p.195; quoted by Heyting 1971, p. 34):

> If we repeatedly are in the same situation, in a relatively invariant environment, two things happen. One is that if we have consistently to perform a similar task in that environment, the task becomes fairly automatic. i.e., we become efficient. We say the organism ... has learned to perform the task; he has formed *habits* regarding it. But at the same time the subject habituates..; he no longer notices the events that endure, are constant.

The further types of learning are based on my interpretation of the present state of neuroscience, and this may be speculative, and in need of testing. But to the extent that they are justified, it is interesting to note the similarity of these forms of learning to the stage theory of conceptual development in the developmental ('genetic') epistemology proposed by Jean Piaget (Piaget 1970, 1974; for a survey of Piaget's work, see Flavell 1967; for an application to the development of organisations and markets, see Nooteboom 1989, 1992). According to this, development occurs in an ongoing 'assimilation' of experience in cognitive structures, and adaptation of those structures ('accommodation') to experience, with the following stages:

1. cognitive structure at first is indeterminate, and by recognition from one context to another, and repetition, it becomes more determinate and efficient;
2. once established, a cognitive structure is generalised to different contexts;
3. in generalisation differences in application are recognised, which leads to a differentiation of the concept;
4. in this process connections are found with other structures;
5. from this 'reciprocation' novel structures tentatively emerge, in a development that starts again at step 1.

It might be worthwhile to take this sequence of stages as an hypothesis for further neurological research. In the context of the present paper it is relevant to highlight the sources of path-dependence in knowledge. Higher level, complex concepts, including categories of perception, interpretation and evaluation, are formed from modular elements that in turn develop from action, which is interaction with the physical an social environment. Hence our ability to perceive and to learn, in the sense of making new cognitive functions by reconnecting parts from existing ones, depends on past development. Hence, people will perceive, interpret and evaluate differently to the extent that they have developed in different contexts, along different paths.

ORGANISATION AS A SUPERBRAIN

How about organisations? How do they perceive, interpret, evaluate and learn? Let us take up the notion of neural networks as a metaphor, to see what happens if we apply some of its content to organisations, to see whether perhaps this may take us beyond metaphor to a model, or perhaps even the beginning of a theory. Here, we are not using the brain as a metaphor of corporate or strategic planning, which governs the action of the organisational body, which has often been employed in the literature on planning (cf. Morgan 1988, p.79). Following Simon (1947), March and Simon (1958), Morgan (1986), I employ the idea (metaphor, analogy or model, perhaps) that an organisation as a whole may share some characteristics with neural networks.

When we talk of the perception, action and learning by an organisation, it is often said that this does not make sense, because it is individual people, not organisations, that have brains and powers of perception and thought. But, we saw that the cognitive and conative (action oriented) capabilities and the identity of a person are made up from paths of activity in neural networks, in which there is no place for the Cartesian 'homunculus' as internal observer and driver (which would take us into an infinite regress). Then why could not the cognitive and conative identity of an organisation be built up from communicative networks of people associated with the organisation? Or, conversely: if one denies that on that basis organisations can be said to have cognitive identity, how could we maintain that a person has such identity? It seems that organisations and people can both be said to have cognitive identity, or neither. It seems that there is equal justification to speak of organisational as of personal identity.

Of course, with this we have not explained how organisational cognitive identity works. And of course there are many dissimilarities: the neural network metaphor is a metaphor, and perhaps a scientific analogy,[6] but we know that not all items from neural networks are reproduced in networks of people. People are not neurons, and what they transmit between them is very different from electro-chemical impulses. As argued by Smith Ring and Van de Ven (1994), people act privately, 'qua persona', and according to organisational roles assigned to them. Alignment between the two can be a problem, but this duality of conduct can also be an advantage. Personal interest may deviate from organisational interest, and may even lead to corruption or embezzlement. On the other hand, the diversity of personal perception, understanding and evaluation can act as a creative force, to yield novel perceptions, ideas or directions for the organisation. To prevent too strong personal interests of incumbents in functions may require turnover of personnel across roles. This may also be required to generate fresh views and new directions. People may be motivated by self-interest or social pressure to deflect, cover up or delude themselves. On the other hand, neurons also have mechanisms for filtering or transforming signals and adjusting thresholds for emitting signals, partly from its own development, and partly from influence (inhibition, triggering) from other neurons or neural paths. These phenomena are of course not identical to those of people in networks, but there may still be relevant insights to be obtained from a comparison. Another major dissimilarity is that people are subject not only to biological evolution but also to the much faster and quite different process of cultural evolution (within and between organisations).[7] Among other things, this yields fundamental changes in the technology of processing and communicating information. Also, while connectable neurons are contained in the brain, communicative connections between people can easily extend beyond the bounds of any organisation. And fragments can be transferred from one organisation to another by take-over or merger (which does not imply that that is always successful). So, the neural network metaphor or analogy cannot without major transformation be a serious model of organisations. The question now is whether some more general model of cognitive networks may serve as a model.

It does seem that the similarities between brain and organisation go far beyond the mere fact that there are networks of units between which signals are sent. How far do the similarities go? The crucial question is whether there are things like organisational equivalents of concepts and categories that emerge from and guide actions, in the sense that they trigger equivalents of motor mechanisms and receive impulses back from them. Does this model help to reconstruct and explain organisational phenomena? How does it perform in comparison with alternative frameworks?

What are those alternative frameworks? Is the alternative framework that cognitive 'contents' of people in organisations somehow 'add up' to the content of organisational knowledge? This adding up would require 'transport' (communication). Does everyone absorb in his mind what everyone else in the organisation knows? Clearly not. So how does the selection take place? By restricting channels of communication. Is every person able to absorb what another knows? Clearly not. What conditions should be satisfied for a person to be able to absorb what another transmits? Information from the sender should some how trigger cognitive mechanisms in the receiver, and for this there must be some commonality of repertoires of concepts, categories and their triggers. Above all the question is whether patterns of communication between people yield mechanisms of response which do not belong to the cognitive repertoire of any individual. Clearly, this must be the case. No person commands the cognitive potential of all the people together. Actions are triggered that are group actions.

I propose that it would be entirely reasonable to see this, in analogy to brain processes, in terms of thresholds of response, triggering and inhibition. Then 'functions' in organisations would be seen as analogues to specialised functions in the brain: there are cognitive areas of marketing, finance, production, and so on. Accounting would be part of organisational language. Production, logistics, distribution, service would be analogues of motor activities. Higher level concepts would consist of linkages between lower level concepts. This would indeed yield supra-personal equivalents of concepts or categories, which shape and are informed by organisational action. Without pretending that everything in the analogue fits, let us explore how far we can go, and what added insight it yields. What predictions would this view yield, and to what extent are they corroborated?

From this point on we could discuss many connections to the literature on organisations, but I prefer to explore the predictions.

PREDICTIONS FOR ORGANISATIONS

From the brain metaphor I now derive predictions for organisations, to see how they might work out. The predictions are more or less loosely intuited from the metaphor. They are not deduced by strict logic, since we do not yet have any formalised structure for a general theory of cognitive networks. For the analysis, I add the following terminology: an operational pattern of connections between nodes in the network is called a 'schema'.[8] This is synonymous to the term 'pathway' that was used before. Such schemata may have a specialised, localised function, but may also constitute more distributed connections between such functions. They become 'routines' when they haven become autonomous, outside higher level control of stimulus and response.

Prediction 1: situated action. Actions, in interaction with the environment, form schemata, which guide action (cf. Piaget: intelligence as 'internalised action; Wittgenstein: 'meaning as use'. This principle is also the principle of cognitive self-organisation). There are schemata on different levels of specialisation and co-ordination:

Prediction 2: modularity and hierarchy. In order to respond with sufficient speed, to have sufficient robustness to distractions along the process of response (not having to start again when disturbed), and to have ability to form novel responses, then like the brain, organisations should arrange cognitive activities in schemata in a modular fashion. To the extent that the complexity of behaviour increases, there are more levels of specialised functions. This principle was also discussed by Morgan (1988: 102–3), with reference to Simon's (1962) parable of the watchmaker and Ashby (1952).

Prediction 3: connectivity and complexity. To the extent that co-ordination between functions is required more, there must be richer connectivity between them. This point seems almost trivial. Note that co-ordination between functions is required more to the extent that viable response cannot be built into the separate functions. This is the case to the extent that the complexity of response, in response to a more complex environment, is greater. When the technology of connection changes, as in the emergence of information and communication technology (ICT), adjustments will take place in organisational structure. We return to this later.

As in the case of the brain, the three predictions imply a prediction of path-dependence:

Prediction 4: path dependence. Since development takes the form of novel connections of schemata, or parts of schemata, developed before, and those have been developed from interaction with the environment, the potential for development is determined by paths through the environment in previous development. If in the brain language (symbolisation, denotation, connotation, grammar) has developed from connections between motor activities (cerebellum) and conceptual capacities (pre-frontal cortex), in close interaction with action ('situated action') the analogue for organisations might be:

Prediction 5: organisational culture as thinking in action. The means by which organisations conceptualise, identify, refer and trigger action, which

71

may be called its culture, develops in interaction between its thinking and its action. Presumably, parts of this are accounting, performance evaluation, material and immaterial reward systems, role models, primary goals, rituals, etc. The prediction, in the analogy of language in the brain as connection between cerebellum and pre-frontal cortex, includes that organisational culture is ineffective if it is not based on sufficient and appropriate connections between thinking and action. Could there be analogues of autism and William's syndrome in organisations? Conceptually and intellectually strong organisations which are communicatively and socially weak? Verbally brilliant but intellectually retarded organisations? Or are we now moving far beyond the limits of the metaphor? Or is the idea valid from the perspective of a generalised principle of situated action? Learning entails the development of schemata, and this has a number of aspects.

Prediction 6: learning. There are several kinds of learning. One is habituation: an existing schema becomes smoother and more efficient; a routine. A second consists in the break-up and recomposition of schemata, yielding new functions or coordinations and thereby new forms of response. In this we can easily recognise the identification, in the organisation literature, of 'single loop' and 'double loop' learning (Argyris and Schön 1978).

Prediction 7: habituation. In organisations, as in brains, there are phenomena of habituation, where a schema can become a routine, where responses to stimuli that reach the schema escape higher level attention ('consciousness'), to the extent that stimuli conform to an established pattern. When stimuli persistently do not conform, and the routine has not become embedded too deeply, attention is triggered, the routine is disturbed, and attempts are made to recompose it to assimilate the anomalous stimuli. As discussed before, habituation seems to take place by a narrowing of the scope for response of nodes in the schema, and inhibition of the triggering of higher level schemata that constitute attention to the lower level schema. We also noted that, given bounded capacity, this is rational, since it enhances efficiency and allows attention to be spent to the non-routine, provided that deviation from the normal reactivates attention. Quite apart from the analogy to brain physiology, it makes sense to say that in order to achieve effective action, the organisation needs to focus attention, which implies a limitation to perception. In other words: at least part of the function of an organisation is to serve as a 'focusing device', and one may speculate that this focusing is at least part of the role of organisational culture, interpreted as 'mental programming' (Nooteboom 1992). Such influence on scope of attention and reaction has an overall effect, across the whole organisation. A more focused, localised form of control of scope of triggering and response is given by organisational structure, in the form of definition and allocation of organisational roles and lines of reporting and procedures of monitoring. Of course such structures themselves constitute schemata. The discussion leads to the following prediction.

Prediction 8: closure and opening. For efficiency, organisations habituate by establishing routines of narrowed scope of response and action for standard activities ('closure'), unattended by higher level (integrative) functions, but for survival they maintain an ability to retrigger attention and widen scope of response, action and triggering ('opening') when non-standard conditions arise ('crises'). If the Piagetian stages of development are correct, there are intermediate stages between the forms of learning indicated in prediction 5:

Prediction 9: generalisation, differentiation and reciprocation. Successful schemata tend to get applied to widening domains, they tend to get differentiated to match different contexts, and are connected with parts of different schemata, which may provide the basis for the composition of a novel schema. This indicates a path to 'double loop learning'. It should be testable in its own right. It would be interesting to investigate whether innovative shifts within firms follow this pattern.

Prediction 10: functional redundancy. To achieve robustness to damage (by departure of personnel, accidents, take-over of part of the organisation, etc.), by regeneration of lost schemata or parts thereof, and to learn in the sense of adapting schemata by reconfiguration of connections, the elements of an organisation (people, groups of people) should have some redundancy of function. This idea was also put forward by Morgan (1988, p. 100),[9] who also added the next point:

Prediction 11: requisite variety. The extent to which functional redundancy is required is governed by the principle of requisite variety (Ashby): redundancy must be greater to the extent that the complexity and speed of adjustment to required response is greater. We noted before that there is a trade-off between specialisation and functional redundancy: specialisation is more efficient (due to habituation), but less flexible than functional redundancy (due to habituation and the need to redistribute functions across units), and requires more overhead for communication and co-ordination. The latter point implies economy of scale. As a result, greater variability of the environment requires a shift from specialisation to functional flexibility. This yields the following prediction:

Prediction 12: scale effects. Small organisations can afford less specialised functions, and rely more on functional redundancy, which makes them less efficient than large organisations, but more flexible. As the environment becomes more variable, the advantage moves to the smaller firm *ceteris paribus*. This is a well received fact in the literature on small business and entrepreneurship (Nooteboom 1994).

EXTENDED ORGANISATIONS

The question rises what the limits of implementing requisite variety might be. The question is highly relevant to present conditions of firms in markets (Nooteboom 1992, 1995; Zuscovitch 1994). Technology and markets are changing fast. Innovation and competition arise from different regions in the world, with the Far East having emerged as a third block of power. Connected to this, innovation progresses more rapidly, and the life-cycles of products have become shorter. Markets rapidly become global. Technological capabilities are often quite high even in low wage countries, and information can be exchanged massively, conveniently and rapidly. This makes production more footloose. For survival in the ensuing commercial and technological races firms need to excel in most if not all dimensions of competition: low cost, high quality, close market match, flexibility, innovativeness. To escape from extremes of price competition, firms must further differentiate products. Differentiation is also market driven, as a result of individualisation of consumer behaviour. It is also technically feasible, on the basis of more flexible production technology, driven by information technology. But the ensuing complexity and fluidity of required knowledge poses extreme cognitive demands on firms. A dilemma arises (Nooteboom 1992): on the one hand, attention must be focused, in order to have a chance of not losing the race; on the other hand one must scan a complex environment not to miss out on relevant threats and opportunities in shifts of markets and technology. This appears to become an impossible task. In terms of our present discussion, the need to build requisite variety gets in conflict with the need to focus. The problem is especially severe in the light of path-dependence of knowledge. And note that habituation compounds the problem of path dependence. Path-dependence implies that what one can perceive, interpret and learn depends on the path of past development in ones environment. To the extent that for different subjects that environment differs, those subjects will have different

74

categories of perception, understanding and evaluation. For these reasons the solution seems to be as follows:

Prediction 13: external networks. In complex, turbulent environments, cognition will be extended with outside networks. Small firms will sooner seek recourse to external networks. This is a solution to the dilemma of focus versus awareness. By limiting the cognitive scope of the firm, focus is achieved, while the ensuing risk of too limited awareness of opportunities and threats is covered by employing the cognitive, path-dependent specialisation of others. An additional twist to the principle is that outside triggers may be required to break out from habituation. The principle constitutes what can be called 'external economy of cognitive scope': different organisations, with different path dependent cognitive competencies, seek each other out for complementarity in a cognitive distribution of labour (Nooteboom 1992, 1993b, 1995). Of course, this requires a careful selection of those others, so that their competence is relevant and complementary to ones own, with apposite communicative connections with them. Also, optimal networking requires a 'cognitive distance' which is sufficiently large to yield novel insights, but not too large to be unable to understand each other (Nooteboom 1995; Péli and Nooteboom 1995). This is connected with what Granovetter (1982) called 'the strength of weak ties'. Due to their greater reliance on functional redundancy to begin with (prediction 12), smaller firms will sooner develop external networks than large firms. This is again a well known fact in the small business literature (Nooteboom 1994).[10]

One can say that prediction 13 is a special case of the more general principle of predictions 2 and 3: higher level complexity leads to novel forms of organisation in which individual firms are modules. We see this prediction corroborated in the facts and the literature on organisations. The need is recognised to focus on 'core competencies' (Prahalad and Hamel 1990). Increasingly, emphasis is laid on the need to delegate more activities externally. This entails a shift of attention from internal economies of scale and scope, within integrated organisations, to external economies of scale and scope between organisations which are of a hybrid form, located 'between market and hierarchy' (cf. Amin and Dietrich 1991; Semlinger 1991). Activities have to be contracted out even if they are 'sensitive', in the sense that one is vulnerable to lack of conformance to technical standards and supply times, and to risks of dependence, as a result of transaction specific investments, opportunism and bounded rationality, as analysed by transaction cost economics (Williamson 1985, 1989). In view of the above considerations, mergers and acquisitions are poor substitutes for extending the cognitive scope of an organisation:

Prediction 14: problems of integration. Because of the connectedness of parts of a cognitive network, and the path dependence of cognitive structures, integration of fragments from outside is likely to carry problems, and it does not yield the required economy of cognitive scope. Integration of functions would require such a strong cognitive and cultural alignment in the integrated system, that it would detract from the originality and novelty of external sources of cognition. Their value is that they have developed a different path dependent set of categories, which makes integration difficult, and their value lies in continued independence of cognitive development. The difficulties of mergers and acquisitions have in fact become increasingly apparent: about 50 per cent is said not to achieve its aims.The emergence of networks between firms is facilitated by the development of Information and Communication Technology (ICT), which also has other implications, as was noted by Morgan (1986).

Prediction 15: information technology. Information technology improves opportunities for fast connections across large distances, simultaneous transmission to multiple destinations, automated information processing, easy access to large volumes of data. At a given level of complexity, this allows for fewer hierarchical levels. It allows for higher levels of complexity, including extended networks across different organisations. It also allows for more specialisation, thus altering its trade-off with functional redundancy. Now, if organisations can be said to have cognitive identity on the basis of networks, in analogy to personal identity on the basis of neural networks, then:

Prediction 16: industrial districts.[11] Linkages between firms to achieve 'external economy of cognitive scope' yield higher level cognitive entities, associated with the notion of 'industrial districts'. But if this is correct, then other predictions, indicated before, may also apply to the higher level of constellations of organisations. For example:

Prediction 17: evolution of industries and markets. In a system of firms that are interconnected in production, distribution, competition, mutual supply, etc., aggregate phenomena of learning may arise: innovation, 'hardening', generalisation, differentiation, reciprocation (hybridization), innovation, etc. This reads very much like a description of the phenomenon of 'product life cycles' in industries/markets. From this line of thought we might entertain a policy prediction:

Prediction 18: systemic industrial policy. Increasingly, industrial policy will not be oriented towards individual firms or industries but on linkages between firms that achieve external economy of cognitive scope. This point is recognised in the increasing attention that in industrial policy is given to 'clusters' of economic activities (Porter 1990), rather than isolated firms or industries.

CONCLUSIONS

Path dependency of knowledge was explained on the basis of the idea that knowledge, in people and organisations, is based on connectivity between units that receive and send signals, in the form of pathways that are subject to triggering or inhibition from signals from other pathways. Pathways develop from a more or less random exploration of novel connections between units, with reinforcement or weakening of linkages depending on practical success. This is consistent with both the notion of symbolic processing and the notion of situated action in cognitive science. Currently, the literature tends to see these two perspectives as conflicting, but I propose that they can be reconciled. Our perspective is consistent with symbolic processing, interpreted as activation of pathways, and mutual triggering of such pathways in patterns of activation. It is consistent with situated action, because the pathways arise from interaction with the external world.

From this perspective 18 predictions were derived concerning processes of cognition within and between organisations. They concerned the following phenomena: development of cognition, path dependency, types of learning and the role of culture and management; relation of a firm's cognition to its environment, and in particular the role of interaction with other organisations, and problems of integration between different firms; efficiency and conservatism of cognition and action, and the relation between the two; functional redundancy, requisite variety and scale effects; the role and impact of information technology; the notion of 'industrial districts', 'clusters' of firms and industries, and evolution of industries and markets. The predictions appear to yield a fruitful basis for discussion on a number of organisational issues of both theoretical and practical importance: innovation and the dynamics of firms, markets and technology; boundaries of the firm, integration of activities and inter-firm partnerships; industrial districts, 'clustering' of activities and industrial policy. The predictions appear to fit observed reality to some extent, and yield hypotheses that can, in principle be tested.

For further progress, we can go in either or both of the following directions. One is to operationalise the predictions further and subject them to systematic empirical tests. A second is to try and develop a more systematic, more formalised general theory of cognitive networks, which might encompass neural networks, and organisational and inter-organisational networks as special cases.

NOTES

1 A famous example is QWERTY: the arrangement of symbols on a keyboard (David, 1985). It was designed to minimise the risk of entanglement of mechanical keys. Later, with electronic typing, this was no longer needed, and a different arrangement would be more efficient, but large investments in typing proficiency on the old design blocked the switch to a new one.

2 That, of course, indicates why it is understandable, though not justifiable, that economics has evaded the issue: if we are to base our economics on psychology (and sociology), then there is the problem of having to choose one of different schools in those disciplines, and on what basis would we make such a choice, short of becoming cognitive scientists ourselves?

3 One should note, however, that there is much variety of thought within that school.

4 Habituation yields what Polanyi (1962,1967, 1969) called 'tacit knowledge': we have competence outside of our consciousness.

5 This process can be reproduced in 'genetic programming'. This has been used to reproduce learning in the evolution of economic systems. See Lane (1993).

6 For the distinction, see Gentner (1982).

7 Cultural evolution differs from biological evolution in at least the following aspects. In contrast with biological genetics, ontogenetic learning in culture can be transmitted to later generations (Lamarckianism) by cultural transmission. Next to biological parenthood there is cultural parenthood (teachers, role models). Extinct species (technologies, or forms of activity) can be revived. Cross-species reproduction is possible (the novel combinations of Schumpeterian innovation). The scope for errors or drift in cultural transmission is greater than in biological transmission (by means of genes), because human and cultural memory are faulty.

8 I take this term from Piagetian theory, to denote a cognitive pattern of activity, but note that I am giving it an amplified meaning, for it to apply also to communicative connections between people.

9 The notion of redundancy of function, as opposed to redundancy of parts is attributed to Emery (1967); cf. Morgan (1988, p. 359).

10 This is not to be confused with the concept of firm's reach in terms of markets: smaller firms serve less extended and fewer markets, but nevertheless use external sources more than internal specalized functions.

11 Perhaps with this we are stretching the original meaning of 'industrial districts' (which goes back to Marshall) too far.

5. Strategic Lock-in as a Human Issue: The Role of Professional Orientation*

Michael Dietrich

INTRODUCTION

Strategic lock-in is usually defined in economics in terms of choice of technology. Examples of this tradition are, of course, David's (1985) account of the dominance of the QWERTY keyboard and Arthur's (1988a, 1989) seminal theoretical ideas. The latter's approach is based on choice of technology following a random walk and increasing returns to lock-in a particular technology. Similar to this is Dasgupta and Maskin's (1987) suggestion that a free market encourages excessive correlation among R&D projects in cases where a firm's R&D costs are reduced if its efforts are closely correlated with those of its rivals.

These general ideas can be broadened out beyond firm-industry-based technological choice in a number of ways. An equivalent logic can be applied to other areas of economics. For example Dosi (1988) defines a 'technological paradigm' that, it is argued, governs long-run economic evolution by selecting the principles and rules used to generate new knowledge. Alternatively (foreign) direct investment and location decisions can produce geographical lock-in when agglomeration externalities or infrastructure synergies exist (Best 1990; Porter 1990). A different way of developing the idea of strategic lock-in is to suggest that choice is not random but may be influenced by strategic leaders (Dietrich and Schenk 1993). This can be complemented by an approach that adopts an intra-firm perspective as when Dietrich (1994) suggests that organisations have idiosyncratic productive opportunities that generate organisational strategic lock-in. These latter two threads are drawn together in this contribution in which the nature of organisational lock-in is examined in terms of the strategic leadership of particular professional groups that can dominate organisational activity.

The structure of the argument is developed as follows. Initially the literature that links professionalism and organisational activity is briefly reviewed. Following this, organisational functioning is examined more conceptually and the theoretical rational for linking professional dominance and organisational lock-in is derived. Having derived this link and discussed its general characteristics a more formal theoretical framework is developed that is used to generate a number of specific conclusions about professional behaviour and organisational dynamics. The final substantive section attempts to link the organisational-professional analysis of lock-in to the more traditional framework based on technological decisions and a black-box organisational logic. Finally concluding comments are made.

PROFESSIONALISM AND ORGANISATIONAL ACTIVITY

The central hypothesis of this paper is that a particular professional dominance is an inevitable aspect of organisational coherence and that this locks-in organisational strategic orientation. This claim seems to be consistent with organisational literature and empirical evidence that examines cross-cultural and historical differences in professional dominance (Lane 1989, 1991; Whittington 1993). The highly influential views of Miles and Snow (1978) suggest that different organisational characteristics and strategies can be conceptualised in terms of the dominance of particular functional-professional groups: R&D, production, accounting or marketing. Particular functional-professional dominance produces characteristic organisational types. In addition the recent study by Richards (1995), based on case studies of UK companies, draws out the implications of not only the dominance of particular professional groups but also stresses the way in which alliances between these groups channel organisational functioning. These perspectives would suggest that there is no 'natural' professional dominance.

Fligstein (1990) compares the background of corporate presidents in the US with that in France, Germany and Japan. In the former country finance has come to dominate, in terms of functional background, whereas in the latter countries finance professionals are far less prominent. To some extent the UK appears to adopt a US professional logic but we should be aware of Chandler's (1990) study that classifies the US, UK and Germany as respectively managerial, personal and cooperative capitalism. The differences involved are based on particular organisational and institutional histories. Within Europe a stark difference is apparent between, on the one hand, France and Germany and, on the other, the UK (Lane 1989). In

France, engineering has a long tradition of dominating management, not least because of close links with the *grandes écoles*. In Germany, engineering and science dominate top management.

The differential influence of particular professional groups can profoundly affect organisational strategy. Armstrong's (1987) discussion of the shift, in the UK, from a dominance of engineering to an accounting logic indicates the way in which particular areas of expertise become defined as the norm and hence dominate strategic orientation - a process that is actively pursued by an emergent dominant grouping. An engineering logic concentrates on building value creating activity, that of accountancy exploiting existing businesses. According to Fligstein (1987), as accountants rise to the top of their organisations (in the US) they define success in their own terms and structure strategies to exploit their particular perceptions and areas of expertise. In the light of this discussion it is perhaps of no real surprise that Hamel and Prahalad (1994), two influential strategic management theorists, emphasise the importance of 'strategic intent' rather than 'strategic fit' (a distinction that mirrors that stressed by Armstrong) as a means of generating competitive advantage. Strategic intent is characteristic of Japanese companies rather than the characteristic Anglo-Saxon use of strategic fit.

The literature just discussed appears to suggest the existence of a link between the dominance of a particular professional grouping in an organisation and a locked-in strategic orientation. Such dominance occurs in what might be called direct and indirect ways.[1] Direct dominance exists because any particular organisation requires a degree of strategic coherence for effective functioning (Dietrich and Al-Awadh 1995). Different professional groups will have different perceptions and define in different ways the nature and success of appropriate strategies. To avoid organisational anarchy one of the perceptions must dominate. But this direct domination does not change professional aspirations which are exogenous to the organisational processes involved. Indirect dominance exists because a particular professional grouping creates the context of organisational decision making and hence defines the framework that is used by other professionals. This context endogenises the aspirations of organisational actors.

The links between direct and indirect dominance and organisational lock-in will be discussed theoretically in the remainder of this paper. But in general terms such links can be established in a straightforward manner. Arthur (1988a, 1988b, 1989) makes reference to four self-reinforcing mechanisms that generate lock-in: large set-up or fixed costs; learning effects; co-ordination effects which confer external benefits from co-operation; and adaptive expectations where increased use enhances belief of further use. As will be substantiated below, these four mechanisms apply equally as well to the dominance of a particular organisational logic as to choice of technology. To develop these points we must analyse the nature of professionalism in more detail.

It is possible to describe professionalism in terms of certain key characteristics that might include a high degree of autonomy and control over work activity, and a high degree of trust between those that act professionally and those who interact with them (Friedsen 1983; MacDonald and Ritzer 1988). When these characteristics take on a concrete institutional form we have the so-called professions as a social group that can be described in terms of three relevant features: self-regulation and the control of entry and quality standards; the existence of a professional ethic rather than a single-minded pursuit of financial reward; and that professional activities have significant externalities (Matthews 1991; Dietrich and Roberts 1995). In terms of intra-organisational activity professions as institutions are less significant than professional activity more generally defined. But, for reasons that will become apparent, the three institutional features become important intra-organisationally if a particular professional group is to promote and sustain an organisational strategic leadership position.

Descriptions such as those just presented are useful as an introduction to the significance of professionalism for organisational activity but in terms of a link with strategic lock-in we must move beyond description of professional activity and professionalism to stress an analysis of its rationale and significance. The key to understanding professional activity is to view it as a response to (organisational) principal-agent problems. If we follow the logic of neo-classical economic theory principal-agent problems can be solved using optimally structured arms-length contracting (see, for example, Gravelle and Rees 1992). In such circumstances professional activity, as just described, has no rationale, and issues of service quality and externalities similarly do not require professionalism (Dietrich and Roberts 1995). The construction of optimal contracts relies on a principal being uncertain of agent characteristics (with hidden information/adverse selection) and/or agent actions (with hidden action/moral hazard). But, and rather counter-intuitively, a principal must have knowledge of outputs produced, agent utility/aspirations and the transformation processes involved. Incomplete knowledge in one, or more, of these latter areas will exist when decision making is characterised by complexity. It follows that complexity (and the attendant ignorance) erects a barrier to the management of principal-agent problems using arms-length relationships. Correspondingly, ignorance, rather than principal-agent problems *per se*, provides a justification for organisation based on professional activity and expertise.

Following Winter (1987) we can define complexity (or its converse simplicity) in terms of the amount of information that is necessary to make effective decisions. In turn complexity will depend on three factors: the extent of tacit (rather than communicable) information; the extent to which an element of information is independent or part of a system; and the observability of information.[2] Tacit information can only effectively be acquired while undertaking an activity, with an emphasis on learning by doing. An important characteristic is that such information can only be understood in the context of particular actions and may be shared to a significant degree by individuals who have a common (organisational) experience. Hence the acquisition of tacit information requires the development of particular skills and expertise (Nelson and Winter 1982) with the complexity this involves. The systemic (or independent) nature of information has obvious relevance for any activity that requires training; the complexity of an element of information will increase depending on the required extent of such training. Finally information observability depends not only on secrecy and monopoly control but also on the extent of disclosure that occurs with use of an activity. Non-observability implies that information acquisition involves additional (search and acquisition) activities, with their own decision making requirements, and hence indirectly increases the complexity of decision making.

When decision making is complex effective information acquisition requires the development of particular areas of expertise and experience that are therefore sunk costs of decision making capability. To some extent these sunk costs will be non-specific for any organisation, as is the case with general accounting, marketing and engineering training and expertise. But, in a particular organisational context, such activities will also have significant externalities, or organisational non-separabilities (Dietrich 1993) in the Alchian and Demsetz (1972) tradition. For instance, accounting expertise provides a general financial framework for an organisation, or marketing and engineering expertise directly impact on each other and other organisational activities. Each organisation is likely to be idiosyncratic with regard to these detailed intra-organisational linkages/externalities, depending on particular unique advantages and product-market characteristics.[3] Hence the sunk costs of expertise development and decision making capability will have significant organisationally specific elements. In such circumstances a 'relational team' (Williamson 1985) becomes appropriate in which employee self-motivation, rather than detailed monitoring becomes important. This 'relational team' is equivalent to Ouchi's (1980) 'clan' which becomes relevant when 'goal congruence' is a significant issue and 'performance ambiguity' high. The non-congruence of goals will be a (potential) problem with particular professional orientations. In addition performance ambiguity will be high when decision making is complex and activities have significant externalities because of the difficulty of constructing reliable and organisationally valid output measures (Ouchi 1977).

While the above discussion indicates the importance of professional activity in an organisational context it gives insufficient consideration to two matters that are important for our discussion: the link between sunk costs and power and the centrality of organisational coherence. The development of professional expertise, in terms of learning and system understanding, is a means of managing the inherent complexity of individual and organisational decision making. But professional decision making inevitably introduces sunk costs of expertise development. As with all sunk costs non-contestable economic relationships will result with resultant monopoly power (Baumol 1982). From a resource-dependence perspective (Pfeffer and Salancik 1978) the power and influence of a particular group will be a function of how reliant an organisation is on the services provided by the group. A particular organisation will be more resource dependent on a profession if strategies cohere around a particular set of professional services. But this coherence is only viable, in the long-run, with complex (and non-contestable) organisational relations.

It follows from these comments that the more effectively an organisational principal-agent problem is resolved by the development of 'professional attitudes' the more entrenched will be professional activity. Conversely, the more contestable organisational activities are made the greater will be management costs aimed at controlling the effects of badly organised principal-agent relationships. In this light the importance of trust and continuing relationships (as key aspects of professionalism) become clear. But the centrality of trust to professional regulation does not remove power differentials, it makes them more manageable. An implication of this perspective is that principal-agent relations are not uni-directional with a principal having an *a priori* right to set the parameters of agent activity (Perrow 1986; Broadbent, Dietrich and Laughlin 1995). Information asymmetries run from both principal to agent and agent to principal; and organisational principal can act opportunistically because of its powerful organisational position. This important complexity will be reflected in later discussion.

This centrality of differential intra-organisational power takes on an added significance when the importance of strategic coherence is recognised. Different professional activities are likely to adopt differing strategic objectives because of divergent learning and problem solving experiences. The avoidance of organisational anarchy therefore requires the dominance of a particular profession and the corresponding strategic orientation. To understand the importance of organisational coherence, which forms the basis of co-ordination benefits that underlie the development of lock-in, we can initially examine behavioural perspectives on the firm that minimises its importance.[4] At a superficial level the discussion presented above might appear to have much in common with behavioural perspectives on the firm. In particular both emphasise the firm as an administrative unit rather than a black box; but important differences are evident. The central shortcoming is the short-run emphasis of behavioural theory (Devine 1985; Kay 1979). Individual aspiration levels and standard operating procedures are essentially exogenous and respond to immediate problems. In addition, immediate problems, and goal adjustment, are viewed in terms of responses to exogenous environmental changes. Senior managers are one party to the ongoing organisational bargaining processes but with the advantage of control over 'side payments'. This control provides the limited degree of organisational coherence suggested by behavioural theorists based on what was called earlier direct dominance. But this coherence is less structured and dominating than the framework suggested in this paper because of the exogeneity of key variables.

Behavioural theory does not recognise a strategic perspective to organisational functioning that endogenises aspiration levels and operating procedures and defines the way that an organisation interacts with its environment (Baumol and Stewart 1971); rather it seems to accept the 'buffeting' of outside forces. A recent contribution in this tradition emphasises this point clearly. March (1988) develops his 'garbage can' model of choice in which solutions are linked to problems because they just happen to be present simultaneously. In short, behavioural theory presents a perspective on the interaction of individuals in an organisational setting rather than a theory of organisational functioning because the firm has no real identity in its own right, i.e. no strategic coherence. In more sociological terms, Perrow (1986) makes an equivalent criticism of March (and more generally behavioural theory) and claims that the perspective is essentially neo-Weberian, and hence limited, in character. From this view organisations lack central conherence and direction.

A way to link the firm as a strategic unit with the firm as a combination of interacting alliances (professions) is to recognise that change may have an internal as well as external dynamic. To use Penrose's (1980) terminology: the firm can be described in terms of an evolving productive opportunity that has both objective and subjective perspectives. Objectively, the firm exists in a real environment with real opportunities and threats. Subjectively, a firms' productive opportunity is based on particular perspectives and expectations, which using the logic introduced earlier is defined in terms of a dominant professional grouping and the way that this interacts with other organisational actors.

A subjectively-objectively defined productive opportunity allows us to recognise the importance of learning as a generator of internal change. This is not possible within behavioural theory. As Bianchi (1990) points out, the assumed separability of aspirations from search procedures is only possible when the parameters of a problem can be well specified *ex-ante*. If this specification is not possible search will involve learning which will in turn affect aspiration levels and goals, to the extent that the latter shift with discovery and development of issues and the knowledge and understanding this implies. In short the behavioural theory's treatment of individual decision making (as a response to exogenous change) rather ironically has to assume that bounded rationality (one of the central conceptual pillars of behavioural theory) does not exist because of the necessary *ex-ante* specification of individual understanding. If the parameters of a problem cannot be well specified *ex-ante* learning processes will endogenise change.

Once this critique of behavioural approaches to the firm is recognised the link between organisational functioning, professional dominance and strategic lock-in can be recognised. Individual learning does not occur in isolation but rather is channelled by the indirect domination of a particular professional perspective and hence creates the subjective productive opportunity of an organisation. This is recognised in recent strategic management theory. Prahalad and Hamel (1990) refer to an organisation's accumulated learning creating an idiosyncratic 'core competence' which is the basis of competitive advantage, and more importantly for our argument, is only subject to change in the long-run with concerted strategic efforts that in many cases are not successful - particularly for accounting dominated Anglo-Saxon organisations.

As a summary of this section we can refer back to the four self-reinforcing mechanisms that generate lock-in. Significant set-up costs are involved with the development of any organisational control framework. A framework based on a particular professional orientation involves significant learning to generate effective organisational control and to exploit the possibilities offered by internally generated change. Co-ordination effects will exist which confer external system benefits from co-operation because of the externalities generated by professional expertise. Finally, adaptive expectations will lead to increased use enhancing further use; the firm as an organisational (rather than a set of interacting individuals) will only exist if expectations and perceptions are endogenised. These conclusions are based on a rich but informal discussion of the importance, and implications of, professional organisation and dominance. A complementary discussion is presented in the next section that adopts a more formal analysis of strategic lock-in within organisations.

PROFESSIONALISM AND STRATEGIC LOCK-IN

Casson (1991) has presented a formal leader-follower organisational analysis of business culture in which local equilibria are derived based on efficiency advantages of informal rather than explicit control. These equilibria, in effect, define locked-in responses to organisational problems. A similar approach will be adopted in this section but rather than an oligopoly informed framework a co-ordination framework with a principal-agent logic will be adopted. We will assume two strategies exist, that will be called later an existing orientation (S1) and an alternative (S2). Two relevant professional groupings exist that adopt the role of principals in their respective strategies. We can think of strategic orientation being determined by the nature of an organisational alliance between these two groups of actors, with detailed strategies being determined by the particular dominance (i.e. principal-agent) relationships. But we will not be assuming uni-directional (agent) opportunism that a principal must accommodate. The relevance and importance of this approach should be clear from earlier discussion.

Returns to either strategy will depend on two factors: exogenous environmental opportunities and threats (which includes market conditions for non-professional human inputs) and organisational characteristics. The latter are captured by the extent to which a strategy is supported by the active organisational actors, i.e. the members of the professional groups. Returns are divided between principal and agent groups based on a simple rule of thumb: a strategy specific proportion of total returns are allocated to the agent grouping by the relevant principal. In practice this might be thought of as income being based on a profit sharing rule that is defined by the organisational principal. An increasing proportion of professionals (both principal and agent) that supports a particular strategy leads to an increasing total surplus being generated from that strategy. The reasoning involved here follows from the discussion presented in the previous section. All the professionals from both groupings are equally necessary for effective organisational functioning. Deviations from a clearly defined strategic coherence therefore implies reduced organisational effectiveness.[5] These ideas suggest that the payoffs to the two strategies can be described as in Table 5.1.

Table 5.1

		Professional Group Two	
		S1	**S2**
Professional Group One	**S1**	$p(R_1-r_1), pr_1$	$0, 0$
	S2	$0, 0$	$(1-p)r_2, (1-p)(R_2-r_2)$

Notes

The first payoff in each pair is that received by professional group one;
p = the proportion of professionals (from both groups) that follow strategy 1;
R_1 = the maximum gross return from strategy 1;
r_1 = the amount of the maximum gross return that is allocated to the agent group;
R_2 and r_2 have equivalent definitions for strategy 2.

Table 5.1 can be interpreted in the following way. To generate positive returns requires some degree of strategic co-operation, hence the S1, S2 and S2, S1 payoffs are zero, the extent of this co-operation is defined by the variable 'p'.[6] It is convenient to imagine the playing of this game in terms of professionals meeting randomly and playing a series of two person co-ordination games. Wider meetings do not occur during play, but might be an aspect of pre-play negotiation of income sharing rules. A methodological point is that this formulation, if taken literally, assumes no environmental uncertainty (the returns are fully specified), but strategic uncertainty exists to the extent that interaction between the groups determines payoffs and decisions. This implies that the framework suggested here stresses the key, but not all, characteristics of earlier discussion. To generate predictions from this framework we can use the idea of an evolutionary stable strategy (ESS) proposed by Maynard-Smith (1982), which is defined in terms of no alternative strategy being able to change the prevailing equilibrium. The resulting equilibria and associated dynamics can be most easily explained in the context of Figure 5.1.

Figure 5.1

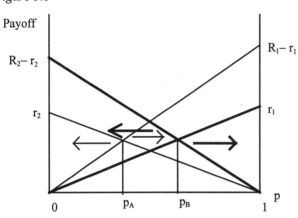

The non-bolded curves in Figure 5.1 describe payoffs to professional group one, the bolded curves to professional group two. So, for example, with full support for the existing strategy (S1) payoffs to groups one and two will be respectively $R_1 - r_1$ and r_1. As support for this strategy declines, i.e. as 'p' decreases, the payoffs from S1 decline and those from S2 increase. The dynamics of this system can be understood in terms of a learning process in which agents change their strategies according to relative payoffs (with no forward looking behaviour). In very general terms:

$$p(t+1) - p(t) = f[v(p, R_1, r_1) - v(p, R_2, r_2)] \qquad [1]$$

where: v = is the value of any payoff, and $f(0) = 0$, $f'(.) > 0$.

The nature of the resulting dynamics are indicated by arrows in Figure 5.1 (bold, once again, indicating the second group of professionals).

We are now in a position to draw out the important implications of this formulation. Given an existing strategy (S1) the agent professionals will prefer this as long as it has the support of more than a proportion p_B of the active organisational agents. This is the required support that is necessary to

89

make a change in strategy a recognisable possibility. But strategic change must also involve the current principals who will agree to change only if a proportion p_A of the organisational actors decide on such a course.[7] In short this simple formulation would seem to indicate that strategic lock-in, based on professional orientation, is a logical possibility given organisational dynamics based on a simple learning process. But this strategic lock-in is not absolute. It is always possible to shift towards an alternative strategy given appropriate (measured in terms of p_A and p_B) organisation support. Note that this strategic stability (or its converse) is not directly reliant on relative returns from the two strategies.

Apart from the simple observation of Figure 5.1 we can see this point clearly by deriving p_A and p_B. The former can be derived from the equality

$$p(R_1 - r_1) = (1 - p)r_2$$

hence

$$P_A = \frac{r_2}{R_1 - r_1 + r_2} \qquad [2a]$$

Similarly we can define

$$P_B = \frac{R_2 - r_2}{R_2 + r_1 - r_2} \qquad [2b]$$

It is clear from [2a] that it is the payment group one receives from strategy two (rather than potential returns) that determines support. Note that there may be a credibility issue here: how can group two credibly signal to group one the payment forthcoming from strategy two given an *ex-post* incentive for a principal to minimise transfers to an agent? An additional point that follows from [2a] and [2b] is that group one can 'bribe' or 'threaten' stability by increasing r_1 and/or r_2; the former being actual payments to strategy one agents and the latter being strategy two prospective income. But there is likely to be a complex bargaining game here because similar tactics may be employed by group two by increasing r_2 and/or r_1. The existence of this bargaining potential is the reason why earlier discussion emphasised the way in which professional power becomes institutionalised by self-regulation, control of entry etc., because this influences actual and/or prospective payments. If credibity problems and bargaining disrupt agreement between the groups, strategic change relies on a 'collapse' scenario in which $p_A = p_B = 1$; in this situation (from [2a] and [2b]) $R_1 - r_1 = 0$ and $r_1 = 0$.

Besides the existence and stability of locked-in strategies the second point that is of interest in Figure 5.1 is the potential region of disagreement or conflict in which contradictory dynamics exist i.e. between p_A and p_B. There is only one class of solutions to this game characterised by universal agreement. This will be the case when $p_A = p_B$, which will occur when

$$\frac{R_2}{R_1} = \frac{r_2}{R_1 - r_1}$$

[3a]

and by implication

$$\frac{R_1}{R_2} = \frac{r_1}{R_2 - r_2}$$

[3b]

Equations [3a] and [3b] suggest that universal agreement will exist when principal and agent returns depend only on exogenous circumstances rather than intra-organisational power relations. Equation [3a] indicates this for professional group one and [3b] for group two. In short the elimination of disagreement relies on a co-operative or partnership arrangement between the active organisational actors. In turn this would seem to rely on subordinating professional identity to organisational functioning, which while not being impossible is a special case.

A partnership/co-operative arrangement will not eliminate strategic lock-in; the absorbing equilibria still exist. Of critical importance in this situation is the nature of organisational learning, as described (in general terms) by equation [1]. If this proceeds in sufficiently 'small steps' strategic lock-in will be stable (ignoring a collapse scenario). The upper limit here will be globally rational agents that can overcome strategic uncertainty by assuming away the possibility of learning. In which case a co-operative/partnership organisation will always choose strategies to maximise returns; i.e. the neo-classical ideal. With bounded rationality existing over strategic matters professional orientation will become significant. In this regard the earlier discussion of the way in which professionalism is grounded in complex information becomes significant.

This complexity implies an inability to communicate and control plans and actions which in turn suggests the existence of strategic uncertainty.[8] In such circumstances professional orientation becomes significant which is likely to undermine the co-operative/partnership requirements of our 'harmony solution'. In addition, such circumstances will slow down the pace of learning. In short, actual or potential disagreement is likely to accompany professional orientation. Actual disagreement or conflict seems to be a common characteristic of UK organisational functioning (Richards 1995). It is revealed in terms of an inability to achieve clear agreement about functional leadership; or in terms of the framework suggested here, an inability to define the professional group that takes on the role of principal (and, by implication, agent).

ORGANISATIONAL AND TECHNOLOGICAL LOCK-IN

In the final substantive section of this contribution we will explore the possible implications for, and links between, the arguments presented above and more traditional views of technological lock-in, because arguably both are empirically observable. If we have many firms, each characterised by particular and idiosyncratic professional alliances, the combination of organisational and technological lock-in is possible but they cannot be simply juxtaposed. The case of many different firms, each characterised by its own organisational trajectory undermines the assumption in Arthur (1988a, 1988b, 1989) that choice of technology follows a random walk; rather, choice of technology will be channelled by organisational characteristics. Hence to generate technological lock-in (given organisational lock-in) mechanisms, processes or structures must exist to undermine the diversity implied by the idiosyncratic nature of decision making and promote convergent technological choices in a way that substitutes for a random walk assumption. In principle we might explain this convergence in two ways: market or institutional driven.

A market driven link between organisational and technological lock-in can draw on the arguments presented by Alchian (1950) and Friedman (1953) that only the fittest organisations will survive in a market economy, i.e. they invoke a crude Darwinian principle. The Alchian and Friedman arguments are based on different principles (Hodgson 1990). Friedman suggests that organisational behaviour can be (not necessarily is) random. For Alchian less efficient organisations imitate the more efficient. If organisational lock-in exists imitation can be a difficult process because, if we follow the framework set out in the previous section, any attempt at strategic change might generate (disequilibrium) disagreement and conflict rather than improvement. For this reason it might seem more appropriate to link organisational and technological lock-in by invoking a random rather than a universal systematic process.

The main difficulty with random selection processes are the implications of environmental and organisational diversity. As well as being a necessary result of organisational lock-in, such diversity must exist for selection to occur. With environmental diversity different aspects of the environment can involve different survival pressures that require contradictory organisational practices (Seal 1990). Therefore, in principle, with idiosyncratic firms we may have a number of different firms existing, each accommodating a different aspect of the environment. Given this possibility, and an ability to innovate there is no unique, stable equilibrium that will select out inefficient firms. In short, we cannot rely on the market to produce technological lock-in if organisational lock-in exists. For this reason stress will be placed on institutional explanations, as will now be discussed.

The discussion of national differences in professional organisation, introduced earlier, skirted over a centrally important differentiating characteristic. The nationally based differences nest into and result from more general institutional characteristics. Armstrong (1985, 1987, 1991) argues that the dominance of the accounting profession in Anglo-Saxon countries results from the importance of auditing and external stock market funding. In Germany and Japan, on the other hand, long-term relations with particular banks are important. Taking the example of Germany we can further explain the general organisational-professional characteristics in terms of the role of the Lander and vocational education and training (Lane 1989). In addition, and as cited earlier, Chandler (1990) stresses differences between corporate functioning in the US, UK and Germany that are organisational-institutional based.

These very simple examples illustrate that characteristic professional orientation nests into wider institutional characteristics that encompass legal, accounting, financial, educational, and so on, relations. This implies, therefore, that within a given society differences in professional orientation are likely to be less significant than differences between societies. In terms of a link between organisational and technological lock-in this can be conceptualised in terms of a two layer co-ordination game. At the first level we have organisations that are institutionally grouped. These groupings produce a second level co-ordination game between technological leaders.

At both levels decision making will revolve around the management of small numbers rivalry. In this regard we might like to remember Schelling's (1978, p. 14) suggestion: 'People are responding to an environment that consists of other people responding to *their* environment, which consists of people responding to an environment of people's responses. Sometimes the dynamics are sequential ... Sometimes the dynamics are reciprocal.' This shifts the analysis of technological lock-in away from a random walk, chance, based process (in which technologies are not sponsored, to use Arthur's (1988) terminology) towards one based on strategic leadership sponsoring particular technologies (Dietrich and Schenk 1993). Based on the arguments suggested here, the strategic leaders are key firms in particular institutional settings.

The link between organisational and technological lock-in therefore involves three sets of dynamics: intra-organisational, industry-technological, and the links between these two. We might like to suggest that effective technological leadership requires effective organisational functioning, i.e. a characteristic locked-in organisational response based on key professional actors. In addition it might seem appropriate to suggest that just as there is an important 'region of disagreement or conflict' in organisational relationships this will also be the case for technological supremacy. Given that organisational lock-in may lead to inflexibilities in firm responses it seems logical to suggest that payoff differentials between strategies will be high, which implies that the scope for conflict between existing and new leaders will be large.

We can apply and illustrate these ideas using two recent examples: VHS video technology and UK satellite television (Kay 1993; Dietrich and Schenk 1993). With regard to the first of these examples, Sony, the developer of the Betamax system, appeared to rely on its existing market dominance. JVC, the VHS developer, adopted an open licensing policy that faciltated rapid diffusion of its system. Although the two systems coexisted for a decade, the benefits of JVC's first mover advantage became increasing significant, even though Betamax was a technically more advanced system (Arthur 1988). The rivalry between Sony and JVC can, therefore, be seen to revolve around organisational links and in particular the way in which the marketing was allied to upstream functions. In addition, without an explanation of organisational lock-in it is difficult to understand why Sony did not change its strategy in the light of implementation issues. This would seem to be a more complete explanation of video system standardisation than accounting for technology choice as a result of a random walk process. Turning to the example of UK satellite television a similar story is illustrated. BSB was the approved broadcaster, but this sponsorship involved the use of a European Community standardised technology that generated higher quality pictures than the alternative. This support contributed to delay in commercial application that was to result in Sky Television establishing a base of subscribers and the advantage this involved. Hence (once again) market credibility was more powerful than a more developed technology. But this credibility must be understood as a strategic, rather than stochastic, issue. In this latter example, in addition to the importance of the marketing function we can also draw attention to the way in which Sky Television viewed the technology in terms of a financial logic. Once again, without organisational lock-in it is difficult to see why BSB did not change its financial-marketing focus by learning from the Murdoch experience. Eventually, of course, this was forced on it by takeover.

CONCLUSION

This paper has attempted to develop a framework that can shift the analysis of strategic lock-in away from a unique reliance on technological matters towards an organisationally based logic. To this extent the importance of professional dominance has been stressed for reasons that are both empirically based (i.e. professional dominance is apparent in reality) and for theoretical convenience (i.e. professional dominance is a useful analytical device). Initially the analysis was structured in an informal way, that involved the development of a rich framework. Specific predictions, however, were derived from a more narrowly focused game theoretic rendering of the same issues. Here strategic lock-in was seen to be likely, but not inevitable. In addition, the formal analysis suggested that conflict-disagreement is likely to accompany professional dominance in all organisations based on professional identity. This conclusion marginalises the 'harmony' solution that is appropriate in co-operative/partnership arrangements.

The final section of the paper linked the analysis of organisational lock-in developed here with the more traditional variant based on technology. Here a shift away from chance events causing lock-in was deemed necessary. After rejecting selection of technologies based on market processes an institutional analysis was suggested that involved interaction between two co-ordination games at organisational and technological levels. The comments developed here were highly speculative implications of the framework developed and were intended to be no more than suggestive. Clearly there is a rich potential research agenda that is possible here, involving a role for empirical and more formal investigation. The particular path dependencies that are generated by the interaction between organisation and technology would seem to be particularly important (North 1990). Technological decisions will have organisational implications as well as causation running in the reverse direction. This suggests, among other things, that technological decisions may be deflected or diverted by organisational responses, in the spirit of Schelling's view cited earlier. This would seem to have the potential of placing an active human agency, that is structured by institutional circumstances, at the centre of lock-in research.

NOTES

* This paper was prepared for the conference *Evolutionary Economics and Path Dependence*, Uppsala University, May 1995. Discussion at this conference, and comments by the editors of this volume have led to refinement of some of the arguments in this contribution. The efforts of all concerned are much appreciated. Obviously any remaining mistakes, confusions, etc, are the author's responsibility.

1 Perrow (1986) makes reference to three types of control: direct, bureaucratic and unobtrusive. The first and third are equivalent to direct and indirect dominance. Bureaucratic control, involving specialisation, standardisation and hierarchy, is not considered in the text because organisational form is ignored in the discussion.

2 Winter's (1987) presentation of these matters differs from that presented in the text. Winter highlights complexity as a separate, independent factor along side tacit, observable and systemic knowledge, as determinants of information problems, rather than an overarching factor that depends on the three characteristics of information.

3 This uniqueness of organisational capabilities is a standard aspect of modern business strategy (Kay 1993; Hamel and Prahalad 1994; Pettigrew and Whipp 1991).

4 This discussion of the behavioural theory is based on that presented in Dietrich (1994). The behavioural theory of the firm is, of course, based on Simon (1955), March and Simon (1958) and Cyert and March (1963).

5 To simplify technical detail we will assume constant returns to professional participation; this has two implications. First, it implies that strategic lock-in is generated by coordination advantages and adaptive expectations, increasing returns to use not being relevant. The second implication is that there is a strightforward mapping from group to individual returns. Individual returns from a particular strategy are constant. The dynamic of the framework is provided by the possibility of meeting someone with whom an actor agrees (i.e. the expected value of individual returns). This simplification implies that the analysis can be conducted at the level of the group rather than the individual.

6 There is a limit problem with this formulation that can be noted. The first professional to adopt a particular strategy generates a (small) surplus which is shared between this person and a non-existent other person. This is obviously logical nonsense, but can be ignored because it is irrelevant for organisational functioning. To generate a shift away from a particular strategy will involve the participation of more than one actor for reasons that will become clear in the text.

7 The analysis in the text will ignore the possibility of $p_A > p_B$. This will occur when strategy payments are greater from agent rather than the principal status. More formally we can show this by setting $p_A > p_B$ (using [2a] and [2b]) from which the following can be derived:

$$\frac{r_1}{R_1} > \frac{R_2 - r_2}{R_2}$$

or

$$\frac{r_2}{R_2} > \frac{R_1 - r_1}{R_1}$$

8 In Dietrich (1994) it is suggested that individual motivation, in the context of complexity and strategic uncertainty, can be analysed in terms of inputs from social psychology and in particular the dissonance resulting from differential power in an organisational context. Essentially equivalent conclusions are drawn as those in the text.

6. The Microfoundations of Path Dependency

Salvatore Rizzello

INTRODUCTION

Framework and Goals

The purpose of this paper is to contribute to the identification of the microfoundations of path dependency. It is my firm belief that this represents a crucial passage towards the full understanding of this category's potential. My hypothesis is that, once the microfoundations are identified, the analyses of path dependent kind will be strengthened and become more easily extensible.

In order to reach this goal, it is above all important to refer to the context in which this category has been used. It has risen within that literature which we may define as heterodox, and which has tried, among other things, to refute the predominant model of Walras and Pareto, from its foundations. This operation did not take place in a systematic way, but through gradual developments, which I certainly cannot account for here. An extensive conception of the heterodox approach should, in fact, include authors of the stature of Menger, Keynes, Schumpeter, etc. (to consider only the first ones or the ones chronologically closer to Walras and Pareto) and the schools they have founded.

Actually, the objective I am pursuing is not to rebuild exhaustively the heterodox approach in economics, nor to point out all the weaknesses of the traditional conception. My objective is first of all to recall only some of the criticism which has emerged, and particularly that criticism which may help us to identify the microfoundations of path dependency. As I shall try to demonstrate, it is my firm belief that these foundations have a psychological nature. And, in order to identify them, it is better to start with the most effective criticism to the neo-classic paradigm.

I will try here to recall what, in my opinion, are the most important points of criticism of the neo-classic paradigm: the ones concerning the scarce or non-existent empirical evidence of its axioms (Hayek 1937, 1945); and, in particular, the assumption that the economic agents are characterised by perfect knowledge and substantive (or Olympic) rationality (Simon 1972, 1979).

The heterodox approach has looked for support in empirical evidence, and this has made it possible, among other things, to elaborate new models of choice on the demand side (just think of Simon's elaboration of the satisficing approach)[1]; it has made it possible to formulate the theory of market failures[2] leading eventually to the full recognition of the institutional framework as a necessary dimension for the carrying out of the transaction processes.[3]

Furthermore, on the supply side, the new approach has allowed the role of the firm and its hierarchical nature to be explained (Coase 1937), but it has also allowed to be cast lights on the processes of organisation and learning within the firm itself (March and Simon 1958; Nelson and Winter 1982), and on the mechanisms of technological change (David 1985, Antonelli 1995).[4] More recently, economic theory has been focusing on a joint analysis of the role of organisations and institutions, and of the relationship between them (North 1990).

In this framework of analysis, path dependence is being used to explain a crucial concept of the heterodox conception: change, be it technological change or institutional change. After the formulation of this concept (David 1985), path dependence has mainly been used within the context of industrial economics. More recently, it has been extended also to institutional change (North 1990).

I am convinced that at the basis of path dependence lie many of the aspects pointed out in today's literature, such as the problems concerning individual rationality, and the processes of the acquisition of knowledge, as well as those of problem solving. It is my intention to make explicit reference to these categories in order to grasp the relationship between them. I will begin with a short illustration of the applications of path analysis.

At first, I will briefly refer to the literature in which this analytical category is used. I will then deal directly with the problems of the microfoundations. Concluding, I will try to point out some relevant implications for economics of innovation and neo-institutional theory.

Path Dependency in Economic Theory

Path dependency was first found in natural history, in the analysis of the evolution of the species, as a characteristic trait which affects future development in a relevant way. In other words, this concept implies that every successive act in the development of an individual, an organisation, or an institution is strongly influenced by, and dependent from, the path (experience and evolution) previously covered.

It is some authors' belief that path-dependence is also present in human history, and that it consequently has a natural as well as a social dimension (Arrow 1994b).

In a weak conception, path-dependence can simply be viewed as an influence of the past upon the present. In a stronger one, it can be considered as a fixed course followed by individuals and organisations in their evolution. In the latter case, we mainly put stress on the limiting aspect of the category, which, in an extreme interpretation, can decline towards some kind of causal determinism: in principle, if everything is strongly path dependent, everything becomes predictable. On the other hand, the first kind of approach emphasises the specificity and the potential which a certain course allows individuals and organisations to reach. In other words, it underlines the structural differences which may or may not allow the evolutionary process to move in certain directions.

The underlying general idea is that the structure of organisations (the functioning of the productive processes, reorganisation, and evolution) and the structure of the institutions (genesis, development, and evolution) derives from a process of sedimentation which influences in a more or less binding way the future development in a precise direction, along paths which are in turn the result of past adaptations of primary conditions, at times resulting from completely casual events; but the idea is also that some form of development and evolution may occur right where a specific concentration of elements and a just as specific background are present, as in the case of localised technological change.

The Application in Industrial Economics

The introduction of path dependence in industrial economics has allowed economists to reach remarkable results in the ambit of innovation economics. In particular, this has allowed the normalisation of the analysis of technological change, no longer conceived as exogenous and perfectly malleable, according to the precepts of the standard economic theory, but strongly localised and mainly endogenous (Antonelli 1995).

Technological change is one of the crucial aspects of all industrial economics. In order to point out the new developments introduced in this literature through the approach 'path dependence', let us trace back, in a very general way, the most relevant steps of the economics of innovation.[5]

In the standard conception, technological change is exogenous, it homogeneously influences all of the agents, and allows an increase in productivity. The access of the firms to new technologies takes place without costs and without any asymmetry of dimensional, technical, informative, market, and organisational kind (Antonelli 1995, ch. 12). From the 1930s on, Schumpeter has identified the limits of the traditional conception with the static nature of the models. The conception of the Viennese economist aimed instead at developing the dynamic components of the theory of technological change, emphasising the tie between economic development and technological change itself. Against the orthodox tradition, the Schumpeterian approach first pointed out the central role of the entrepreneur as the engine of economic development. He is the maker of innovative choices, in a survey in which these are irregularly distributed in time and space, and are concentrated in cycles (*The Theory of Economic Development*). Schumpeter, however, later made a further step, identifying the endogenous nature of technological change (especially in *Capitalism, Socialism, and Democracy*). He puts forward the following virtuous circle: the introduction of successful innovations brings forth the creation of monopolistic 'quasi-rents', which, in turn, give rise to resources and funds for research and development. These investments lead to new innovations whose application will bring forth further 'quasi-rents', which will allow new investments, and so on.

Directly derived from the Schumpeterian tradition, the theory of evolution has made further steps ahead in this direction. Moreover, considering the role of learning and of externalities, it has pointed out how technological change is highly specific and idiosyncratic, and how, in many cases, it does not have any of the characteristics of a public good. Conversely, the ability to appropriate themselves of innovations and the protection from free imitation are among the basic elements which spur firms to invest in research and development, and to introduce specific technological change.

From this point, there is but a small step to the more recent results of the economics of innovation. These results are due to the full acknowledgement of the path-dependent nature of these processes, which can be synthesised in the expression 'processes of localised technological change'. The term 'localised' has in this context a double meaning: it is referred both to its

101

specific as well as to its endogenous nature. Practically, the process of innovation is internal and depends on the specific dynamics of the firm. It does not derive, instead, from a process by which the firm simply decides whether or not to adopt an invention produced exogenously, which everyone can have access to.[6]

Without pretending to deal with all the complex and numerous aspects which determine technological change (the dynamics of prices, the course of costs, etc.), I can nevertheless state that the recent literature emphasises the rigidity of change, its idiosyncratic character, and its endogenous nature. This new model fully welcomes the path-dependent approach. In fact, it is the latter itself which, resulting from ample empirical evidence, strengthens the former's hypotheses and conclusions. The framework in which the model is elaborated is structured upon the following assumptions: a) agents are characterised by limited rationality and act according to criteria of procedural rationality (Simon 1979b) firms operate in heterogeneous markets and are above all characterised by a substantial diversity in the use of techniques, structures, and organisation, in market behaviour, and in the ability to innovate and learn (Antonelli 1995, ch. 12); c) information is imperfect; and d) sunk and switching costs matter (Stiglitz 1987; Schmanlensee 1992).

Emphasising specialisation and diversification, this approach can account for the competitive advantage which characterises each firm and for all the specific processes of innovation or substitution which are, in fact, highly path dependent (this aspect has also been pointed out by Arthur (1988a)).

Institutional Change

Recently, path dependence has also been introduced in the neo-institutional literature (North 1990). Especially during the last twenty years, following an approach which was critical and different with regard to the traditional neo-classic one, founded on the Walrasian conception, the neo-institutional literature has developed in the firm belief that the economic relationships can only be understood within the institutional framework in which they take place. Special attention has been given to the role of organisations, as well as to the nature, genesis, and the developments of the institutions. In particular, the current literature is dealing with the existing relationship between organisations and institutions, and with the dynamics which characterise them (Rizzello 1995a).

What is the role of path dependence in the analyses carried out in this literature? On a social level (the development of languages and cultures) there are many examples in which it can be presumed that path dependence covers an important role.

The consequences of small events and changes in circumstances, often fortuitous, may determine situations which, once they prevail, can consolidate and establish a certain path. North (1991), in particular, has provided evidence of the deep relationship between historical evolution and the specific evolution of institutions. According to this conception, institutional change has the same path dependent nature as technological change, since in both cases 'ideological beliefs influence the subjective construction of the models that determine choices' (North 1990, p. 103), and the evolution of behavioural rules, the implicit and explicit rules, and institutions derive from a spontaneous interactive process. The institutions are the rules, arising spontaneously, within which organisations move. Organisations are the players (North 1992, p. 4). The continuous interaction between institutions and organisations in a context of scarcity and, therefore, of competition represents the key to institutional change.

There are authors who prefer to consider the dynamic processes between institutions and organisations in a context characterised by increasing returns, rather than in a context of scarcity (Smith, Young, Schumpeter, Nelson and Winter, etc.). In my opinion, the two positions are not incompatible, since there is the unifying element of competition. In fact, we find competition both in a context of scarcity and in one of increasing returns. However, once the context is defined, be it characterised by scarcity, or increasing returns, or both, it becomes important to pick up the dynamics that take place between organisations and institutions. And this interaction can be described here, albeit in very broad terms.

Organisations, in fact, urged by competition in a context of uncertainty, are continuously investing in knowledge and skills in order to respond in the most efficient way to the problems that come from the environment (which is also made of the other firms). These choices, as well as the structure itself of the organisations, are conditioned by the institutional environment. Whenever the institutional rules become too binding for free action of organisations, there rises conflict and request for a change in the institutional rules.

However, one should always keep in mind the dynamics underlying the generation of new rules. As we have seen, individuals, organisations, and institutions all live according to rules, with a few, important, differences. Both individuals and organisations solve problematic situations through learning, according to criteria of procedural rationality. Yet, individuals change their routines in a less 'bureaucratic' way, and faster, within the

103

spaces of free will allowed by the institutional rules and by the organisations in which they operate. On the other hand, organisations carry out changes, which are slower than the individual ones, within the limits of the institutions and of competition.

In short, the changeability and complexity of the environment urge the organisations to reshape their structure and to adapt to changes. Whenever the institutional environment is too binding with regard to the needed changes, there begins a process by which institutions are modified. This process is usually slower than the one needed to modify organisations, which, by their own nature, must be more elastic in responding to environmental changes.

In general, institutions and organisations can be thought of as routines. Therefore, institutional and organisational change can be thought of as a process in which new routines try to take the place of preceding ones. However, in the last analysis, what are the mechanisms that give rise to changes, be they organisational or institutional, and that regulate the dynamics which take place between organisations and institutions? It is my belief that these mechanisms have first of all an individual dimension. They should therefore be searched for in the subjective processes which generate routines, whatever the ambit in which they are exerted, with particular reference to the neurological, psychological, and social processes on which they are founded. It is quite right to expect these processes to have a path-dependent nature.

THE PSYCHOLOGICAL DIMENSION

The Analysis of the Microfoundations

To state that when individuals act they are characterised by path dependence, means to recognise that they are influenced by their own specific characteristics, by their experience (Hayek 1952), by the specific feed-back which is enacted with the environment in the processes of problem solving (Simon 1956), by the personal learning processes, and, above all, by the subjective mechanisms of acquisition of knowledge (Rizzello 1995b). First of all, let us try to understand on the empirical level how the individual actually learns, chooses, and acts. The examples from the heterodox literature are relevant.

Among the most important contributions which the unorthodox approach has given to economic theory, those of F. von Hayek and H. Simon should certainly be included. Hayek has criticised the traditional assumption according to which all individuals act in a situation of perfect knowledge and without costs. He has demonstrated, on the contrary, how knowledge is dispersed among many individuals who, in order to act, use the relevant knowledge whose acquisition depends on a process which entails costs (Hayek 1937). Furthermore, Hayek has pointed out that the mechanism of competition works exactly because individuals have differentiated knowledge (Hayek 1945). However, with his book of 1952, *The Sensory Order*, he has shown how individuals acquire knowledge through a mechanism, also neurological, which, in my opinion, is strongly path dependent. Before explaining this mechanism a bit more in depth, it is however necessary to throw light on another aspect. The results obtained by Hayek and Simon are also the outcome of the growing diffusion of cognitivism, to whose birth they have directly and indirectly contributed.

The Influence of Cognitive Psychology Upon Economic Theory

Cognitive psychology was born in the middle years of this century, and its results have carried some important implications also for contemporary economic theory. Some authors have empirically verified the assumptions of the economic models in the light of the discoveries in the field of psychology, often finding the inadequacy of the assumptions themselves. This fact has given an important impulse to build an alternative approach, whose foundations are first of all consistent with the new developments in the field of psychology (Gardner 1985).

As we have seen, those who have fully accepted the cognitivistic approach have been able to elaborate new models of choice of the satisficing kind, instead of the traditional optimising approach (Simon); to replan the role of the market as a cybernetic instrument, which allows the use of much more knowledge than an individual can actually possess (Hayek); and to begin to explain the role of the firm – and, in general, of organisations – as the site of hierarchic division of knowledge and competence (March and Simon 1958, Nelson and Winter 1982) instead of the traditional neo-classic black box. Furthermore, this approach has recently given life to the neo-institutional literature, which has developed within the economic theory the study of the birth and role of institutions (Williamson 1986, North 1990). The above are only some aspects, even though they are among the most relevant in the heterodox literature, which are founded on axioms of behaviour that are coherent with the results attained by cognitive psychology (Rizzello 1995a). For this reason, it seems useful to describe it briefly.

Cognitivism

In order to briefly explain what cognitivism is, it is necessary to refer to the introduction in cybernetics (Wiener 1948) of the concept of feed back, and then to its extension in psychology. In general, feed back can be defined as a control system which continuously adjusts (in a compensatory way) the present action, on the base of the returning information, in reference to the desired action (Gregory 1987, pp. 297–300).

The application of the concept of feed-back in psychology has entailed the abandonment of behaviourism to the advantage of cognitivism. Behaviourism upheld the necessity of a totally objective psychology, which was to deal with behavioural acts, that could be described in terms of stimulus – response; consequently, all the concepts and terms that referred abstractly to the mind had to be rejected. Such terms as 'image', 'mind', and 'conscience' were, in that context, without a meaning (Schultz 1974, pp. 226–7). In the behavioural perspective, the environment had a central role in determining individual action: the person did not act according to his own ideas and intentions, but passively mirrored the environmental reflections. Conversely, in the view of cognitive psychologists, the behavioural sequences are already planned and organised before the action take place. They are not mere chains of stimuli and responses. The form precedes and determines behaviour, and does not come from without, but from within the organisms.[7]

According to cognitivism, every person is endowed with cognitive functions, which allow him to interact with the environment. The organism does not only adapt itself to the environment, but it *modifies* it according to its needs. The acquisition of knowledge derives from the feed back between the person and his environment, in which a decisive role is played by the perception, reelaboration, and the interpretation of the surrounding world. The person is active and adjusts his behaviour each time according to the information received from without. He owns interpretative schemes, which are inborn. Thanks to them, he perceives the external stimuli through an interactive process of adjustment of the external data to the owned schemes. The latter being hereditary they allow from the time of birth a good adjustment to the external environment. These schemes develop through mechanisms of adaptation and assimilation. If the perceived data is something already known, we are facing a process of recognitive assimilation, in which a scheme is applied to the recognised situation exactly as it is. If, on the other hand, the action or situation is new, we deal with a generalising assimilation, in which the new is perceived through the application (association) of an already owned scheme. When the situation is complex, the scheme is each time adjusted through adaptation. The same scheme modifies itself by 'adapting' according to the new experience it is perceiving.

Hayek's View

The pioneering articles of Hayek on the importance and the use of knowledge in economic processes represent one of his major contributions to economic theory (Hayek 1937; 1945). He has maintained that the processes of acquisition of information and the use of knowledge respond to a spontaneous and autonomous adjustment of individuals, who, in order to act, use relevant information only (Hayek 1945, p. 527). Hayek has often stressed the prodigiousness of the market as a cybernetic instrument, which enables the agents to use correctly much more knowledge than they actually possess. In making this point, he often emphasised two fundamental aspects: the impersonal nature of the market and the individual limits in processing information.

Let us come to the relevant aspects, which concern path dependence. It is my firm belief that the methodological coherence of Hayek's approach is already verifiable in one of his early works, *The Sensory Order*, written in the 1920's, but published only in 1952.[8] Let us try now to expound in a systematic way the most relevant aspects of the process of acquisition of knowledge, according to Hayek. As we shall see, it is much more similar to the one elaborated by cognitive psychology, which occupies a central position in all of Hayek's works (from the mechanisms of interaction to the emergence of norms); but, above all, it has a strongly path dependent nature, on which I shall dwell, since it represents the pivot of this article's entire analytic construction.

Classifier System

The main thesis maintained by Hayek in *The Sensory Order* is that every fragment of cognitive action is a subjective act of *interpretation*, based upon the experience previously acquired by an individual and his species. The mind is a framework that orders the perceptions of the world through neurological phenomena of classification and association of classes of stimuli into classes of responses. The mind does not receive sensations in a passive way, but through an act of *interpretation*. Every perception and every action (presented in an indissoluble bond) are influenced by an individual's genetic structure and by his previous classifications and associations (the past experience that varies according to each individual). The central elements in the cognitive process are therefore the synchronous multiple classification of perception, and the feedback between the individual and his environment. Thanks to the latter, the mental structure is not rigid and presumptive, but continuously evolving according to spontaneous mechanisms that are supraconscious and therefore unknowable.[9]

Perception

The impossibility to predict subjective behaviour is deeply rooted in the perceptive activity. The latter is part of a continuous process by which, through subsequent approximations, the brain's microcosm comes to the reproduction of the external macrocosm (Hayek 1952, p. 108; Hayek 1963). Perception is founded *upon the experience* of a person. All that is perceived is immediately confronted with classes of already recorded data. Every perception of a new stimulus, or class of stimuli, will be influenced by previously implemented classifications. A new phenomenon will always be perceived in association with other events with which it has something in common (Hayek 1952, pp. 142–3). Every individual stores different experiences and creates a different system of connections of stimuli. Consequently, it is impossible for the same phenomenon to be perceived in exactly the same way by the same individuals, because each person will associate that particular stimulus to his own class of stimuli which obviously differs from that of everyone else.

Therefore, according to Hayek, even the sensation is *essentially dependent* from experience, since even at this level there appears a process of interpretation based upon an individual's or a race's experience (Hayek 1952, pp. 41–2). Hayek resumes Kant's model of the mind and speaks of a *framework*, belonging to each person, which contains patterns that give order to the world view. The framework is a representation of the kind of world in which the organism has existed in the past and within it come together the classifications and the interpretations given to past stimuli. The schemes have a semipermanent character. In fact, being the result of the gathering of a long past experience, they are stable with reference to the experience of the moment. However, they are in turn conditioned by past experience and slowly modify themselves according to the adjustment of individual action in response to new external stimuli. Hayek's schemes, therefore, differ from Kant's categories of the intellect, which are rigid and presumptive. They are rather the result of dispositions, perhaps even inborn, but continuously remodelled and fitted (adjusted) to experience.

The mind is a system of abstract rules which, like a 'grill', gives order to our perceptions of the world. All sensations, perceptions, and images are the outcome of a superimposition of many 'classifications' of events perceived with a diversified meaning. Abstractions are dispositions that make the organism inclined to respond to certain stimuli; and, in turn, readiness for action comes from the superimposition of many of these dispositions. The general models of action work like moulds in which external perceptions are shaped. The framework, however, also has a collective valence. In fact, a person does not have only his own individual experience, but also all the experience which he receives unintentionally from the group and the environment. His individual action, when repeated in a routine, consolidates the collective custom; when innovative, it contributes to the evolution of the collective framework.[10]

Perception – Action

The phenomenon of perception is strictly connected with action in a bond of adaptive kind. The perceptive schemes conform to (are influenced by) the schemes of behaviour, and, at the same time, the latter are caused by the perceptive ones. Therefore, between perception and action there is a continuous process of feedback, and the resulting sensory order is contemporaneously input and output of the activities of the superior nervous centres (Hayek 1952, p. 90). If, in the past facing a problematic situation, a person has experimented effective schemes of action which have shown themselves to be effective, he will be ready to use them again when he associate these already selected schemes to the newly perceived phenomena. Association is therefore the main phenomenon of knowledge; it is strongly present in perception as well as in action and is tied to *historic* events and to the *specific experience* of every individual.

These 'different' individuals are able to communicate thanks to the common elements which they possess, and which characterise the subjective schemes that have developed through a process of imitation (Hayek 1952, pp.192–3). The social co-ordination, instead, is guaranteed by the institutions. These are a set of rules, arising more or less spontaneously, which simplifies the framework of human rationality, standardises behaviours, and guarantees the social order of a complex reality like that of an open society (Catallaxis) (Hayek 1967).

Already at this point we can make the very first remarks about the implications of this theory on the mechanism of competition. This mechanism works not only because individuals have access to different relevant information, but above all because they *interpret*, in a different manner, the same data, since classification and feedback are entirely subjective processes based on the *genetic tradition* and on the *experience* acquired by the individual. The foundation of the differentiation of individual action in the processes of choosing lies therefore on this diversity in the interpretation of the external stimuli, which derives from the neuronal structure.

Simon's View

Drawing on the results of cognitive psychology, Simon has elaborated a concept of rationality, which points out how every individual is characterised by bounded rationality. These limits concern the computing and cognitive ability, which is typical of the human mind (Simon 1982). However, Simon has also emphasised the potential of human rationality by pointing out that, in spite of their bounded rationality, individuals act according to criteria of procedural rationality. In short, when facing a problematic situation, individuals deal with it by applying an already tried routine, or by generating new routines.[11]

Some of these processes take place unconsciously, others require instead strong concentration and the full use of the individual faculties. Thanks to Simon's contributions, the most recent literature has obtained important results in this field. In particular, there has been the elaboration of models of choice characterised by imperfect imitation (e.g. Alchian's model),[12] which I have referred to above; but there has also been the conception of models of generation of routines in three different directions. The first one is the one that starts from the research made by Newell and Simon on problem solving, which we have described above (Egidi 1992); the second one is tied to models of neural networks (Terna 1992; Fabbri Orsini 1991); and, finally, the last one is based on genetic algorithms (Holland, Holyoak, Nisbett and Thagard 1988).

The most interesting applications of this new perspective surely concern the theory of the firm. According to the evolutionist view (Alchian 1950, Winter 1964), the firm is a complex subject, which modifies its internal structure in order to adjust to the uncertain and changing environment in which it operates. Within the firm take place learning mechanisms, mechanisms by which knowledge is passed between the actors, and mechanisms by which new skills are acquired. This entails the problem of co-ordinating existing routines; but, most important, it entails the possibility of generating new routines (Nelson and Winter 1982).

If we unify Hayek's and Simon's positions, we find the microfoundations of the individual economic behaviour utilised in the heterodox approach. I will try now to define it in outline, and to explain why I feel it is strongly path dependent. At this point, the most important aspect is to understand how individuals elaborate the routines which they utilise to solve problematic situations. Let us set aside the mechanisms of imitation and concentrate on the mechanisms of the original formulation of new routines. They derive from mental mechanisms of perception of external data through the association with already codified data.

As Hayek (1952) has pointed out, and as the most recent neurologic studies have confirmed (Calissano 1992, Patterson and Nawa 1993), individuals build up their own knowledge giving and interpretation of sensorial data according to criteria of classification, which depend on an individual's innate characteristics, on his mental categories, and, above all, on acquired experience. Since experience varies from one individual to another, its sedimentation subjectively modifies and characterises the interpretative schemes of the sensorial data.

According to the most recent discoveries in neurology, already perceived by Hayek, it can be stated that external information, made up of objective data, becomes knowledge which can be used by the individual through endogenous processes (Rizzello 1995b). Individuals who face the same data could give a different interpretation of it, precisely because the processes by which knowledge is acquired are personal and vary from one individual to another.

Path dependency in the processes of acquisition of knowledge is evident. Its acquisition depends in fact on history, on upbringing, and above all on the experience which the individual has acquired and is continuously acquiring. Every single perception of external data depends on subjective characteristics which, in turn, derive from the original paths of data interpretation and, first of all, from inborn characteristics.[13]

Let us see the implications of all this in Simon's conception. I have already said that the individual acts in situations of problem solving by enacting processes of imitation of already tried procedures, or generating new routines. Simplifying, we can state that firms, too, act using more or less the same mechanisms. The teachings of Hayek and of cognitive psychology show, however, that also when imitating, agents enact subjective processes of interpretation of the observed data. Knowledge is the adjustment to situations which do not correspond to what has previously been acquired. In other words, knowledge is an operation of continuous adjustment of perceived data, which does not correspond to the preceding experiences.

This explains in part the different performances of firms that have similar characteristics whenever they enact processes of imitation. But this path-dependent approach also explains that innovation is first of all an original act of data interpretation, whose specificity and eventual effectiveness is founded on the personal learning skills of the individual or the firm, which strongly depend on their own history and corporate culture.

Environmental mutability and complexity spur the organisations to restructure and adjust to changes. Whenever the institutional environment becomes too limiting with respect to the room required by firms for development, there begins a process of modification of the institutions that is generally slower than the one needed by organisations. The latter, in fact, for their own nature, must be more elastic in responding to the environmental changes according to efficiency criteria.

In general, institutions and organisations can be thought of as routines. Therefore, institutional and organisational change can be thought of as a process in which new routines try to take the place of the preceding ones. But which are, in the last analysis, the mechanisms underlying the individual, organisational, and institutional changes, and underlying the dynamics that takes place between organisations and institutions? I believe that these mechanisms should be identified in the subjective processes that generate routines, whatever may be the ambit in which they are exerted with particular reference to the neurological, psychological, and social mechanisms which underlie the processes themselves. Since these processes have a path-dependent nature, this justifies, at a micro level, the assumptions and analyses about technological and institutional change.

IMPLICATION FOR ECONOMIC THEORY

Technological Change

Following the approach of Nelson and Winter, we can consider the technology used by firms as routines, which are the result of previously experimented and codified knowledge that is continuously applied in the same way (Egidi 1991). On the base of this definition, if we consider the organisation in general terms and not only with reference to its technological structure, we can locate the presence of routines at every level: organisational, productive, technological, commercial, etc. Let us now ask ourselves, in general terms, how the change takes place, and why it can be considered path dependent, also in consideration of what I have stated on the microfoundations.

We can start from a given situation in which a firm or an organisation uses routines. Whenever a problematic situation occurs, for example an erosion of profits, losses of market share, an increase or decrease of costs, etc., the firm is induced to solve it. As already stated above, it can carry out processes of imitation or else generate new routines. In both cases, the change it will bring about is likely to be of a path-dependent kind, all the more so if the firm is characterised by bonds, such as the levels of sunk and switching costs, the particular conditions of the market, the presence – or absence – of available internal capital for investments in research and development, and the level of access to credit.

An ever growing body of empirical evidence (Antonelli 1988), has shown that these bonds of firms are in two ways fundamental in the process by which an innovation is adopted: as bonds, precisely, but also as potentialities.

The more a firm is characterised by high sunk and switching costs, by particular market structures, by particular dimensions of the plants, or by the availability of capital for research and development, etc., the more in the processes of imitation it will tend to adopt an innovation by fitting its configuration (adapting it) in the best possible way to its specific situation, holding back as much as possible the costs of the adoption. All this will allow it to take into the process of adoption-adjustment some changes to the innovation, which will be specific and idiosyncratic, and will become in turn objects of further imitation. However, as in the case of the genuine generation of new routines, the process is path dependent and probably stronger. Also in this case the spur toward change derives from a problematic situation (it could even be a very general problematic situation, such as that of keeping a leadership). The greater the above-mentioned characteristics (sunk costs, etc.), the more specific and path dependent will be the innovations.

Before moving on to the next paragraph, let me make a last, but fundamental, point. First of all, it is easy to see the analogy between the individual processes of acquisition of knowledge through the imitation or generation of new routines, and the processes of imitation or genuine innovation of the firms. Yet, there is more. It should be remembered that, even though they are structured in hierarchies, it is individuals who act within organisations. These individuals have the psychological and neurological characteristics described above, and their decisions derive from the process of feed-back between the problematic situation, the existing bonds, environmental complexity, acquired experience, and learning ability. At this point, the path-dependent process becomes evident also in the framework of what we may define in general terms as technological change. The conclusion is the following: the more the markets are characterised by firms that are heterogeneous, specific, idiosyncratic, etc., the more we see processes of path dependent change. As can be inferred from the analysis of the microfoundations, there is perfect coherence between individual and organisational learning processes. It is possible to identify this coherence, in spite of a few differences, also within the institutional context.

Institutional Change

I feel that many of the above statements concerning technological change are also valid for institutional change. For this reason, in this paragraph I shall only point out the small, but significant, differences. Institutions too, can be thought of as routines. However, in comparison with the routines of organisations, they have a slightly different foundation. In fact, the rules adopted by firms must fulfil criteria of efficiency, since a competitive market punishes those who adopt inefficient innovations. Institutional rules, on the other hand, must fulfil criteria of effectiveness. In fact, every institution, as long as it is effective and in harmony with the other institutions, will continue to exist. Therefore, we can recognise two moments through which a set of rules can assert itself as an institution. In the first one, as we have seen, there is a spontaneous formation of a behavioural model, which, once it has proven its effectiveness, spreads by imitation (Hayek 1963 and Horwitz 1993). It is what North calls 'informal constraints'; and is the element which introduces the predictability of the conduct of others and the simplification of the environmental variables, allowing them to surmount the limitations of individuals. In this phase, the respect of 'normal behaviour' is guaranteed by a network of informal sanctions.

In a second moment, the rules thus set, i.e. the informal institutions, need some sort of 'protection', to defend themselves and guarantee their functioning. Here, we can identify the process of institutionalisation: the spontaneous rules are now supported by other rules, which are formal, planned, conceived in such a way as to allow the survival of the former and to enhance their effectiveness. However, the relationship between the two is not necessarily linear. The informal institutions have in general a spontaneous nature, but their normalisation is also the result of mediations and of conflicts of interests. The context in which they are generated is substantially limited by two bounds: effectiveness and the harmony with other institutions. Within the scope of these two bounds take place the conflicts of interests.

Between informal and formal institutions there is a relationship by which they mutually affect each other (feedback). The effectiveness of the formal institutions results directly from the characteristics of the informal ones: the fact of being conventionally recognised and of being perceived as 'right behaviour' (tacit conventions); however, at the same time, the objective of the formal rules is just to stabilise and defend a mechanism, which has proven effective. The informal institutions are therefore strongly influenced by the formal ones.

Although the effectiveness of the two kinds of rules has different sources and characteristics, there is a common element which allows us to maintain the oneness of the concept of institution: the ordering function. If the characteristic of being a norm is a fact for the informal institutions, it is an act for the formal ones, in the sense that the latter are the result of choices directed immediately and consciously toward the creation of rules. As already stated above, I also consider valid for institutional change what I have said about the similarities between the individual and organisational processes of imitation, of learning, and of generation of new routines.

However, I believe that in the case of institutional change there is need to distinguish two different path-dependent processes. In the spontaneous rise of institutions (as it is described by Hayek), path dependence derives mainly from the individual processes by which problematic situations are perceived and by which knowledge is acquired and communicated to other individuals; path dependence derives also, but a little less, from the history and the traditions of a country (North 1991). In this first case, it seems to me that the individual dimension prevails over the holistic one.

Conversely, in the case of the processes by which institutions are formalised, the situation seems to be completely reversed. Generally, normative processes seem to prevail in tradition and history (think, for instance, of the differences between common law and civil law), as well as the solution of power conflicts, which also take place in a path-dependent way; while the spontaneous, individual dimension, which was prevailing in the first case, is here of smaller influence.

The conclusion on the subject of institutional change is the following: here we also find path dependence in the processes of change, and a strong connection with the microfoundations previously described. However, in this context it is necessary to distinguish between two types of path dependence: the first, tied to the spontaneous process of the emergence of norms, is easily linked to the processes of acquisition of knowledge and adoption of routines by individuals; the second is more closely connected to the cultural tradition of the normalisation of norms, which has a more holistic dimension and is more dependent on the society's history.

CONCLUDING REMARKS

In this contribution I have tried to pursue three goals. First of all, I have tried to point out the central and fruitful role of path-dependency in all hetherodox literature. Next, I have systematically analysed its microfoundations, and from this study have emerged at least two important aspects: their psychological nature, and their connection with two heterogeneous trends of contemporary economic theory, that were developed in the last fifty years on the basis of Hayek's and Simon's studies. Finally, as a third goal, I have attempted to examine some implications of the achieved results, that are relevant for economic theory, particularly for the theory of innovation and the neo-institutional one.

In this context, I would like to point out what, to me, is the most significant result of these studies: at the neuronal level, path dependency can be traced back even to the mechanisms of perception and, consequently, to the mechanisms that underlie the use of information and the generation of knowledge. These processes can produce different interpretations of external data, thanks to each person's genetic differences and different wealth of experience. All this allows us to apply the concept of path dependency to the above mentioned theoretical contexts and suggests its development in quite precise directions. For instance, some recent analyses of path dependency (Arthur 1989, Rizzello 1995a) question economic theory's predictive ability. There is certainly a great deal more to explore in this field, but the right direction seems to have been pointed out.

In conclusion, I would like to return briefly to two aspects which are in my opinion of great momentum for the subject dealt with in this paper: the endogenous nature of change, and the psychological nature of the microfoundations of path dependency. The first is not a new idea: endogenous change, in fact, is characteristic of the evolutionary tradition (Witt 1992, p. 405). However, among the problems in this literature that are still unsolved, there also is the need to understand how change is generated;

and the solution should go beyond the intuitive answers that refer to human creativity (Witt 1992, p. 407). My hope is that this contribution may give at least a partial contribution to the identification of the way to a more satisfactory answer.

For what concerns the conception of the psychological nature of microfoundations, this idea comes from the traditional theory of subjectivism, according to which the generation of knowledge is a highly individual process, in which new notions emerge from the specific processes of interpretation of data and from individual experience (Witt 1992, p. 402, stresses this point, referring to Shackle 1972 and Loasby 1976). In this context, however, this paper strongly asserts Hayek's central role as the founder of the subjectivist approach. This role is not always acknowledged; if it were, his thought would be the object of interpretations of more consequence.

In short, it can be stated that: i) path-dependency is a powerful analytical instrument for the understanding of the processes of change considered by economic theory; ii) the microfoundations have a psychological nature, which confirms the findings of the tradition of subjectivism; iii) the achieved results are the product of the analyses that integrate Hayek's contributions on the generation of knowledge, seen as a process of endogenous elaboration of information, and Simon's contributions on the generation of innovation as a process of feedback between the individual (or the firm) and the environment, in the attempt to adapt the levels of aspiration on the basis of tradition and past experience (satisficing approach).

It can finally be stated that iv) the source of human creativity and, thus, of the process of change has been located in the neuronal perceptive processes and, in other words, in the imperfect predictability of human behaviour, based on the above-mentioned neurological mechanisms. The innovation may derive from processes of perception, planning, and implementation which certainly are path-dependent, but maintain an important degree of free will, which results precisely from imperfect information and procedural rationality.

NOTES

1 Regarding this aspect, starting in the 1950s, with Simon's studies on the rationality of the economic agents, a new model of choice, alternative to the orthodox one has gradually emerged. While the orthodox model followed an 'optimising' approach, Simon's one has proposed a satisficing behaviour (Simon 1969).

2 Especially Arrow (1962) and Akerlof (1970) have pointed out that, because of the nature of certain goods such as information and innovations, and because of the presence of asymmetrical information, the market would fail in allocating certain resources in the traditional terms.

3 The acknowledgement of market failures, the presence of asymmetrical information (Akerlof 1970) and of transaction costs (Coase 1937 and Williamson 1975) have led to the birth of a new paradigm, the neo-institutional one, whose purpose is to analyse the economic phenomena in close connection with the institutional structures and within the institutions themselves.

4 This has resulted in the birth of the by now boundless literature on the new theory of the firm, which has studied the nature, role, genesis, organisational processes, power dynamics, contractual relationships, learning processes, etc.

5 For a systematic reconstruction of the whole evolution of the economics of innovation, with particular reference to technological change, see Antonelli 1995, particularly chapter 7.

6 Actually, this approach gives account of both kinds of adoption. However, it considers the localised ones as being better able to describe the dynamics of the firms.

7 We have acquired this knowledge thanks to the developments of Gestalt psychology.

8 This text is little considered by most scholars. Yet, as Hayek himself has later remarked (1988), many considerations worked out in the field of psychology and included in *The Sensory Order* are fundamental for his whole social and economic theory. This simple fact would be enough to emphasise the book's importance. Even though it was published in 1952, its conception can be dated back thirty years. This work was conceived and written (in German) in the 1920s when, having completed his law studies, Hayek was hesitating between economics and psychology (Hayek 1994).

9 These aspects have been further developed by Polanyi (1967).

10 Even though in the context of methodological individualism, in a recent article K. Arrow has pointed out the importance, ever-growing in time, of the social component in the individual processes of acquisition of knowledge and technical information (Arrow 1994a).

11 The term 'routine' means here 'codified knowledge'. In this context, this term refers to those problematic situations already faced and solved before, to which the same, previously utilised, procedures are applied...(unconscious level, generation, etc.).

12 Alchian (1950) was the first to consider the principle of imperfect imitation between firms as an important source of innovation.

13 If brought to its extreme consequences, a view of this kind could lead to the impossibility to communicate. Yet, as Hayek points out, individuals can communicate and live together thanks to affinity processes and to the co-ordinating role played by the institutions (Hayek 1963, 1973).

7. Paths in Time and Space – Path Dependence in Industrial Networks

Håkan Håkansson and Anders Lundgren

INTRODUCTION

Time. Time wears upon everyone and everything. It is the nature of existence that it changes. Existence changes and so do also the preconditions for existence. Yet, in the midst of all metamorphosis there is a grand perpetuity. People change, they age and bring forth new generations, but they remain people, living in families in smaller or larger societies. Objects change, they possess the world yet innovations make them obsolete, but they are still based upon the same elements. Societies change, the people and the human-made objects of society change, but the basic structure of society remains the same. Reading the phenomenon of transformation we must be able to understand both why change occurs and why it does not.

The fundamental problem of reading and anticipating change is that people, objects and societies are linked together in several ways. Our primary focus is these linkages and how they affect particular processes, in time and space. More specifically our point of departure is the linked realities of industrial networks and our aim is to discuss how the past affects changes in industrial networks (Axelsson and Easton 1992; Ford 1990; Håkansson and Snehota 1995 and Mattsson and Hultén 1994). We begin by drawing an image of the subject of change, industrial networks, which is followed by an outline of the nature of change. The main discussion, path dependence in industrial networks, is divided into two parts, paths as structures and paths as processes. The paper ends with some concluding remarks.

Industrial Networks

Network theories are becoming increasingly recognized as analytical tools applicable to the analysis of the nature of industrial production and consumption (e.g., Nohria and Eccles 1992; DiMaggio and Powell 1991). Network theories rest upon the observation that buyers and sellers develop long-lasting relationships. Economic actors do not yield to the price mechanisms of the market, nor do they choose to internalize the exchange. Actors handle the uncertainties of exchange by developing relationships built on trust and mutual interest. In industrial networks actors (firms, organisations or parts thereof) develop long-lasting relationships which define what activities of transformation and transaction are to be performed by whom and what resources are to be employed in doing so. So far this is an extremely deterministic view of firm behaviour. A relationship is, however, always reciprocal. It defines the behaviour of both sides, but not in the same way. There is nothing that says that a relationship is symmetrical. On the contrary the assumption is that it is asymmetrical. A specific relationship is likely to look very different, depending on from which actor's perspective it is viewed. Here we have the basic variables and entities of industrial networks; activities, actors and resources and firms, relationships and networks (Figure 7.1).

Relationships are multi-layered, they link activities, bond actors and tie resources. This multi-layeredness is reflected both in the firms and in the network. A relationship bonds the organisational structures of two firms and through the connectedness of relationships a web of actors is formed and thus activity structures are linked into an activity pattern and resources collections are tied into a resource constellation. Relationships are developed by the firms. They are created voluntarily, but when they are established they induce constraining elements for the same firms.

What do network theories in general suggest? If the theory of the firm should state factors that determine or control firm behaviour, then network theories state that firm behaviour is controlled by its relationships to other firms and neither by internal factors nor by aggregates of unspecified units, such as competitors and markets for supply and demand. At the core of industrial networks are the relationships that define the behaviour of individual firms. This is, however, only one side of the coin. On the other side is the fact that relationships through actors are connected to other relationships and that they thus constitute the building blocks of the macro-concept industrial networks. The evolution of the whole industrial network is then defined by the specific pattern of relationships connecting several firms. What begets change in industrial networks is thus relationships defining the possibilities and limitations of both individual firms and of sets of interconnected firms.

Industrial networks are as frozen structures and thus we must look beyond the singular in its singularity and see it as it is: as an entity connected to other entities and underscore the multiple in its multiplicity. The industrial network of personal transportation is not only manufacturing of cars: it is connected to the production and distribution of other vehicles, roads, bridges, town planning, parking facilities and gas stations. Not even these entities are invariable: the manufacturing automobile is yet another set of interconnected activities involving; wheels, steel, engine, glass, electronics and clothes, which are combined into what we know as both Jaguars or Skodas. The story does, however, not end here: each of these activities is in its turn connected also to other sets of entities. Altogether industrial networks consist of intricate webs of nodes and connections. Hence, changes in the production of steel might require corresponding changes in road construction. Yet, on the other hand the same change might affect combustion technology, inducing more fuel-efficient engines, which in its turn will certainly feed back into the petroleum industry. Since networks are connected we know that change in one part of the network will affect, positively or negatively, other parts. The problem is that we rarely know where these effects will surface or whether they will be positive or negative.

Figure 7.1 Industrial networks; activities, actors and resources in firms, relationships and networks

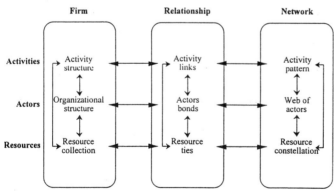

Source: Håkansson and Snehota (1995), p. 42.

121

The historical roots, traditions and corporate culture of a business enterprise defines its development and thus also the evolution of the setting to which it belongs. Relationships developed in the past facilitate the exchange between buyers and sellers, they channel information and they provide impulses for redirection and change and thus they define the behaviour of the firms (Glete 1994, p. 23). But since relationships do not only define individual behaviour but also the collective behaviour of the network the control strikes back: the relationships cannot escape from the pattern created by their own development. There is a path dependence in the development of relationships and networks. The actors of the network structure will have some discretion in certain areas and at the same time be entirely locked into others. 'The network of business relationships is both a prison and a tool' (Håkansson and Snehota 1995, p. 42). It is this path dependency in networks we will address in the remainder of the paper, but we will begin by discussing change and path dependence in general.

Perspective on Change and Path Dependence

Change is problematic, especially if it is to be brought about through deliberate action. It does not follow automatically from the balancing of underlying factors. Nor is it striving towards a future balanced state. The winds of change will rage. It has no beginning nor end and it comes from nowhere and blows everywhere and it changes the world. Or better, it changes somethings in the world: at any moment in time most things are untouched by the ever raging wind. Processes of change are always filled with episodes and events, with temporary successes and failures, and they are enclosed by futile attempts and unexplored routes and the outcomes will neither be optimal nor conclusive. Change, thus, results from a series of connected activities and events, both advancements and set-backs and the outcome of these activities and events is not necessarily moving towards a final optimal or balanced stage. Small, seemingly insignificant events in the past might flip the coin over and alter the direction of change. The past matters and future outcomes are controlled by the specific course of events. Anything can happen and anything will happen, which might have momentous effects upon future development. The issue then is: how can these processes of change be understood, especially since neither the present nor the future seem to provide satisfactory answers?

Change is the business of historians and during the last ten years there has, in almost every field of social sciences, been increasing attention to history when addressing issues of change. History is the science of men in time and time has two dimensions; change and stability. A special problem of time is the difference between history as we experience it and history as we know it. History is manifested in the frozen structures of the past: the human-made and organized world of the past influences future action. History is also in the mind of the people and as such it is subject to both perfection, revision and distortion. While the historical science might aim for perfection, the understanding of change necessitates the reading of the past both interpreted and experienced by the actors. Only by approaching change from several angles can the knowledge of the influence of the past, present and future be transformed and perfected.

In every development some things will change while others will remain untouched. An excellent example is the case of the Qwerty keyboard. While typewriters and other technologies of typing have undergone a tremendous development, the keyboard has been the same. Not because it was or is the most efficient, but because it early became the standard keyboard (David 1985). In understanding why we still have qwerty at our fingertips it is necessary to turn to the past. What were the carriers of history and how can the future escape from the past? The past and the future are connected in the present and thus history is made through the recurrent connection of the past and future. A history which leaves its mark on the present frames a future that cannot shake loose from the past. What is holding them back - and also pushing them forth - is the inertia of past achievements.

Path Dependence

A recently expressed metaphor explaining the previously unexplained in change is path dependence. Paul David discusses models associated with path dependent dynamics of economic systems, in which the role of history is strong. According to David path dependence connotes the fact that, 'the influences of past events and of the states they bring about must be communicated - like the deepening of the wheel-ruts by each successive vehicle - through some definite chain of intervening casual events, effects and resultant states - down to the present state, whence they can be passed on to future events' (David 1988, p. 17). Path dependence does not preach historical determinism, where the totality of the present is derived from the totality of the past. It simply suggests that every event has its past, its present and its future, where irreversible events or activities effectively disconnect some regions of the state space from the rest. All roads do not lead to Rome but as way leads onto way, the particular path 'chosen' will make all the difference.

David discusses two explicit forms of path dependence; lock-in by small historical events and path dependent transitions. The first refers to dynamical processes, which can be locked into particular evolutionary paths through seemingly insignificant and entirely random events. The work of Brian Arthur shows that issues, like competing technologies and industry location, can be analyzed as processes locked in by small historical events (Arthur 1986, 1988a, 1988b). And even if the event shaping the future is random and initially insignificant it is possible to make statements regarding the probability of the possible outcomes, one of which is sure to emerge (David 1988, p. 20).

Path dependence of transition probabilities refers to a class of models where history really matters in the sense that knowledge of the present is not sufficient when it comes to predicting the future: some knowledge of the past is also necessary. The dynamics of a system are not only governed by where it is, but also by where it is coming from. In path dependent dynamics, history is transmitted through a series of positive feedbacks through which the system gains momentum: pushing it forward in a direction set by the past, thus carrying the past into the future. Yet some forces - technological innovation, economic conditions or political ambitions function in the present inducing the system to drift. These forces do not affect the system directly, but through particular sequences of events, which slowly break history. A third class of models in which history plays a significant role is the evolutionary models suggested by Nelson and Winter (1982). Note that in these models processes can shake loose from their origin and thus they are not really path dependent models.

Path dependence has its major strength in the explaining of change once it has occurred. The past sets the possibilities, while the present controls what possibility is to be explored and any change can be explained *ex post*. The issue most often addressed is how change travels through time. The initial change is often random and what is shown is how a certain process is reinforced through different types of positive feed backs. What, then are the carriers of history? Paul David (1988, pp. 26-8) identifies two major classes of variables carrying history, institutions and technology. Expanding on these, Arthur (1988, p. 591) identified four major carriers of history and sources of feedback and reinforcement: 1) economies of scale in production; 2) learning which always favours the existing (David 1975 and Rosenberg 1982); 3) technological interrelatedness creating indivisibilities and 4) network externalities which suggest that the economic value of one service is dependent on the number of users of that service (Katz and Shapiro 1985). Other carriers of history not listed directly are rules and routines, which for instance Nelson and Winter (1982) uses as core concepts when explaining industrial evolution. These sources of positive feedback are obviously not mutually exclusive. They influence and interact with each other in intricate and complex ways creating a decisive momentum pushing the dynamics of systems into path dependent evolution. These mechanisms reinforce past achievements and thus preserve pre-existing structures and counteract novelties.

The risk with all metaphors is that they might turn back at us as explanations. Once a metaphor has been discovered or expressed it loses meaning. To extract the gist of a metaphor such as path dependence it is necessary to go beyond the simple statement or to explore the possibilities of modelling. Studies of path dependent processes have in general focused on the carriers of history and the issue of how to escape history has been of little interest. Once an event has occurred, path dependence enables us to understand how it is reinforced. Causes of reinforcement have been explored and modelled. Causes of change, on the other hand, are still left in shadow. Thus they cannot be assumed, they must be looked for.

We know how paths are reinforced, but how are they paved? Given the assumption that change is path dependent, what are the possibilities of escaping the path set by the past: of escaping history. Do models of path dependence offer suggestions when it comes to explaining for instance what innovation will surge from the endless stream of inventive activity? Can path dependent processes be manipulated? The aim is not to find alternative explanations, but to explore the possibilities of making and breaking history. To do this we must first look into what path dependency is and then discuss both the carriers of history and the possibilities of breaking new ground.

PATH DEPENDENCE IN INDUSTRIAL NETWORKS

Can changes in industrial networks be explained as path dependent evolution? Most studies of industrial networks deal with changes over time. Some focus on the development of individual firms in a network setting and others look at the evolution of the network itself (e.g., Laage-Hellman 1989; Waluszewski 1989; Dubois 1994 and Lundgren 1994). The studies share the common view that history matters and that to understand a phenomenon we must understand its history. When it comes to articulating the perspective of change the studies do, however, differ. The aim of the remainder of the paper is to articulate our perspective on path dependence and what makes changes in industrial networks path dependent. We do this because path dependency seems to provide a perspective that captures much of the essence of change. A problem is, however, that it seems to make change intelligible only in hindsight and apart from saying that the future will contain more of the same it offers no directions. It is like Søren Kierkegaard has said about life: it can only be understood backwards, yet it must be lived onwards. Even if change can only be fully understood backwards we must learn to cope better with change in the present, but maybe we should be more cautious when using the hindsight understanding of change. Does abiding to the rules of path dependency mean that nothing can be said about future directions and to what extent does intentional action shape the future?

To answer this question it is necessary to explore the rules of path dependency in industrial networks and to discriminate between different sets of rules.

It is possible to distinguish between at least two different definitions of what constitutes a path. What first comes to mind are the paths made in the forest by the frequent or habitual use of men or animals. The second possible definition focuses attention on paths.

These two concepts of paths point at different aspects of path dependency. Aspects that can also be related to an ongoing discussion in physics are the confrontation of the 'particle theory' and the 'wave-theory'; both theories are important in observing phenomena in physics, but they cannot be observed simultaneously. The first definition points at the spatial dimension and it suggests that a path is a structure. We are talking about paths in space, which result from the relationships between several elements. A path is the elements or parts of an entity or the position of such elements or parts in their external relationships to each other. It is the result of collective and repetitive behaviour and it appears as a part of an existing structure, something that exists and is used again and again over time and which will continue to exist as long as it is being used. History is in this case carried indirectly through the structure controlling or governing individual action.

The second definition on the contrary highlights the time dimension and thus provides us with a totally different concept of path dependence: with paths in time which point at the individuality of paths. From this perspective a path is a link in the endless interlocking chain of causation and concomitance that constitutes the process of history. A path is thus summarized as a process, relating a series of episodes to each other, linking experiences. Of course this can also be related to structure but in another way than in the first. A path as a way of life is closer to the word

126

structuralize; to put into a meaningful frame of reference; to establish the relationship between elements. Paths in time suggest that history is carried directly by the actors. The memory of past actions and events will coincide with actions or events in the present and thus control or govern future actions and events. Anything can happen and it will. The influence of these often random elements on the process is, however, mediated through the way of life. The same element will have different effect on different lives.

Schumpeter makes a similar distinction when he sets the circular flow of economic life against development. The circular flow is a structural perspective explaining the function of an economy and its continuous change. It aims at what holds economic life together. Development on the other hand deals with change that arises by its own initiative, from within, and which does not appear continuously and which changes the framework of the traditional course itself. This perspective aims at explaining what changes economic life. But while Schumpeter (1983 pp. 61-3) ends up with one perspective explaining stability and another explaining change we believe that we have change and stability in both structure and process. The nature of change and stability should, however, come up differently in the two definitions suggested.

Let us now discuss these two different definitions of a path in order to find different sets of rules of path dependence in a network setting.

Paths as Structures

Paths in space; paths as structures focus attention on aspects existing in the industrial structure, paths which are used again and again and paths which can be used by several actors together or separately. One example can be repetitive activity patterns in relation to the production steps of a certain type of product. Through such linked activity patterns, producers are bonded to each other. The bonded actors create a web which is a second type of structure that will control behaviour. Actors invest resources to construct and to support the activity patterns and resources which in their turn also form a structure in terms of resource constellations. The total effect is an industrial or network structure with a highly specific organized structure, in which paths are elements of organized network configurations.

Paths as structures are characterized by features which can be analysed by the tools developed within economics. One important economic factor is economies of scale or in Richardson's words, the taking advantage of 'similar resources' (Richardson 1972). Another path dependency accrues through coordination in order to take advantage of complementarities.

Investments in similar and complementary resources pave broader and broader paths, enabling both rationalization and innovation. Resources and technical solutions are developed in accordance with these paths of links and nodes, where larger nodes represents special combinations of technologies or production processes.

A number of economic issues are related to paths as structures: 1) What is a path, what are the carriers of history? 2) How are paths related? 3) How do paths change, how do we escape from the past? 4) How is a company related to paths?

Carriers of History

Spatial paths carry history through the fact that the pre-existing structure controls or governs future action. It hinges on the fact that individual actions are dependent on the actions of others. It will seem profitable to wander the paths others already have trod and history is carried through systems of action. The dynamics of a system are not only governed by where it is, but also by where it is coming from. In path dependent dynamics, history is transmitted through a series of positive feedbacks, through which the system gains momentum: pushing it forward in a direction set by the past. What are the carriers of history in industrial networks: what are the structural elements?

Looking more closely at the inertia of industrial networks, we have already identified the main elements of structural paths in organized networks; activity patterns, webs of actors and resource constellations. We need, however, to say more about how these carry history. In order to do so we distinguish between strong and weak structures and between large and small overlapping. Strong and weak are related to how well-established the structures are. A complication is that time might move differently in the different structures, that is, that the structures are stable to different degrees. We could for instance think of an industrial activity, where the resource constellation has remained the same for a century, whilst the web of actors has been constantly changing. The problem is, however, that it is not evident that this follows specific rules. Even though we could hypothesise that resource constellation is the deepest structure and the web of actors the one most subject to change, the opposite might well be the case. The time horizons of structural elements must be left to empirical studies. Overlapping should be understood as the extent to which the structures are superimposed on each other, that is, to what extent the three different structures are similar. Resources can be part of more than one resource constellation, activities part of more than one activity pattern, and actors members of more than one web. With large overlapping we thus mean a situation where the three structures are matched and where the connections to other structures are few. Combining structure and overlapping we can identify four classes of structural paths in industrial networks, see Figure 7.2.

Figure 7.2 Structure and overlapping as carrier of history

		Overlapping	
		Large	*Small*
Structure	*Weak*	*Medium history* Stable situation with a clear direction. Behaviour directed towards rationalization in the use of resources will be reinforcec. Drift towards strengthening of structure.	*Weak history* Unstable situation, many changes but no direction, low economic effiency. Behaviour not reinforced. Exogenous shocks necessary to provide direction.
	Strong	*Strong history* Stable situation with efficient production and little room for endogenous change.	*Medium history* Stable situation but without any clear direction. The network could tip in several directions. Inventive behaviour will be reinforced

The critical observation is that history is carried to a different degree in different paths. The reinforcement as well as the causation of change will be different, in different industrial networks. All networks are not equally equipped or prone either to reinforce change, adapt and prosper on innovation or to generate change, foster innovation. In modelling path dependence, the models should ideally be made to represent the structure reinforcing the processes they aim to explain.

The Crossing of Paths

How are paths related? A path cannot exist in a vacuum, it must in some way be related to other paths, other structures. The critical issue must be: what constitutes a crossing? Given the basic definition of a path, a crossing should be where actors, activities or resources meet and habits or routines are confronted or combined. A crossing could be one actor connected to different activity patterns and resource constellations. It could also be one resource which can, and perhaps is, used to perform different activities. Hence, the degree of overlap is a measure of the degree of crossings. It is at crossings that structures meet: where different technologies or different flows of products are confronted. Along a path the aim is to increase economic efficiency while at the crossings the opportunities to develop new combinations are higher. At crossings the probability of random events is higher. Higher is also the likelihood that these random events will be reinforced. Hence, we can aim for crossings, but since we do not know what will be there, the outcome cannot be controlled. It is at crossings, that the opportunities of breaking new paths are the highest. Even if we still cannot explain what changes will occur, we can identify where they are likely to surface.

Breaking Paths – Escaping History

The second question deals with the escape from history and the emergence of new paths. How do paths come about, what induces the structure to drift? Starting out with what he labelled Wieser's principle of continuity, Schumpeter wrote that; 'the economic system will not change capriciously on its own initiative but will be at all times connected with the preceding state of affairs' (Schumpeter 1983, p. 9). Yet, as he entered his path of industrial dynamics he asserted that the new structures would emerge beside the old. He wrote; 'new combinations are, as a rule embodied, as it were, in new firms which generally do not arise out of the old ones but start producing beside them' (Schumpeter 1983, p. 66).

The economic structure in the western world of today is in many respects different from the structure experienced by Schumpeter. The technological systems have grown larger and become more integrated; industrial networks have been extended globally and specialization and division of labour have become more apparent and distinct. Almost every economic field has become dominated by a few large multi-product firms. As a consequence economic activity has increasingly become embedded in socio-technical structures. A more potent social and technological momentum has been accumulated causing the emergence of new industrial structures to be more aligned with the pre-existing structure than Schumpeter had reason to anticipate. Changes emerge from pre-existing structures and if viable, they will eventually be reintegrated with the structures from which they originated. To realize changes the semi-autonomous actors of industrial networks are dependent upon the support of others. But others will also induce changes which require reactions. Hence, the emergence of a new path is neither purely cumulative nor purely revolutionary. It results from a combination of accumulation and revolutionary change, where previously independent paths are being linked into one larger structure.

Structural paths results from collective and repetitive behaviour and thus the breaking of new ground also necessitates collective and repetitive behaviour. The process must, however, be started, someone has to start to walk and others have to follow. The change must be set off and it must be reinforced and thus directed. Given the significance attributed to the pre-existing structures, a reasonable assumption must be that the start will be from one of the existing paths. In order for the process to end up somewhere it must also go in the direction of another path. What is between paths? We might suspect that also between paths we have some sort of structure, this would, however, by necessity be what we have labelled weak history, which itself is incapable of transmitting direction. Clearly, no-one will know a priori what will be between paths, what kind of terrain has to be covered, before connecting or crossing with other paths.

Companies and Paths

The final question is how companies should be viewed? We suggest that a company should be seen as a nexus of paths. This nexus will contain both paths and crossings and while some relationships and exchanges are located along a path others will represent crossing. The different path settings demand different types of efficiencies and involve different types of exchanges, on both the input and output sides. Critical issues for a company are how many paths it can hold together and how they can relate paths to each other, and what the role of their counterparts is. Developing and maintaining paths often requires massive investments and a company can either travel the path frequently and habitually or it can encourage others to travel the path with them. As new paths, through different acts of innovation, diverge from the paths of the established industrial networks, the innovators undertake to accumulate resources to transform the innovations into self-sustaining economic enterprises (Van de Ven and Garud 1987, p. 10). Simultaneously, new infrastructures, new industrial networks, connecting the interrelated parts of the emerging path must evolve. The performance of individual actors is therefore to some extent contingent upon the performance of the whole.

Paths as Structures: Summing Up

The world is filled with humans and with human-made objects and people and objects hang together in intricate ways. Formed in the past are intertwined and heterogeneous structures, which will affect the present. If we want to understand change, we must begin with how the structures are intertwined and how they change. It is these structures that sets the rules of path dependence: what can be changed depends to a large degree on the existing structure. New paths will very much be a product of the earlier structure of existing activities, existing resources and existing actors. The ties, links and bonds existing between these three categories give obvious 'path dependence' features carrying history, containing technological, economic, social and knowledge barriers to exploiting new avenues. Viewing paths as structures inevitably leaves us with history as a restriction. But we believe that there is more to path dependence then an inability to shake loose from the past. To explore that avenue we turn to the second definition of path dependence, following from perceiving paths as processes.

Paths as Processes

The travel through time leaves its specific track and viewing paths as processes points at totally different ways in which history matters. A path is laid by taking one rock at a time. In this way the past holds a stronger grip over progress than all the future opportunities combined (Håkansson 1989, p. 37). Neither technology nor society are advancing towards any particular future state. They are both evolving from their present states. Change is not enclosed in the shadows of the future, but in the ambiguity of the past. This does not imply that the present is derived from the past and the future from the present: we are not slaves of the past, but we are its children. Progress is propelled by circumstances embodied in history and in this sense every process is unique and it is in these unique sequences of events at explanations to the outcome of dynamic processes should be sought. The particular path travelled, with its uniqueness and dependency on chance, will make all the difference.

The path dependence has in this case some features different from the first case. Here it is a possibility, something that can be exploited. The question is how much an individual actor can and will take advantage of it. This ability is related to the structure identified earlier, but now in a structuralized form. This means that it has been translated or framed into a

132

picture which is partly determined by how the individual organisation reads its past and present.

Carriers of History

What are the carriers of history in paths as processes? The notion that it is a path in time suggests that everyone, individuals as well as companies, will follow unique paths - a path is absolutely individual and history is carried directly through the path. The path travelled by provides a specific history, specific experiences and a specific sets of attitudes. Surely we are learning from others but it is always the individual, person or organisation, which carries history, makes the picture a whole picture. Again, this is obviously the case for individual persons but is important for organisations such as companies. One question is how the past is interpreted and how it is carried on; how the memory functions; the actor's own memory of past achievements and other actors' memory of the actor's past behaviour.

The past, or rather the path through the past, defines the range of possible actions, while the decision of what action to take is always determined by the perception of the present state of affairs. One important aspect must be our ability to exploit the past and what we learn of own experiences. But since we ourselves are the carriers of history we have a choice - we do not have to learn. We can continue as if nothing has changed. History may be mutable and it can be subjected to discontinuous revisions. In the sake of action history might be rewritten. A critical part of our memory is the relationships we have with counterparts. These give us a set of social bonds, mutual identities and more or less of mutual sentiments. Thus, a company can take care of its own experiences, of everything it has been through. The higher their ability is to exploit the past, the stronger is their path dependence. The path dependence is in other words to take advantage of already made experiences and investments. History can mean everything or almost nothing! Previously having invested in a new machine, which is currently is running at a loss, a firm can either choose to forget it; see it as sunk cost, or it can state that the machine is important and to exploit the investment in another context. Change is about breaking with the past to establish a new future; a new technology, a new industry, a new firm or a new life. Prior investments determine the rate of return on future investments. The accumulation of investments is thus more critical than the absolute level of a specific investment. The logic of this would be to build investments gradually. In building history small wins and the creation of traditions would be more critical than innovativeness. The new future must

133

be built on the old and the question should be how to exploit the past in escaping from it?

The Crossing of Paths

A second important feature is that individual paths are related to each other. During different time periods we have been more or less related to someone following another path. It is by definition impossible to follow the path of someone else. However, the paths can be related and be crossing each other in different ways. How does that influence the unique paths of the individuals? We have no clear answer. If we were romantics we would say that a meeting can be a possibility of, if only for a blessed moment, escaping from ourselves. For a moment the small space around us on the path becomes so much larger, carrying another past and with it new opportunities. We - because in that moment the two meeting must feel as we - will be deeply influenced by the meeting and can pass through an important transformation. If we on the other hand are realists, a meeting is at least an occasion to exchange some thoughts or physical items. It is just an occasion and it will always be marginal. It will have no effects on the basic features of the person. Reflecting on a brief encounter Paul Auster (1995, p. 35) says: 'The whole incident had taken place in a flash: ten seconds of her life, an interval of no account, and none of it had left the slightest mark on her. For me, on the other hand, those seconds had been a defining experience, a singular event in my internal history.' This suggests that a crossing can be of different importance for different actors, such as how we are affected by the crossing of others' paths dependence on our own path and how we interpret the crossing.

This for the personal level, what about companies? If we overlook the emotional aspects there are obvious analogies. A meeting is always a confrontation of different pasts and thus an opportunity to exchange experience and knowledge. By actively changing the industrial network, by seeking new relationships, actors can alter their past: they can enter onto new paths, previously unattainable. Through relationships the past is changed and thus also the set of possibilities and furthermore also the present is changed, which will alter the decision of what possibility is to be explored. The effects can be both tremendous and marginal. It is, however, impossible to take over someone's history; on the contrary, every entity is transforming the past of others when they are relating it to their own. As we have not travelled the same path we are reframing the results which the travel has given the other. It can be specific experiences, products, knowledge or others and the reframing leaves us with a choice of taking or not taking the opportunity to escape our own history.

A company is constantly crossing the paths of others and these crossings could be anything from a brief encounter to a lifelong relationship. A normal day in a large company life could involve as much as thousands of encounters and the issue is what encounters will be critical to the foundation of the company's future path.

Breaking Paths – Escaping History

What can we say about future paths? It depends on how the individual exploits its own and others' pasts. Here there are different types of possibilities. Furthermore, we can also choose which type of terrain we want to cover. We will never know where a certain route will take us, but we can choose the more general types of terrain. Some are trying to choose easier routes while others are trying to climb high hills. Here we can certainly choose, but there is an important limitation for the company. It has to try to find places where it will meet others. It has to find partners to have commercial exchange with later on. A company can freely choose the direction - it is free to invest in anything, but in some directions the possibility of encountering others is infinitesimal. On the other hand there can be too many travelling in the most popular direction. In deciding on direction, here are two alternatives a company can choose between;

1. Travel with someone - or try to go in the same direction as some others.
2. Identify some future meeting places, i.e. try to forecast how others will move which probably is a function of how they perceive the terrain.

A major benefit and also possibility is that the existing structures do not change so dramatically. Earlier investments provide stability and they also point at possible directions. The terrain is to a large degree given. Earthquakes do happen but they are rare.

Companies and Paths

As the path is individual it is not possible to distinguish between a company and its path. The path does, however, contain certain elements such as specific activity and organisational structure as well as resource collection. A major reorganisation represents a revision of the company's past. But more than that it also represents guidelines for future encounters. The company is reshaping its borders to others. Another way of revising the past would be to merge with another company. If successful the merger creates a new past of the company, which would result from negotiation between the different pasts

Paths as Processes: Summing Up

Reading path dependent processes means reading individual entities following unique paths. Relating unique paths to one another suggests that we must learn to face the heterogeneous whole and acknowledge that similar points can be reached following different paths. There is not one, but many paths to fame and glory. Success is built upon a number of factors and different endeavours might have been successful for different reasons. It is impossible and also dangerous to single out specific factors making the process drift. Every historical process is unique and in fostering a specific process, we must look into the nature of the process. No statement regarding how to foster change should thus be made general.

CONCLUDING REMARKS

Time wears upon us in different ways. The past shows its face as both restrictions and possibilities and the problem is that we cannot see both at the same time. We have distinguished between paths as structures and paths as processes and discussed how path dependence works in the different cases. Where paths as structures point at the collective past functioning as a restriction in the present, paths as processes highlights the individual past which represents possibilities to be exploited. Of course there is always both sides, but we can only look at one at a time. Even though they stem from the same source, relationships, the link between structure and process is an imaginary crossing of totally different types of paths. The other side of this is that a relationship looks different depending on if it is a view from the individual company or the collective network.

Development is subject to change through collective as well as individual action. Action matters, it makes a difference. It does not make the difference and it does not govern change. History matters, it makes a difference. It does not make the difference and it does not govern development. It is against this backdrop of voluntarism and determinism that individuals, governments and firms take measures and act, and it is only against this backdrop that the outcome of individual and collective action can be fully understood. Individual action can always be directed, but the outcome can never be controlled, it is mediated through structures established in the past. Actors create structures and structures create actors. Industrial networks are heterogeneous and heterogeneous should also be the attempts to understand changes in networks, both collective and individual. Instead of trying to melt the both pictures together in the same pot we suggest that our understanding of the influence of the past will be higher if they were kept separate. The aim should be to generate several, not single, images of change.

8. The Making of National Telephone Networks in Scandinavia. The State and the Emergence of National Regulatory Patterns 1880-1920

Lena Andersson-Skog

INTRODUCTION

The elements of institutional transformation have for a long time been a major field of research in economic history, due to the historical experience of rigidity in the change of political and economic institutions. Most analyses have, however, been empirically oriented. Ideas regarding the impact of past and present power structures, traditions and personal relations along with economic and technological rigidities have been vital in analysing the shaping of the context where human interaction takes place, and as a result, conditions the framework of economic development; yet explicit theoretical approaches have not often been used. However, in recent heterodox economic discourse, economic historians, such as Douglass North (1981, 1990), have been seminal in attempts to narrow this gap between theory and history.

Lately, path dependence has become one of the frequently used concepts in research efforts trying to analyse the behaviour of the firm and different historical market-hierarchical configurations (Nelson and Winter 1982, Dosi *et al* 1992). But at the present stage, we are still very much lacking an integrated analysis of relations between the governmental bodies, economic organisations and path dependency processes on the one hand, and the implications on the political arena or on the market on the other. [1]

This is true both with regard to the nature of institutional change, and to the conditions triggering the process of transformation. Hence, it is important to describe when a historical process or event can be labelled as the result of a certain path dependency process at work. This may be done by tracing the impact of path dependency when equal or better alternatives evidently exist, but are not chosen in strategic decision making. We also have to distinguish between informal, everyday changes, taking place in a firm or a line of business within a distinct institutional setting, and the more radical changes of formal institutional arrangements due to exogenous processes, such as new technology or new laws enforced by political bodies. In the first case, the decisions made can be the result of a path dependency dominating that particular firm or business line. In the latter case, the outcome will most probably be the result of decisions and deliberations external to the firm.

To analyse the interaction and dependence between these two spheres is a task of great importance in the path dependency approach. Important issues are which relations actually make the economy flourish in some institutional settings, and why other contexts seem to petrify economic and social relations, thus creating lock-in situations slowing down the growth of economy and wealth. If the new institutional approaches are to succeed in making the concept of path dependency an analytic tool with a greater explanatory value than just the historical reference to habits, traditions and culture, we have yet to carry out additional investigations concerning the empirical and theoretical complexity of the concept.

One way to handle these questions is to emphasise the analysis of the State as an agent of institutional transformation. Here, decision making and the regulation of economic activities are biased by institutionalised political practises in a specific political context. Thus, economic institutions are the results of political regulatory processes, sometimes determined by an ideological bias far from the market conditions. Political decision making takes place in a complex web of individual preferences, economic institutions and political obligations. This context differs even in contemporary situations, depending on the issue. Several codes of conduct and loyalty may co-exist, and as a consequence they sometimes result in conflicts between different traditions of path dependencies. Thus, access to political power is necessary in institutional construction or change outside the specific context of the firm.

Hence it can be argued, that cross-country analyses are vital to the future development of institutional theory. A broad comparison may make it possible to distinguish between the general transformation of institutions during industrialisation – such as company laws, changes in the educational system and property rights with regard to private property- and the shaping of sector-specific institutions regulating economic activities by political decisions. Here, the emergence of sector-specific regulations and the impact of path dependency processes may be a rewarding subject of study.

The long perspective implications of state regulatory behaviour have previously been analysed in the field of transport and communication, especially in the railway sector. In many countries the State, promoting the building of canals, roads and railways, has actively engaged in the industrialisation process. Variations in the rules of property rights, contractual arrangements, regulations of the services supplied, tariffs and so on, are examples of political decisions that have influenced the practices of companies in different countries, irrespective of whether they were private or state-operated enterprises. The political context thus accounts for the financing of technological renewal and change, infrastructure investment, organisational patterns, regulations and politics. For example, in a study of the Prussian and American railway sector, Dunlavy argues very strongly the overall importance of the power of political structure in shaping the organisation and industrialisation (Dunlavy 1994).

This article is an attempt to interpret, in the context sketched above, the role of the State in the emergence of sector-specific institutions in telecommunications in Scandinavia, viz. Denmark, Norway and Sweden from 1890 to the beginning of the inter-war period. One reason for a comparison of these countries is the mix of similarities and differences in and between the respective nations during the period investigated. The three countries were very similar in respect of social structure and ethnic homogeneity, and they were to a great extent economically dependent on their export of agricultural products and raw materials to the world market. At the same time, there were differences with respect to geography, population size and population density, natural resources, external relations, sovereignty and political structure, etc. These features together conditioned the creation of economic institutions during the industrialisation era.

It is a debatable issue whether the common features led to similar communication policies, noticeable in the case of diffusion of the telephone systems in the respective countries. Evidently, the telephone networks in the region showed a remarkably rapid growth compared to Europe at large. At the turn of the century in 1900, there was on average one telephone subscription per 74 inhabitants in the region. This differed widely from the continent. In Germany, for instance, the figures were one per 197 and in France one per 553 (Mitchell 1992). This indicates that in Scandinavia favourable conditions on the telephone market were somehow established right from the start. What may have conditioned the regulation process here?

In discussing the relations between government structures and subordination in the State-market configuration, the impact of non-economic considerations on economic regulations are in focus. Economic and political incentives were created by the existing national framework and existing power structure in the national context (Dobbin 1994). In short, the way agents tend to organise an industry depends on incentives provided by institutions and the strength put up by the government to implement a certain policy. As a consequence, national experiences led to the emergence of a wide variety of institutional patterns, furthering growth in different ways. My intention here is to examine this aspect of institutional change and path dependency.

THE DORMANT STATE AND THE RISE OF THE TELEPHONE IN SCANDINAVIA

When the Bell telephone was invented in 1876, a triumphant series of victories all over the world was initiated. In Scandinavia, the 1880s was likewise a period of rapid expansion in this field. However, the governments made little or no efforts to actively stimulate the emergence of telephone systems. In contrast, the national telegraph networks had rapidly developed in the hands of the Scandinavian State administrations from the 1850s onwards, with one exception. In 1869, a privately owned company, The Great Northern Telegraph Company, was founded in Denmark. The company obtained a thirty years' concession to operate on the international market, transmitting telegrams from Western to Eastern Europe in co-operation with the different Scandinavian State administrations concerned. Thus, the national communication systems were considered a matter for the State, whereas private capital could cultivate the international market. The neglect of the telephone in its infancy can be understood very much in the same way: as a local means of communication with little direct effect on national economic performance, it was less important to the State than the telegraph.

A number of telephone networks emerged all over Scandinavia, due to local initiative and demand. Hence, co-operative societies and telephone companies set up by local business and local politicians became the common organisational form for resource allocation and operation. But in spite of the similarities during this early period, the Scandinavian countries followed different trajectories in establishing specific institutions in telecommunications. The divergent paths can be traced back to the 1890s, the period when the national State agencies definitely entered the arena. The following section will describe the divergent patterns established in each

141

country, and the way they were successively transformed. The focus is on the role of the State in establishing regulations. The relation between the State and private business life is also discussed. Comparing these, what indications are there that the national settings did imply different paths of institutional change? Finally there are comments on the impact of institutions on the prolonged development of the telephone sector in the countries studied.

THE MAKING OF SECTOR-SPECIFIC INSTITUTIONS UNTIL 1920

Denmark

In Denmark, the telephone market was characterised by the rapid growth of regional telephone companies and associations. One of the pioneers in the Danish telephone business was the famous merchant capitalist and industrial entrepreneur C.F. Tietgen, one of the founders of The Great Northern Telegraph Society mentioned above. In 1879, a local telephone company called the Copenhagen House and Town Telephone was established in Copenhagen. A year later, in 1880, the International Bell Company also established a telephone network in Copenhagen after negotiations with the former one. In 1882, Tietgen, at the time a Cabinet minister, negotiated to purchase the Bell network. An agreement was signed and a new company, the Copenhagen Telephone Society Ltd, started its business with Tietgen as chairman of the board. An early strategy was to co-operate with or to merge with other local telephone networks, in order to internalise the expanding regional market. At this time, the interest shown by other companies was fairly limited, but in 1886 the local network in Helsingör was connected with that of Copenhagen. The ongoing expansion and the growing need of investment capital resulted in the floating of a new issue of shares in 1894. The company was also renamed the Copenhagen Telephone Company Ltd and became a major agent on the Danish telephone market (Jarlöv 1956).

Concurrently, the Danish parliament tried to enforce a law excluding private companies from operating any kind of electric communication. This failed, and instead, in 1883, a regional restriction was imposed upon the market of the existing private companies. To defend their positions, the regional companies tried to merge in order to consolidate the regional markets. From the turn of the century in 1900, the private sector was dominated by four large regional companies, constituted in the major islands and the peninsula of Jutland (Tholstrup 1992). This development was partly due to business conditions and partly to the fact that the State had altered the rules of the game.

From the mid 1890s, the Danish State started to engage in the telephone business. The State telegraph agency developed long-distance lines connecting the various regional companies, thus strengthening the national telegraph infrastructure by adding telephone lines. In 1897, the Danish parliament instituted a Telephone and Telegraph Act containing new rules. The decision in Parliament resulted in the imposing of a general concession period of twenty years from 1898. The concession procedure was introduced to limit the entrance of new companies. Public authority over the performance of private companies was also expanded. The State telegraph agency had the right to run local telephone networks inside the dominions of the concessioned areas in the few cases where publicly owned networks already existed. However, to comfort private business, the State could not just take over single profitable lines in the concessioned areas, but had to nationalise the company network in total. The purchase price was decided to be set on the basis of the estimated value of the assets at the time of nationalisation (Tholstrup 1992). The attempts to widen the political control over telephone companies thus resulted in a situation where the company structure before the Act was maintained.

From this time on, the telephone communications fell under the newly established Ministry of Public Works. In establishing regulatory practices, the Minister in charge decided to make it possible for the existing regional companies to put in a plea for concessions to run the networks as before. Since for a short period the minister in charge of this issue had been a member of the board of the Copenhagen Telephone Company, accusations of corruption were heard. The deal upset the public as well as some members of parliament. As a result, whenever the pricing policy of the companies was discussed in parliament, new debates on this issue followed (Jarlöv 1956). Furthermore, in these cases the governing minister usually decided in favour of the private companies. Thus, the pricing of telephones was generally high as compared to Sweden.

In the period 1918 to 1920, when the telephone companies were either to be nationalised or the concession to be re-negotiated, the government, after a parliamentary investigation, decided in favour of the latter. A purchase was considered too expensive, due to the high price level after the First World War. Instead, a new period of concession was agreed upon, this time for ten years. This time the terms of purchase were more clearly defined.

The bonds were to be sold at a fixed rate related to the market value. If the financial situation was such that the State could not fulfil its commitment, the concession was to be prolonged by five years at a time. During this period, the State could purchase shares in the companies until all stocks were in the hands of the State. Thus, the State telegraph agency gradually moved in as the owner of the shares in the regional telephone companies during the mid-war period. At the same time, the composition, technical standards and price tariffs of the companies differed. The companies saw little advantage in making investments in new technology under these circumstances. As a result, property rights were not definitely set, and the State gradually became the passive owner of local networks.

Norway

In Norway, the initiative on the telephone market was also taken by private telephone companies. Thus, a number of local networks developed during the 1880s. In Oslo, the capital (at the time called Christiania) in 1880 telephone lines between public sites were concessioned to the International Bell Company. As early as one year later, a Norwegian company, the Christiania Telephone Company, was constructed and established a local telephone network. In 1884 the two companies merged, and constituted the Christiania Telephone Association (Rafto 1955).

In 1881, the Bell company wanted to set up a line between Oslo and the important industrial town of Drammen. The attempt by the Bell company thus interfered with the arena of national interest in infrastructure guarded by the State since the 1850s. As a result, in the same year, the Norwegian parliament passed a Telephone Act, prohibiting the establishment of privately owned national telecommunications whenever they could be expected to threaten the revenue of the state-owned telegraph. But even if private companies could not establish national telephone lines, the Crown could give concessions for five year leases if the interested party compensated the State telegraph for the calculated loss of revenues. At the same time, similar to Denmark, privately owned telephone networks were regionally restricted. However, in Norway the market was restricted to the town limits and the immediate surroundings. The local networks could also be connected with the telegraph infrastructure, which at the time was combined with telephone lines in order to improve the telegraph services (Rafto 1955). These opportunities were often used to widen the area accessible to local subscribers.

During the 1890s, the regulation of the private sector was slack. This ensured a continued expansion of local networks, but at the same time private mergers were restricted by the Act of 1881. The State telegraph agency also tried to expand its national lines. In 1892, the first telephone long-distance line was opened between Oslo and Stockholm. The same year, the new managing director of the State telegraph agency started to engage in telephone networks as a mode of communication of its own. This time, not only the national and often non-profitable investments in infrastructure were emphasised, but the board expressed a wish to also operate the profitable local networks. In 1894, a National Telephone Building Plan was passed by Parliament. According to this, the State was to build long-distance lines to the main towns in southern Norway using Oslo as the nodal point. In this scheme, nationalisation was vital. Opposition from the private telephone companies was strong. The local companies organised in The Norwegian National Telephone Association. This organisation was successful in raising support in parliament for opposing and slowing down the process of nationalisation (Rafto 1955).

In 1899, however, the Norwegian parliament passed a Telephone Act restricting the construction of local telephone networks in towns. Thus the foundation was solidly laid for a future expansion of the Norwegian telephone network in the hands of the State. This was in accordance with the conception held by the State telegraph agency and parliament, claming that only the State could grant the telephone market to be nationwide, since profit-seeking companies would never attend to the link between the sparsely populated areas far north and the networks in the south (Rafto 1955).

However, there was still another obstacle to the plans of the State authorities to pursue national expansion, namely the power balance between oppositional groups in the parliament. On several occasions, the State agency introduced investment plans for a national telephone network, but these plans were rejected by various regional interests represented in parliament. There was generally strong opposition in parliament against raising state loans for infrastructure investment (Hodne 1984). Instead, there was stiff regional competition for scarce capital resources, where the amount depended on the state finances and the trade balance. Regional hostility made it extremely difficult to reach political consensus on areas that should be invested in. A common opinion was also that the national railway lines had to be given preference to telephones. parliament also opposed to the nationalisation of the private telephone companies, since many of them were considered unprofitable.

However, during the first decade of the 20th century, a number of private telephone networks were in fact taken over by the State agency. The most important purchase was the private network in Oslo in 1896. With this important nodal point in the hands of the State, the power balance started to change. In 1911, there was enough support in parliament to ensure a plan of furthering the national telephone lines to the northern parts of Norway. At this time, the importance of the telephone system to the Norwegian economy was apparent, and the priority of railway financing was deranged. This was partly due to the strategy of the government to nationalise the telephone networks, thus altering the regional conditions by improving the quality of telephone technology and services provided in some areas, but not in others. Not until the early 1920s, in 1922–23, was a united national telephone network established in Norway.

Sweden

As opposed to the other Scandinavian countries, where political intervention was needed to ensure the State agency's position on the market, Sweden witnessed a rapid expansion of the telephone system in the hands of the State. This was not due to a political intention to conquer the market, but rather the result of the State telegraph agency acting at its own discretion. Contrary to the other countries as well, Sweden had a quarter of a century of stiff oligopolistic competition between the State and private companies on the most important market – the market in Stockholm.

In 1880, the International Bell Company established telephone networks in Stockholm, and Sweden's second largest city, Gothenburg. The endeavour to conquer the Swedish market was not very successful and lasted only for a decade. From 1891, Swedish interests controlled the telephone market. The major challenge to the Bell system came from the Swedish engineer T.H. Cedergren, founder of the Stockholm General Telephone Company in 1883. From the very beginning, Cedergren initiated close co-operation with L.M. Ericsson, the inventor, who started his own telephone production in the L.M. Ericsson Company, still world famous. In a few years time, the General Company was the largest agent on the telephone market in Stockholm (Johansson 1953).

At the same time, local entrepreneurs dominated the country outside the biggest towns. In 1892, 158 different local telephone associations existed in Sweden (Bennett 1895). All in all, some 200 private telephone networks were established until 1920. These companies or associations bought their know-how and equipment, mostly from the L.M. Ericsson Company, and from then on lived their own life on the basis on self-subsistence. The long-term problem, however, was the difficulty to ensure technological renewal and thereby develop long-distance telephony on this financial ground. To some extent, the problem was solved by mergers between local networks. The most common development however, was that a local association contacted the State telegraph agency and negotiated in order to sell its local telephone network in exchange for access to the national network. As a result, in a few years time the State agency operated a vast, almost national, system of telephone networks connected to the telegraph system. Here a difference between the Swedish and the Norwegian development may be pointed out. In Norway, the political system shaped the formation of the national network a high degree, tying the hands of the State agency by political decisions, whereas the unification in Sweden was the result of processes on the market, where the State agency acted at its own discretion in response to the market.

It is an interesting question if the Swedish development was the result of regulations and judicial obstacles to private enterprise or not. During the 1880s, the State agency had started to engage in telephone services as a means to improve the capacity of the electric telegraph. The aim was to avoid a disastrous decrease of telegraph revenues because of the telephone competition. A government bill resulted in a parliament decision in 1883, prohibiting private companies from placing telephone posts on common land without a concession. However, obedience was weak. Ten years later, only about 15 per cent of the most expansive regional networks were concessioned (Storckenfeldt 1893). If the authorities showed little interest to implement the restrictions, a more severe blow to a private national telephone network was the 1888 decision to reject a proposal to connect the private networks in Stockholm, Gothenburg and in the industrial town of Sundsvall up in the north by long-distance telephony. Parliament instead accepted an almost identical plan for a National Telephone Network proposed by the State agency. But contrary to the situation in Norway and Denmark, political decisions were not taken in order to give the State agency a monopolistic hegemony as entrepreneur on the national telephone market. Though some attempts in this direction were made by the State agency, they were rejected. As a consequence, private interests were not stopped by any legal restrictions prohibiting the expansion of a competing national network – there was never a monopoly position by law in Sweden.

So far, the telephone had been of secondary importance to the State compared to the telegraph. It was not until 1896 that someone, actually one single person, was employed to be responsible for telephone matters on the

147

board of the State agency. The relative lack of formal regulations can be explained as a reflection of the alleged minor importance of the telephone for national economy. The initiative to develop the telephone systems in the hands of the State did not emanate from political decisions in parliament, but from what the board of the State agency considered necessary to do in order to consolidate its position – sometimes even by using dubious methods. By being indifferent, the uninterested State had given the board great opportunities to act on its own discretion in the case of telephony. One example to illustrate this: the board could freely dispose of its surplus as long as it was reinvested to improve the operation of the telegraph network. During the 1890s, the board used the surplus to promote telephony. This created some tension between the board and the Treasury. In spite of repeated demands, the board refused to submit any accounts where the telephone and telegraph investments were separated. The agency management considered it better to keep the books in such a state, that parliament did not get too clear a view of how things were. (Storckenfeldt 1893) Obviously, the board was more eager to compete and to develop the telephone system than the State, and during the 1890s the strategy became even more offensive.

During the 1890s, the State agency had been busy consolidating its expanding national telephone network. In Stockholm, competition had been regulated according to an agreement of intercommunication between the networks. This agreement terminated in 1900. Then, a decisively oligopolistic pattern was established: private companies dominated the telephone market in Stockholm, and the State agency dominated the national market. In 1902, almost two thirds of all telephones in Sweden were connected with the State network. Outside of Stockholm the percentage was 97 per cent. The bottle-neck situation in Stockholm had to be resolved before the growth of a national telephone network could be completed.

At that time, Cedergren clearly saw that the exclusion from the national market made private competition hopeless in the long run. He thus initiated negotiations with the State agency about a purchase (Johansson 1953). In 1902, a request from the board of the State agency to purchase the General Company was dismissed by parliament. Negotiations between the board and the General Company resulted in another bill in 1906. This was also turned down by parliament, since the purchase was regarded as too expensive. Not until 1918 did parliament approve of a purchase. This resulted in a functional monopoly on the national market in the hands of the State agency.

NATIONAL REGULATORY PATTERNS ON THE THRESHOLD OF THE INTER-WAR PERIOD.

The telephone markets in the Scandinavian countries at the beginning of the inter-war period can be positioned on a scale between State and market regulation. In Denmark, large private regional companies dominated the market, while the State telephone lines connected their respective areas. A regulatory mode was not chosen definitively, since the concession system existed. As a result, the private companies tried to maximise the revenues but did not improve the technological standard. In Norway at the beginning of the 1910s, the strong private sector was step by step bought up by the State, but the national network was not unified until 1923. The need of technical improvement and standardisation was then a main question. In Sweden, the national telephone market outside Stockholm was united in the hands of the State agency in 1900. When the Stockholm telephone network was purchased in 1918, it was well equipped as a result of efforts to stay on the market in the stiff competition. The technical variations within the system were of a minor problem due to the early dominance of one owner only.

National Trajectories of Institutional Transformation Until 1920 – a Discussion.

What, then, can be said about the role of the State in setting up institutions in the telecommunication sector in the Scandinavian countries, and how did this intervention impact the respective fields? Should the development in the respective countries be considered as the result of a national path dependency process? In Denmark and Norway, the spheres of governance were divided along a national-regional line between the State and private business, where the State operated the national arena and the private companies the regional market. This was not the case in Sweden. Here, even in the 1880s, the State agency had taken over, and operated a great number of local telephone networks. As a result, the Swedish market outside Stockholm was mainly a matter of public operation. Thus, as early as in the 1890s, different national patterns existed in the Scandinavian countries. This was the result of an interplay between the governmental bodies, the State agency and the private telephone industry. This process eventuated in political decision making, and a more or less definite choice between public regulation and a solution adjusted to the conditions on the market.

Actions taken by parliament and the government clearly differed in the way power was invested in the public economic organisations, the State agencies in telecommunications. In Denmark, the telephone market was divided between a few large regional companies and the State agency operated a national network connecting the various regional ones. The political decision to hold on to a concession system created a high degree of uncertainty about the future during the period. The lack of long-term stable institutions made short term decisions dominate in private strategic decision making. Individual relations between the Copenhagen Telephone Company and the government to some extent eased the pressure of the concession system. In Norway, a similar kind of uncertainty as in Denmark existed regarding the development of a united telephone network. However, from the turn of the century, private businesses knew that mergers were excluded as strategic alternatives. Still, the plans on nationalisation were hampered by the struggles in parliament over the financing of the telephone infrastructure. The State agency tried to get a number of national plans accepted, but this did not succeed until 1911.

Interestingly enough, Sweden, the country with least judicial restrictions to private enterprise, showed the fastest development of a State operated nationwide telephone network. A possible interpretation may be that in Norway and Denmark, if the companies wanted to be able to stay on the market, private business was forced to, and succeeded in, slowing down the expansion of the State agency by restricting its freedom of action. This was not the case in Sweden. Even if in 1888 parliament decided on a national telephone plan and tried to make it illegal for private companies to place telephone posts on common land, parliament never actually tried to restrict the private business by prescribing concession periods or by passing other laws.

This development may in one respect be considered as constituting a path dependency process. From the time the State entered the arena around 1890, the respective national trajectory was designed by the original way of regulation, even if the extent of regulation differed. Thus existing rules restrained the directions of decision making. At the same time, it may be argued that it is more questionable if it is possible to identify equally good strategic alternatives that were not chosen, and hence in a more thorough way evaluate the impact of path dependency.

More interesting is perhaps the fact that even if different institutions emerged, their effect on the diffusion pattern of telephones and the outcome on the consumer market showed great similarities. In 1920, there was one telephone per 13 inhabitants in Denmark, one per 15 in Sweden and one per

18 in Norway (Mitchell 1992). The most marked divergence was a higher price level in the Danish case, but in other respects the regulatory solutions seamed to be equally effective for expanding the telephone system during the period studied. However, this is not to say that institutions and regulatory modes do not matter. Rather it is important to emphasise that due to existing institutional frameworks, the efforts needed to cope with future challenges – technical as well as political – actually did vary in decisive ways. This can be illustrated by a hasty extrapolation of the development in telecommunications in these countries.

On the threshold of the 1920s, the technological knowledge in telecommunications made it possible to automatise the local networks, thus improving the quality of services provided. Automation also meant an increase in excessive capacity. This was a challenge the Swedish telephone industry was well equipped to meet and in some respects had helped develop. From the late 19th century, research had been promoted both by the State agency and by the L.M. Ericsson Company. The two competitors often co-operated in trading know-how (Attman *et al* 1976). These different roles of the State agencies may also explain the early efforts to cope with long-distance transmission, thus encouraging technical research in the hands of the State in Sweden. This differed from the development in the other countries. In Denmark, no telephone industry emerged at the beginning of the century besides the production of cables and telephone cords. Instead the technology was bought from foreign, mostly German and Swedish, suppliers. In Norway, the active State agency promoted a domestic telegraph industry from the 1860s. In the 1910s, the leading Norwegian telephone industry, The Electric Bureau, started to co-operate with L.M. Ericsson (Hodne 1985). Thus the L.M. Ericsson Company became one of the leading suppliers to the Nordic market. It amounted to 20 per cent of Ericsson's production in 1900 (Attman *et al* 1976).

From the 1920s, the major importance of the private telephone business in Sweden was to equip the national telephone market rather than to run telephone networks. This functional symbiosis secured the home market to the L M Ericsson Company, thus raising the barrier of entry to other competitors. It may even be argued that these early established specific sector regulations in Sweden may constitute a most significant watershed in the future contribution of telecommunications to the growth potentials among the Scandinavian economies. Hence it is a delicate matter to choose the right perspective of agents as well as the historical period, if we are to explore the full impact of path dependency processes embedded in institutional changes.

151

There are also other variables, not mentioned here, which are worth discussing in the interpretation of national regulatory patterns. One important factor in the case of network industries is the geography in itself – the size and shape of the country in question. Somewhat oversimplified, it can be argued that the technical and economic problems, needed to be resolved in order to establish a national telephone network, are so essentially different in each of these countries, that the diversities themselves may explain the way the spatial organisations were set up and regulated. In Denmark, a fairly small country consisting of islands and one peninsula, the distances were short and the capital needed for the investments could easily be raised on a regional basis. In Norway, with its high mountains and fjords cutting deep into the coastal areas, the distances were long and the technical problems hard to solve. This naturally led to the growth of regional networks, financed by local interests, whereas the expensive long-distance lines were considered a matter for the State. As the largest country of the three, Sweden had the longest distances to cover and the most widely spread population. This led to a need of vast investments by the State just to keep the national telegraph lines in order, and thus local networks could easily be attached to the national lines. This of course is only a lucid sketch of a possible interpretation, but it suggests that some fundamental path dependency processes may emanate from very general preconditions in a country.[2]

CONCLUDING REMARKS

The divergent patterns of regulation in the telephone sector in Scandinavia can be dated back to the 1890s, when political decisions opened different trajectories. Here the Swedish experience stands out from the others. The main difference is that the State did not constitute the national telephone market as an arena closed to economic actors and assigned for political domination as was the case in Denmark and Norway, this was the case with the Telephone Acts 1897 and 1899. From then on, the national telephone market was locked-in to actions taken by political interest groups in parliamentary decisions. In Denmark, private companies were concessioned on time limited leases. The result was that stable and favourable property rights did not emerge. In Norway, political antagonism in parliament over the use of national financial resources hampered the development of a national telephone network.

A vital condition for the evolution of national telephone systems was the relation between the State as a political body and its economic agents, in this case the State agencies. It is obvious that in Sweden, the State agency was the most powerful and determined agent in constituting a national network. This was possibly due to the lack of regulating instructions. This, in combination with the advantage given by the telegraph network, helped in uniting the Swedish network in the hands of the State. Only in Sweden, sector-specific regulations can be said to have emerged before the 1920s. From this period on, a functional symbiosis emerged between the State agency and the L.M. Ericsson Company.

Another difference impacting the regulatory process can be found among the entrepreneurs. Broadly speaking, in Denmark and Norway, the telephone companies emanated from local demands or from national entrepreneurs, trying to maximise the opportunities given by new technology. Contrary to this, the dominating Swedish private telephone company was founded in intimate interaction with the growth of a domestic telephone industry. Hence, technological knowledge and inventions were made only at arm's length distance from the needs of the market. In this process the State agency as a major customer, and also as a promoter of research, helped create a national telephone sector in the late 1910s.

The transformation of the national patterns followed different paths from the 1890s. They were even more diverged and rigid at the end of World War One. In spite of the different trajectories, the expansion of the telephone did not show any remarkable differences in the growth patterns. This shows that different institutional settings can promote similar developments – at least for some time. But at the same time, dissimilar regulatory structures implied different opportunities for future developments. This is to say, that different institutional settings put a certain stress on the kind of effort needed to change those regulations and to meet new challenges. In the case of the Scandinavian countries the challenge from the 1920s on, with a rapidly growing diversification of the telecommunication technology, took place in different institutional settings. Whether this technological shift was strong enough to alter the paths of institutional transformation in Scandinavia from the interwar period is an interesting issue in this respect. To answer it, more empirical research and a continued national comparison are needed.

NOTES

1   The concept of path dependency was borrowed from the history of technology, where it explains the rigidity in the change of technical systems. Douglass North most explicitly admitted his indebtedness to the article by P.A. David and to the work of B.W. Arthur in his adoption of the concept North (1990). Hughes (1983) also works with similar problems.
2   One point in favour of the impact of geography is that similar solutions were chosen in railway and telephone regulation in each of these countries during this period, see Andersson-Skog (1994). For a discussion of national regulatory patterns due to a general 'bias', see Dobbin (1994). He does not discuss the geography as a driving force in industrial policy making, but rather the habit of copying existing institutional patterns to solve a problem defined as similar.

9. Institutions as Determinants of Institutional Change – Case Studies in the Field of EEC Transport Policy

Juan Bergdahl and Jan L. Östlund

INTRODUCTION

In this article, the Common Transport Policy of the European Community is used to illustrate a theoretical discussion on institutional change. It is shown that fundamental parts of the Common Transport Policy, stated early in the integration process, were not realized until the Single European Act went into power, making substantial changes in the decision-making process of the Community political organisations.

The concept of *meta-institutions* is introduced to label such rules that are devoted solely to governing the process of formal rule making. Meta-institutions appear both in informal and formal shapes, the latter including major parts of constitutions.

Using two case studies from the Common Transport Policy, we argue that certain forms of meta-institutions may severely diminish the ability of decision making within a system of political organisations. We call these meta-institutions *perverted*. Deterioration of decision making may occur, even when the formal meta-institutions are apparently adequate, if perverted informal meta-institutions hamper the effect of the formal ones.

Until the the Single European Act changed certain perverted meta-institutions of the EEC, unanimity voting, combined with the unwillingness of some member states, forced the integration process to stay on a path that apparently did not lead to a common transport market. This historical process shows an example of path dependency that concerns institutional development.

At the heart of modern institutional theory lies the distinction between institutions as constraints on human interaction and organisations, as groups of individuals united by aspirations toward common objectives, a distinction made by Douglass C. North (1990, pp. 4-5).

If institutional theory is to be used on historical data there is an obvious need to include dynamics, that is, a theory of institutional change. In this line of reasoning, the ever-continuing process of institutional change depends on organisations as well as institutions formed at earlier stages. Thus, the evolution of history is never free of path dependency.

In the concept of organisations North includes political, economic, social and educational bodies (North 1990, p. 5). All these have a part in the process of institutional change within any constitutional democracy, however, for the development of formal institutions the political bodies are in an exceptional position. Other bodies can use whatever means they possess to exercise influence on political decisions affecting the formal institutional framework. Economic organisations generally have the strongest incentives to influence politics through lobbyism. Members of the other bodies mainly use their vote to influence formal institutional change.

When economic bodies lobby for certain institutional changes, their prospects of turning impulses of change into real institutional change depend mainly upon political considerations. A union of industrialists may, for example, have a hard time trying to gain the attention of a government which has strong ties to the labour unions. The prospects of the industrialists may however improve as voter preferences change over time and democratic rules of the game come into play (Easton 1965, pp. 11-12; North 1990, pp. 47-50).

Nevertheless, the fact that some organisations may have a harder time than others in influencing a political organisation like a government, does not usually mean that no decisions are made. What happens is that other organisations get preferential treatment in the political process. The institutional framework should continue to develop since national western democracies seldom are politically paralyzed over prolonged periods of time. Problems such as parliamentary deadlocks are usually resolved by changes in the political preferences of votes.

Decision making within political organisations, whether or not economic organisations interfere, is a process demanding both money and time. If the decisions must be agreed upon by all parties in consensus, it is possible that a portion of them may be delayed, for a long time or for ever, by people or groups fearing negative effects while disregarding overall positive effects for all involved. This may be rectified by rules governing the process, for example prescribing majority rule voting for all but a few categories of decisions (cf. Olson 1982, pp. 53-5). The implication here is that the political bodies themselves, in their work of changing institutions, must follow the rules of the political game. Such 'higher' institutions may be formulated in order to facilitate the decision-making process by prescribing the methods by which political organisations are allowed to change and develop institutions. They can also be used to safeguard certain values which are perceived central to the democratic structure and not easily changed by a few decisions of a single political organisation. To distinguish these rules about the making of rules from other institutions, in the absence of an established concept, we choose here to call them *meta-institutions*.

We will show that meta-institutions as well as other institutions can be both formal and informal. The formal meta-institutions include the constitutions of states, while the informal meta-institutions can best be described as a part of the prevailing culture within the policy-making system.

Needless to say, the way meta-institutions are structured directly affects the ability of a country's political system to change and develop formal institutions. An alternative treatment of rules constraining the changing of rules has been advocated by Brennan and Buchanan (1985, p. 6). Meta-institutions that support rapid, well justified institutional development may very well contribute to prosperous economic development. On the other hand, meta-institutions may also hamper institutional development, for example if consensus decision-making is prescribed. We will here label meta-institutions perverted if they, with an *ex post* point of view, obstruct the institutional development required for reaching economic and political goals that *ex ante* were agreed upon as desirable.

In the light of these circumstances, the doubting-Thomas within us cannot avoid phrasing troubling questions. What happens if the political system is bound by perverted meta-institutions? And, perhaps more important, can such political systems exist in the late 20th century?

This paper reviews how both formal and informal meta-institutions of the European Community, between the years 1958 and 1992 influenced the rate of institutional change and development in the field of transport policy.The chronological scope of the study (1958-92) encompasses the institutional development from the Treaty of Rome and up to the official date for the realization of the internal market as stated in the White Paper.

After a general section introducing the Common Transport Policy, we use two cases to support our argumentation. The first is the introduction of rules under which non-resident carriers can operate national road haulage services within the member states and the second is the creation of a Common Market for air transports. In the conclusions we return to the effect of the rules governing the decision making process. The empirical case studies are illustrations of the fact that the Council, for almost 30 years, failed to fulfill the transport policy intentions of the Treaty. It was not until the meta-institutions were reformed in 1987 that institutional changes started to take place in this area.

The European Transport Policy

The fact that the founding members, when they signed the Treaty of Rome, agreed on specific rules governing transport, serves to highlight the special status they accorded to this area of policy. Instead of resolving the question of transport by the application of the Treaty's general provisions on access to the market and freedom to provide services, the originators of the Treaty developed special provisions for transports by rail, road and inland waterways under the heading of a Common Transport Policy. However, transports by sea and air were *not* included in the provisions of the Treaty. Instead the Council was given the right to decide if, how and to what extent, regulations were to be set up to cover these modes of transport.

Using the words of degli Abbati (1986, p. 19), transport, like agriculture, fell into the realm of *lex specialis*. The key to the understanding of this discriminative treatment can be found in the attitudes of the national governments towards transport policy in general and road haulage in particular. The attitudes towards a more liberalized transport market varied significantly between member states. Some governments wanted a European transport market based on the principle of *laissez-faire* while others preferred an interventionist approach (degli Abbati 1986, pp. 18-19).

National transport systems and transport policies had often been used as tools for the attainment of other national policy goals outside the field of transport. Some member states hesitated to surrender control of an important national policymaking tool to essentially supranational political bodies.

Behind these careful attitudes also lay a well developed suspicion that a European road transport market, unfettered by quantitative restrictions and national boundaries, would seriously threaten the national railroad undertakings. This scepticism was particularly well developed in countries where rail transport had a more substantial role in the overall transport system (Erdmenger (1983 pp. 6-7; degli Abbati 1986, pp. 18-19). The perceived need of protecting rail transport against road-borne competition became a powerful incentive for the preservation of the more regulated market structure present in some of the member states.

The result of what can be described as a clash between two principles of market organisation - one that wanted to avoid destructive competition by

158

limitations in the access to national markets and another that wanted to promote a transport market where the market mechanism could be brought into play relatively freely (Erdmenger 1983, p. 7) - became a grand political compromize. As a result of this, transport fell under the heading of a dedicated Common Transport Policy.

After the adoption of the Treaty of Rome the implementation of the principles concerning the integration of Europe did not fall out equally well within all fields. The development of transport policy was especially slow. When the transitional period of twelve years had passed, the transport sector was still far from liberalized. In some specific areas the regulations were perhaps even more bureaucratic than before since the roles of national and Community bodies were far from well defined.

As the years passed without any progress in the field of transport, the European parliament in 1983, with the active support of the Commission, initiated legal actions against the Council of Ministers. This unprecedented act was set to run its course through the European Court of Justice, which had to assess if the Council indeed had neglected its duty regarding the creation of a Common Transport Policy. Even if the outcome of the legal action was inconclusive, it nevertheless emphasized the discontent fermenting within certain Community political bodies (Court of Justice of the European Communities, Case 13/83)

The assault on this Eurosclerosis of the policy making process continued with the launching of the Commission's White Paper. In this document, the development of a free transport market throughout the Community was subsequently stated as a task of substantial importance, emphasizing the fact that transport services had a 7 per cent share of the gross domestic product of the Community.

The Commission also called for an extension of the Common Transport Policy to include air and sea transport. The Commission even went as far as to warn the Council of the consequences if it failed to make progress towards the establishment of competition in the air and sea transport markets. In this case the Commission would use its rights according to Article 89 of the Treaty of Rome, i.e., make its own decisions and authorize the member states to take the necessary measures in order to comply with the White Paper.

The Introduction of Road Cabotage

From the very beginning, one of the clearest operative goals of the Common Transport Policy, as stated in Article 75 (1b), was the introduction of a system of road cabotage within the Common Market. The Treaty of Rome clearly required the Commission and the Council to take positive action to establish the conditions under which non-resident carriers could operate transport services within another member state, i.e., the establishment of a Community-wide system of road cabotage. Article 75 (2) furthermore stipulated that it must be implemented within the transitional period, spanning over the first twelve to fifteen years after the date of conception of the EEC.

Despite the lucid formulations of the Treaty, the member states kept careful attitudes towards transport. This was also clearly evident when it came to road haulage. The chaotic and predatory situation in the road transport market of the inter-war years was still a relatively recent memory (Despicht 1969, p. 13). For this reason, and considering the member states' sometimes dipolar attitudes concerning transport policy in general, competition on national transport markets was not always welcomed in all quarters.

The Council thus never fulfilled its Treaty obligations regarding road transport. A system of road cabotage was not implemented during the transitional period and time continued to pass without any regulations forthcoming even after the end of the period. The uneasiness felt by other Community political bodies over this fact found its expression in the parliament's 1983 Court action against the Council. Furthermore, the White Paper of 1985 stated that a system of cabotage must be completed no later than 1988 (Completing the internal market: White Paper, § 109, p. 30, see also annex page 27).

Not until December 1989 did the Council decide upon a regulation allowing road haulage contractors established in one member state to operate services within other member states (Council Regulation no. 4059/89). This first regulation was anything but comprehensive. It did not enable all carriers to compete freely on the domestic markets of other member states. Instead the strategy was to incrementally open the national markets to foreign competition. The European transport market continued to be partitioned as regarded the freedom to provide services. The regulation in question was therefore seen as transitional in nature and only a pathfinder for future regulation that would lay down permanent rules for essentially unlimited road cabotage.

This limited transitional system revolved around a Community cabotage quota, initially consisting of 15 000 cabotage authorizations, all valid for one vehicle during two months (with some possibilities to convert one authorization into two one-month authorizations). The quota was allocated among the member states, which in turn were to issue authorizations to carriers applying for them. To illustrate the limited nature of the system it is sufficient to say that the total number of goods motor vehicles operated for hire or reward in Germany alone was 161 000 in 1990. On the other end of the scale, the number in Denmark was 17 000 vehicles (Eurostat 1993, p. 70). The requirements made on the applying carriers were that they were established in a member state, operated in accordance with its regulations, and were prepared to operate road haulage services on a temporary basis in another member state subject to the laws, regulations and administrative provisions in force in that nation.

The regulation entered into force on 1 July 1990 and applied during a transitional period of two and a half years until 31 December 1992. After this date the intention was to implement a definitive cabotage system, drawn up in compliance with the Treaty. The specific responsibility for this was given to the Council.

The level of the aggregated quota was to be raised by at least 10 per cent per year from 1 July 1991, through decisions by the Commission. The level was also raised on 1 January 1991 by 298 authorizations as a result of the unification of Germany (Council Regulation no. 296/91).

Despite these preparatory regulations, the Council failed to agree on a definitive cabotage system before the internal market went into force on 1 January 1993. In a regulation of October 1993 the Council instead extended the transitional cabotage system (Council Regulation no. 3118/93). It both extended the quota in the number of authorizations, now doubled to 30 000, and in the future rate of increase to, raised to 30 per cent per year. However, the number of authorizations still remain negligible compared to the total number of vehicles used for hire and reward in circulation within the territory of the Community.

The regulation mentioned above entered into force on 1 January 1994 and is to cease on 1 July 1998. The intention is that it will be succeeded by a fully free cabotage system allowing all carriers established in member states to compete on the domestic transport markets of the other member states.

Even if we disregard the obvious fact that the system described above was severely limited we can still maintain that at least *some* headway was finally made towards the introduction of road cabotage. With this in mind it instead becomes interesting to focus on the fact that it took the political organisations of the Community more than thirty years to generate legislation in this area. When the first regulation concerning road cabotage finally appeared, it was extremely overdue and sorely needed if the

161

principle of the freedom to provide transport services should gain any foothold within the Community.

The Inclusion of Air Transport in the CTP

In contrast to road haulage, no clear operative goals were set up for air transport within the Treaty of Rome. The Treaty's original provisions regarding transport, in Article 84 (2), merely stated that the Council was at liberty to decide whether, to what extent and by what procedure provisions were to be set up to cover air as well as sea transport.

The fact that air transport was excluded from the Treaty's provisions has been explained on the basis of the member states' lack of interest for the inclusion of air transport into the process of integration. The large air carriers of Europe were often undertakings containing substantial state interests, not unlike national railway undertakings. It is easy to see how national flag carriers like Air France, Lufthansa, *et al.*, became something of the airborne prides of the countries they represented. In view of this special relationship between the member states and their flag carriers it was only natural that protectionist attitudes appeared. In this context the member states had a tendency to try to reserve certain international air routes for their own flag carriers, something that ran contrary to a number of guiding principles underlying the Treaty (Erdmenger 1983, p. 7).

An unequivocal inclusion of air transport into the Common Transport Policy would have highlighted the fact that this part of the transport sector operated out of reach of general Treaty provisions concerning, *inter alia*, market access and competition policy.

However, the need for an application of transport policy on the area of air transport could not be neglected forever. The anomaly of an essentially protectionist sector within the European transport market began to develop into a political embarrassment. It became clear that the air transport sector could not be allowed to continue to operate in the shadowlands between national interest and the development of a European transport market founded on the principle of free competition.

By its judgement of 1974 the European Court of Justice also gave the Council powerful incentives to actually include air transport in the Common Transport Policy. By explicitly stating that the general provisions of the Treaty regarding rules of competition indeed was applicable also to air transport, the Court finally set the wheels of policymaking into motion (Court of Justice of the European Communities, Case 167/73). The speed of the process was, however, far from impressive.

162

At the core of any attempt to include air transport in the internal market lay the necessity of creating provisions for the enforcement of the rules of competition. Specifically: if air transport services were to be purveyed by a competitive market system it was essential to guarantee that collusion, cartellization etc. did not threaten competition. In other words: the political apparatus of the EEC had the task of enforcing Treaty articles 85 and 86 on the air transport sector. Despite the importance of such measures, especially with the often dominant market positions of the national carriers in mind, regulations in this area tarried in coming. The years went by without any real headway being made.

As was the case in the road haulage sector, the Commission finally got tired of waiting. The White Paper of 1985 stated that the air transport services between member states needed greater freedom. In particular there was a demand for changes in the system for the setting and approval of tariffs, and limits to the rights of governments to restrict capacity and access to the market. The timetable of the White Paper prescribed that these measures must be taken by 1987 (Communication from the Commission to the European parliament -White Paper on the European Integration, § 109, p. 30, see also Annex p. 27).

To bring about action in this area it was necessary to modify relevant meta-institutions. The Treaty in its original form stated that the Council was to decide unanimously how the air transport sector should be included within the scope of the Common Transport Policy. It therefore also became necessary to change the wording of the Treaty's article 84 (2). Thus, with the aid of the Single European Act, Article 16 (5), qualified majority voting was finally introduced for decision-making relevant to air transport. Following the Commission's urgings and the change in meta-institutions mentioned above, the first substantial step to address questions concerning air transport could be taken in late 1987. Since the Court had ruled that air transport was subject to the general rules of competition, it became necessary to lay down the procedures needed for the application of the rules of competition, something that had been lacking in the years following the Court's decision. The objective behind the introduction of Council Regulation 3975/87 was to supply the Community with the legal instruments necessary to intervene in case of breaches against the rules of competition, concerning international air transport between Community airports, and specifically articles 85 and 86 of the Treaty (Council Regulation no. 3975/87).

Even so, the Community's approach in this area was in no way aimed toward a radical application of the above mentioned articles. Since the

163

European air transport sector had been governed by what was described as a network of bilateral, international and multilateral agreements between states and/or air carriers, the Council felt that any change brought about should be introduced gradually to allow the sector time to adapt (Council Regulation no. 3975/87). Article 85 (3), permitted certain categories of agreements between undertakings, decisions of associations of undertakings and concerted parties. The use of these provisions made it possible to attain a step by step approach toward the elimination of agreements between carriers.

To comply with the spirit of the general rules of competition, while still offering the carriers a smooth transition, the Commission was given the task, through Council Regulation 3976/87, of defining the types of agreements that should be excluded from the scope of article 85 (1). In this context the Commission exempted, *inter alia*, agreements between air carriers concerning joint planning and co-ordination of capacity for scheduled international air services, certain forms of limited revenue sharing and airport scheduling (e. g. slot allocation) (Commission Regulation no. 2671/88, Commission Regulation no. 84/91). In addition, the carriers were also allowed to enter agreements in connection with the common purchase, development and operation of computer reservation systems (Commission Regulation no. 2672/88). In July 1990 the Council also allowed consultations on cargo rates (Council Regulation no. 2344/90). All in all, the application of the competition rules of Article 85 and 86 in the field of air transport was substantially weakened by all these exemptions, made for different reasons.

Nevertheless, the scope for application of the rules of competition was eventually broadened in certain respects through a pair of amendments. In May 1991 the Commission was given more power to hinder practices that directly jeopardize the existence of an air service (Council Regulation no. 1284/91). This was followed in July 1992 by a widening of the application of regulation 3975/87 from 'international air transport' to all 'air transport' between Community airports (Council Regulation no. 2410/92).

The above exemptions from the application of article 85 (1) was originally intended to expire before the realization of the internal market, that is, at the latest on the 31 December 1992. However, as the Community drew closer to that date, these exemptions were granted an extended stay of life (Council Regulation no. 2411/92, Council Regulation no. 3618/92). It was now apparent that the Community's political organisations were far from prepared to let loose the forces of competition on the air transport sector in any manner resembling the original intentions of the internal market.

In the above we have seen how the developed provisions in this particular field of the Common Transport Policy became less the tools for the introduction of competition within the air transport sector than an escape from the Community's rules of competition. Even if this is an interesting observation in itself, let us for the moment concentrate on the fact that regulation was indeed introduced to cover this sector of the transport market. Disregarding more qualitative appraisals of the Community's efforts in this area, we can still conclude that headway was finally made in the area of air transport. As in the case with road cabotage, the political system of the Community had finally addressed an area of policy that was long overdue for attention.

An Application of Theory on Empirical Data

This investigation of two significant parts of the Common Transport Policy reveals that the development of relevant institutions gathered momentum at a specific time in the Community's history, i.e. the years following 1 July 1987. Before we turn to our conclusions, we return to the concept of meta-institutions developed earlier. At the focus lies the development of the Community's decision-making process.

On a general level the meta-institutions, as stated in the Treaty of Rome, provided for a voting procedure whereby the Council would act on the Commission's proposals mainly by qualified majority during the transitional period. This was, however, not realized. By way of France's 'empty chair policy' and the following 'Luxembourg compromise' of the middle sixties, the culture of political decision making changed without any formal changes in meta-institutions. The practice of unanimous voting gained the permanent status of informal meta-institution as Community decision making was concerned (degli Abbati 1986, p. 60, 74). This had, as degli Abbati duly noted, disastrous effect on the overall Community decision making process, thus this practice may well be called, using our terminology, a perverted meta-institution (degli Abbati 1986, p. 74).

With this in mind it is important to remember that transport had acquired the special status of an essentially separate area of policy, which resulted in the formulation of special meta-institutions for decision making specific to transport policy. Thus article 75 (1) of the Treaty stated that the Council was to adopt the Commission's transport policy proposals on the basis of unanimity during the first and second stages of the transitional period, and thereafter with qualified majority. It is clear that institutional development was severely hampered by the unanimity procedure in use during the early years. Since the members of Council did not always share the same view of the process of integration, unanimity could be difficult to obtain. The rules on Council voting therefore constituted an effective blocking mechanism, useful for member states wishing to hinder the creation of provisions that in some way were running contrary to their interests.

Once again though, article 75 (1) prescribed the Council to make its decisions on the basis of qualified majority voting after the Community's entry into the third stage. As is well known, this did not come about. Article 75 (3) permitted continued use of the earlier voting procedure when the Council was about to act on proposals for regulations that could severely affect the living conditions in specific regions, or the use of assets within transport undertakings. This opportunity to evade the qualified majority procedure was eagerly seized by at least some of the ministers at given times. It became possible for the member states to force a return to the principle of veto, whenever they felt that national interests were at stake, by simply stating that proposed legislation could possibly have the effects described above. The practice of unanimity voting could therefore be continued through an informal, perverted meta-institution in the form of a convenient but erroneous interpretation of Article 75 (3) (degli Abbati 1986, p. 74).

A change in the form of decision making setting this interpretation aside did not come until the Single European Act, which entered into force on July 1, 1987. By signing this document, the member states took a major step forward in the process of integration (Lewis 1993, p. 78). For us the most important aspect is that it restored the use of qualified majority as the principal way of making decisions.

The introduction of the SEA can be seen as the substitution of a perverted informal meta-institution that effectively hindered institutional change for new meta-institutions much more in tune with the need for dynamic policy-making. With restored qualified majority voting, the chance that a Commission proposal actually would be adopted by the Council improved significantly. Since the Council was no longer hog-tied by unanimity voting, the task of producing legal provision for the integration of Europe became a somewhat simpler task.

CONCLUSIONS

If we consider the historical process described here using the theory of path dependency, one interpretation reveals itself immediately. It is obvious that the use of perverted meta-institutions made the European integration take another path than the map drawn by the Treaty of Rome. Unanimity voting, combined with the unwillingness of certain member states, heavily bound the transport market to earlier institutions; i.e. forced the integration process to stay on a path that apparently did not lead to a common transport market. Our two case studies show that only after the Single European Act changed the meta-institutions, was it possible to change onto a path leading to the common transport market.

Behind this change towards more dynamic policymaking were factors such as the political pressure generated by the parliament's court action together with the publication of the Commission's White Paper on the European integration. Seen as a change of formal meta-institutions the Single European Act firmly established qualified majority voting within the decision making system. Furthermore the Single European Act, together with the parliament's legal action, lessened the Council's propensity to make use of article 75 (3), thereby eliminating an informal institution detrimental to the process of integration.

Equipped with new meta-institutions the Community was better prepared than ever for the journey towards the realization of the Common Transport Policy.

167

10. Institutional Change and European Air Transport, 1910-1985

Peter J. Lyth

'... there is nothing more difficult
to plan or more uncertain of success
or more dangerous to carry out than an
attempt to introduce new institutions...'
Niccolò Machiavelli, The Prince (1972, pp. 71-2).

The term *institution* is a broad and rather malleable concept which in the twentieth century has come to mean almost any organised element in society. As Machiavelli recognised five centuries ago, changing institutions is a hard task and those reformers who attempt it can be certain of vigorous opposition from everyone with an interest in the existing arrangements. Once created, institutions seem to be remarkably durable; they may be partially supplanted, or bypassed, or simply added to, but only rarely are they completely destroyed. Where institutions perform a regulatory function they remain in place until circumstances force a change, but the new regime is likely to feature an additional institution rather than the replacement of the first one.

Any definition of a regulatory institution must therefore include the attributes of durability and proliferation, but also the idea of constraint. Above all there must be an historical reference point, a conceptual anchor embedded in the past which ties things down. The application of evolutionary principles to economics and institutional theory has yielded a fruitful literature from which to derive such a definition and is useful in guiding the analysis of how regulatory institutions function over time. Thus Douglass North sees institutions as any form of constraint devised to shape human interaction, their purpose being to reduce uncertainty by providing a stable, although not necessarily efficient, structure to everyday life (North 1990, pp. 6, 25). Change in institutions consist of continuous marginal adjustments to the whole; there may be wars and revolutions which periodically cause sudden and 'discontinuous' change, but normally it is 'overwhelmingly incremental' (North 1990, pp. 83-9). Nelson and Winter concur, describing institutional development as 'a groping, incremental process, in which the conditions of each day arise from the actual circumstances of the preceding day and in which uncertainty abounds ...'(Nelson and Winter 1982, p. 404)

Institutions also exhibit inherited stabilising qualities which are passed on through time, 'the deadweight of social inertia supported by intentionally taught tradition' as Hirschleifer (1987, p. 221) has put it. Social institutions, in particular, have enduring characteristics which reflect conditions as they stood at the time of the institution's creation but which later can cause rigidities or obstacles to modernisation (Hodgson, 1989, p. 80). This historical element, the conceptual anchor, can be understood in terms of path dependency, an explanatory phenomenon which is usually applied to technological change but which is equally helpful in understanding the evolution of institutions (David 1985; Arthur 1989). For Joel Mokyr (1991, p. 134) an important aspect of path dependence is the way it 'indicates the role of accident and chance in forming our environment'; things could have gone differently, other paths could have been taken, but some initial salient condition or event guided evolution down a certain route. For North (1990, pp. 95-9, 103) the choice of route is shaped by increasing returns to the established institutions and by imperfect markets, characterised by significant transaction costs. In other words if a constraining institution yields increasing returns, its path will persist and groups of actors will appear with a stake in its survival. And as Machiavelli observed, those actors will resist change with surprising determination.

This conception of the regulatory institution is applied here to the analysis of one of the archetypal industries of the twentieth century: international air transport. On the eve of the First World War air transport was an entirely new industry which could have followed one of several paths to the mass transport sector we know today; it was so-to-speak pre-emergent with no governing standards or regulations, indeed no substance whatever since no airlines existed. In 1950 air transport was still negligible as means of mass passenger transport yet a comprehensive network of international routes had been established. Aircraft technology had by no means reached the level at which profitable passenger operations could be guaranteed, although aircraft like the Douglas DC4 and the Lockheed Constellation held promise for the future. With the notable exception of the United States, airline organisation was generally focused on the state-owned monopolies with exclusive access to government subsidies. The question arises therefore: in what kind of regulatory regime had international air transport grown up? What was the nature of the industry's regulative institutions, its governing rules, its constraints? How was it that, with little impulse from market forces, a passenger network had been established which in its extent and density was more or less the equal of the route system of today?

In answering this question this paper presents international air transport regulation as an example of path dependency in institutional evolution. A single event – the First World War – conditioned government decision makers to choose a highly nationalistic framework within which the commercial industry could operate. Thereafter, the institutions which they had created rigidified the industry until the experience of another war brought about new institutional growth in the mid-1940s, but growth in the form of additional branches to an original trunk which still stands as the central legal pillar of modern civil aviation. Wars often trigger institutional change. For example the Second World War saw the creation of new international monetary institutions at Bretton Woods, a conference at which the participants were keenly aware of the failure of previous exchange control arrangements in the interwar years and their responsibility for the break down of international trade (Guillame 1977). North recognises that wars do provide the necessary jolt to shift institutional change from the incremental to the sudden and discontinuous. What follows is an evaluation of this effect in international air transport.

I

In 1910, before any air transport services were planned or even technically possible, a group of European lawyers, diplomats and military men gathered in Paris to consider an institutional and legal framework for the future development of international civil aviation. Two opposing philosophies were represented: firstly *freedom of the air*, analogous to the freedom of the seas, whereby commercial air transport would operate everywhere, irrespective of the territory it was overflying, and secondly, *state sovereignty*, the upward extension of the national prerogative over air space, similar, in the opposite direction, to the idea of oil and mineral rights. The military men and those concerned with national security favoured the latter philosophy, on the grounds that the air above a territory was exposed to hostile intrusion in a way which did not apply to an adjacent stretch of sea. Idealists and free trade enthusiasts argued for the former philosophy out of concern that the new transport medium should not be crippled at the outset by restrictive arrangements but should be allowed to blossom and make the kind of contribution to the twentieth century that maritime transport had made to the nineteenth. However no consensus was reached between the opposing sides and the First World War broke out before any further attempts at agreement could be made (Cooper 1947, pp. 17-35; Goedhuis 1942, pp. 596-613).

The First World War settled the question overwhelmingly in favour of the state sovereigntists. By 1918 everyone, including the idealists of 1910, had been made acutely aware of the military potential of aircraft and air travel. More than the heroic dogfights over the Western Front, the use of German Zeppelin airships to bomb England, although ineffectual in themselves, had nonetheless driven home the lesson that nations were now fundamentally vulnerable to attack from a new quarter (Fritsche 1992, pp. 9-58). Although aircraft were hardly beyond an embryonic state of technological development, they were already associated with death and destruction and it was inevitable that civil air tranport was born with strong strategic implications. Within twenty years the cult of the bomber and its supposed irresistability had gripped the minds of a generation in Europe and it took another war to show that this new weapon did not, in fact, signify the end of civilisation (Howard 1976, p. 130; Bond 1984, pp. 150-153). Against this background it is not surprising that at the Convention on the future of civil aviation held in Paris in 1919, the guarantee to every state of total and exclusive sovereignty over its airspace was unanimously accepted and featured early in the ensuing treaty (Cooper 1947, pp. 18-28, 107-11).

The universal adoption of the doctrine of sovereign airspace could, of course, have taken place without the experience of the First World War, but it is likely that it would not have been so early nor so widely accepted. What had happened was that the value of a future form of mass transport had been eclipsed by its perceived military importance before any civil experience had been gained. From the outset, therefore, air transport was laden with strategic and national political implications which blinded governments and policy-makers to its broader economic potential (Lissitzyn 1942, pp. 38-93; Thornton 1970; Wheatcroft, 1964, pp. 46-57). And as civil aviation took off in the 1920s the guiding idea in the formation of its regulatory institutions was nationalist, protectionist and generally 'beggar-thy-neighbour' in spirit. Up until 1944 the ideal of national sovereignty was the cornerstone of international air transport regulation with the traffic rights deriving from that sovereignty treated as the commercial stock of state-owned airlines (Naveau 1989, pp. 25-6, 87). Air space became a national as well as natural resource.

For a very brief period the market for commercial air transport in Europe was open and competitive. In Germany in 1919 no less than 48 firms applied for licences to fly commercial air transport routes within the country's boundaries. However the result was generally disastrous since the industry was too young, the aircraft too primitive and traffic too small to support competition (Birkhead 1960, pp. 133-45). Instead competitive operations were abandoned and an era of state-subsidised monopoly was ushered in with the establishment of famous flag-carriers like KLM (1920), Imperial Airways (1924), and Deutsche Luft Hansa (1926) (Higham 1960; Appel 1993). In the absence of profits, the European industry was controlled by governments, indeed it became virtually a department of government. With air space a negotiable part of national sovereignty, civil aviation developed in an atmosphere where prestige and high politics replaced the usual commercial considerations. For this reason the profitless early airlines were not allowed to succumb to market forces but were amalgamated into Europe's *chosen instruments*. Had the pioneer airlines been required to 'fly on their own or not at all', as Winston Churchill, at the time British Secretary of State for War and Air (House of Commons Debates, 5. Series, Vol.126, 11 March 1920, c.1622), urged in Britain in 1920, then international civil aviation would have taken a radically different path in the the interwar years. It is likely that the only airlines to survive would have been those with the natural advantage of providing services across short but inaccessible tracts of land and sea, i.e. on the northern and western periphery of Europe and in Australia, South America and Canada. The reason that this path was not taken, and Churchill's Darwinian sentiment of 1920 was quickly superceded by interventionist policies, was that once the strict sovereignty of air space had been universally accepted it was a natural development that international air transport generally would take on a strong national orientation and the whole business become prestige-driven. In line with the recommendation of the Hambling Committee, Britain adopted a long-term subsidy scheme with the creation of Imperial Airways in 1924 (Civil Air Transport Subsidies Committee, *Report on Government Financial Assistance to Civil Air Transport Companies*, Cmd. 1811, 1923).

This prestige principle was particularly clear in aircraft procurement and in the building up of route networks. The new *chosen instruments* were supposed to fly locally-produced aircraft, if that was possible, and fly them to destinations where it was important to show the flag. Because of their low cruising speed and primitive navigational equipment, early aircraft had to reach their destination in daylight which meant that their range was severely restricted. In Europe international air routes tended to consist of a number of short hops, for example a flight from London to Stockholm would have been interrupted for fuel, and possibly an exchange of passengers, in Amsterdam, Hamburg and Copenhagen. This would have enhanced the value of Dutch, German and Danish air space in the necessary bilateral negotiations between Britain and Sweden, and further consolidated the institutional regime of national sovereignty. Within a short space of time Western European airlines established spoke networks radiating out from national capitals. Britain, France, Belgium and Holland were soon connected by triangular route taking in the four capitals, while Germany built up a network linking its major cities and extending the system into Switzerland, Czechoslovakia, Poland and Scandanavia.

For Britain, France, Belgium and Holland prestige and strategic considerations demanded that their spoke networks be extended and their flag carriers establish air communications with colonial possessions in Africa and Asia, a sort of twentieth century continuation of the imperial rivalry begun in the 1870s. The exception was Germany which had been deprived of its few colonies by the Versailles treaty and which created instead a dense, Eurocentric network, extended southwards in the 1930s towards what might best described as an *ersatz* colony in South America (Quin-Harkin 1954, pp. 197-215; Burden 1943; Bruettingg 1979, pp. 88-98). These were the first long-haul air routes, but being subject to the same technical limitations as the European networks, they were, in effect, an extended series of short hops. For example, to travel by Imperial Airways from London to Karachi in the spring of 1929 one had to stop en route at Paris, Basle, Genoa, Rome, Naples, Corfu, Athens, Suda Bay, Tobruk, Alexandria, Gaza, Rutbah Wells, Baghdad, Basra, Bushire, Lingeh, Jask, and Gwadar, as well as enduring three different types of aircraft and a train journey (Basle-Genoa) (*Flight Magazine*, 16.4.1954, Imperial Record).

Because of restricted aircraft range and the institution of absolute air sovereignty, the prewar international air transport regime offered frequent opportunities to exploit others wishing to overfly one's territory. Indeed horse-trading over air rights was a characteristic of the period, with bilateral reciprocity the guiding principle in negotiations. The Italians refused to let the British overfly parts of their territory unless revenue was shared with their inefficient local carrier, and Greece, Turkey and Iran also made life difficult for Imperial Airways. On the North Atlantic the British themselves exercised their sovereign rights in Canada and Bermuda and held up the introduction of Pan American's transatlantic service in the mid-1930s by at least three years. They obstructed KLM's plans in 1929 to establish a

173

service between Amsterdam and Batavia by denying en route landing rights (Higham 1960, pp. 135-40; Corbett 1965, pp. 29-30).

Aircraft technology developed swiftly in the interwar years and it is remarkable in retrospect how many of the fundamental problems of transport aircraft construction were solved by 1940. In 1920, with the exception of the remarkable Junkers F-13, passenger aircraft were usually biplanes made of wood and fabric which were slow, aerodynamically inefficient and fundamentally uneconomic in operation. In 1940 aircraft like the Douglas DC3, the forerunner of the modern airliner, were equipping airline fleets across the world (Miller and Sawers 1968). The increase in aircraft range had the greatest political ramifications since it allowed airlines to bypass troublesome states who exacted an unacceptable price for overflying their territory. In practical terms however it probably had more effect in North America than in Europe where most of the important routes were already being operated with short-range equipment. Above all increased range opened up the greatest prize of international air transport: the North Atlantic.

One of the more obvious technological deadends in interwar aviation was the flying boat. The British in particular pursued this hybrid solution, with its comforting associations to maritime tradition, in the development of their Empire routes in the second half of the 1930s. It has been cogently argued that the British decision to concentrate its efforts on air communications with the Empire restricted the horizons of British aircraft builders and led to the production of aircraft which were outdated and inferior in comparison with the American and German competition; the workhorse of Imperial Airways in the 1930s, the stately Handley Page HP42 biplane, is the prime example (Fearon 1974, pp. 249-251). So far as flying boats are concerned, it seems now that they were a technological response to the problem of unrestricted air sovereignty and the obstacles that foreign states placed in path of colonial air routes in Asia and Africa: unable to land under acceptable conditions in countries like Iran, airlines like Imperial Airways landed instead on the adjacent seaboard. Politics and the institutional regime forged with such alacrity and haste in 1919, were dictating the path of technology.

II

Just as the First World War had precipitated air transport's institutional development down a certain path, so the Second World War was responsible for a significant swerve from that path. It brought a 'discontinuous' jolt to the process of incremental change whereby institutional apparatus had been added, bit by bit, to the central pillar of unrestricted air sovereignty. In November 1944 the major powers opposing the Axis forces (excluding the Soviet Union) gathered in Chicago to consider the postwar development of international air transport. Their representatives were aware of the record of abuse that the *philosophy* of air sovereignty had called forth, but there was no serious support for the idea of reverting to the uncontrolled situation which might have existed before the establishment of the *institution* of air sovereignty in 1919. Instead it was agreed that its power would be circumscribed by a set of universal rights, the so-called Five Freedoms, which would guarantee air transport operators the transit and refuelling facilities which were vital to commercial survival.

The dominant theme of the Chicago conference was the commercial and philisophical confrontation between the two major air transport powers of the western world: the United States and Britain. The Americans were on the threshold of superpower status and were immensely powerful in civil aviation; they had the transport aircraft and they had the airlines (notably Pan American Airways) which would use them. The British were impoverished and had few decent aircraft, but they did have a vast spread of territory across the globe, the legacy of the Empire, with which to bargain over future rights. The Americans, with the support of a few likeminded nations like the Netherlands, wanted an unrestricted 'open-skies' regime for air transport supply, the British, with the general support of the Europeans, wanted protection and regulation. The result of this clash between the old and new worlds was inconclusive and settlement of the debate over rights, rates and routes in air transport was deferred until Anglo-American bilateral negotiations in Bermuda (Smith 1991, pp. 146-265; Dobson 1991, pp. 151-72; Stannard 1945, pp. 497-512).

A third possible path of future development for air transport which was proposed at Chicago was the idea of total internationalisation. Under such a scheme, competition would be completely replaced by a single giant airline operated by an organisation similiar to the United Nations. Its supporters tended to be idealists, for example in the British Labour Party, who were strongly influenced by the experience of rampant nationalism in the prewar years (Joensson 1987, pp. 105-6). As a praisal it is interesting for it would have implied a total reversal of the principle of air sovereignty: it would have been hard to deny access to an internationally-owned airline. Whereas the American negotiating position at Chicago rested upon the declared objective of maximum competition between national carriers and the British wanted maximum regulation of national carriers, the internationalists had no need of regulation since there was going to be only one airline and everybody was going to own a share of it. As it turned out the British and Americans shared a common affection for national carriers, although their respective ideas of the playing field on which they would compete, was very different. The internationalists found little sympathy amongst the hard-headed policy-makers in London. In response to an earlier committee report in 1941 recommending 'the complete internationalisation of civil aviation', Sir William Hildred, Director-General of Civil Aviation at the Air Ministry, demolished with characteristic vigour any attempt to rebuild the supporting institutions of the air transport industry:

> Human nature will be much the same at the end of this conflict and to offer internationalism to PAA (Pan American Airways) would be like offering a hymn book to a rattle snake; and just as dangerous. But I would not fight against internationalism because of the ruthless positivists like PAA who know what they want. Its principle danger would be that it would be a pot of honey for the shilly shalliers who don't know what they want, and just as the last war left its weeping misery of vacillation in many spheres, so, I think, would civil aviation policy be imperilled and progress stayed if anyone, at the conclusion of hostilities, tried to talk internationalism in so complex a field as civil aviation. The sponsor would be left talking to a bunch of idealists, whilst Stalin and Trippe [chairman of Pan American] quartered the ether between them. (Minute, 31 January 1942, Postwar Policy for Organisation of Civil Aviation, 1941-1943, Public Record Office, Kew, BT.217/2201)

What was not agreed at Chicago in 1944, was decided in Bermuda in early 1946. There the Americans and the British reached agreement on the routes and frequencies of their respective national carriers in an accord which became a lasting model for bilateral treaties around the world. Eventually a mosaic of interlocking deals was created which formed the legal foundation for postwar international civil aviation. It was a mosaic mounted upon the central trunk of the air sovereignty principle; the prewar accretion of antagonistic nationalism having been stripped away, there was room for a new mechanism of co-operation.

The relative strengths of the Americans and British at Bermuda were much the same as they had been at Chicago: the Americans had the industry, both in terms of supply (strong and numerous airlines) and demand (a high volume of generated traffic), while the British had the 'real estate' in the form of a string of colonial and dominion territories around the world which could be used as refuelling stops for aircraft and therefore as bargaining chips in any deal (Naveau 1989, p. 37; Joensson pp. 44-50). The

Americans got most of what they wanted at Bermuda, i.e. a generous frequency and capacity regime, but in one vital respect they did make a concession in favour of regulation and away from the free market: they accepted the authority of the International Air Transport Association (IATA) to fix international air fares (Thornton 1970; Mackenzie 1991, pp. 61-73; Dobson pp. 173-210).

IATA is a fascinating organisation. It is probably one of the most successful price cartels of the twentieth century and, as an instrument of constraint within an industry, an institution of proven durability. In fact it is an institutional accretion – something built onto an existing framework, an embellishment of the air sovereignty principle, but also a symbol of the Chicago/Bermuda era, and proof that air transport was not going to return to some free market version of its pre-1914 status. An International Air Traffic Association had actually been founded in 1919 at the very birth of commercial air transport, but this was essentially a European club (only in 1938 did its members agree to elect Pan American), and it was not empowered to fix rates (Murray 1953 pp. 265; Brancker 1977, pp. 7-8). The modern IATA, a private trade association established at Havana in April 1945, was much more influential and its authority in postwar aviation can hardly be exaggerated. Since most of the world's international airlines were subsidised or state-owned, and price competition would have meant, in practice, an international subsidy war, most governments were more than happy to see IATA control fares. Moreover IATA reinforced the sovereignty principle and the explicit politicisation of the air transport industry; because it fixed international scheduled air fares at regular tariff conferences where total unanimity amongst the members was required, and every airline had a veto, the adoption of a fare involved a great deal of horse-trading and tended to be set at a level high enough to suit the smallest, and least efficient airlines (Murray 1953, p. 267).

IATA's central purpose was to achieve a high degree of stability in the international air transport industry and protect with high fares the *little guy* who would otherwise succumb to competition from bigger and more efficient carriers. In other words, ensuring the survival of airlines took precedence over raising efficiency and offering the consumer lower prices. In general IATA doctrine led to higher costs, lower load factors and the shifting of competition between scheduled carriers from price to less quantifiable areas of performance such as flight service, cabin decor, seat size and the width of the stewardess's smile (Ellison and Stafford 1974, pp. 8, 11-12).

And because amongst its members small airlines from the Third World outnumbered more efficient carriers from the industrialised nations, IATA's survival was ensured; the small airlines had a strong interest in preserving the exisiting arrangements. They have been characterised by one authority as inefficient, serving no mass travel markets, encountering no competition from charter carriers, facing no demand for innovative fares, lacking the ability to offer a high level of inflight service, and having a strong need to show their national flags and to fly routes for political reasons (Gidwitz 1980, p. 97). Small wonder therefore that they needed IATA to enable them to stay in the air.

The institutional regime represented by IATA and the Chicago/Bermuda agreements suited the air transport industry well in the 1950s and to a slightly lesser degree in the 1960s. Occasionally however the interests of the efficient few amongst IATA members diverged so drastically from those of the inefficient majority, that a crisis was inevitable. The first notable occasion was when fare increases which had been approved by an IATA meeting at Chandler, Arizona in the autumn of 1962 were subsequently rejected by the American Civil Aeronautics Board (CAB). The CAB, which had previously consented to the granting of anti-trust immunity to IATA, appeared now to want to challenge the organisation. It seemed to be a clear manifestation of the potential for friction which had existed since Chicago between efficient American carriers like Pan American and Trans World Airlines (TWA) on the one hand, and the rest of the world on the other. Although it should be noted that in this case the two American airlines actually supported the Chandler rate, nonetheless the CAB, in presenting itself as a champion of lower rates, attacked what it saw as a cartel-ridden (and British-led) industry in the name of efficient American enterprise (*The Economist* 1963, pp. 452-3). Thanks partly to vigorous and highly publicised defence of the Chandler decision by BOAC, which showed up the British flag-carrier's dependence on IATA to maintain its high-cost operations, the CAB was forced to back down and IATA survived with little more to show than the splash from a shot across its instititional bows (*The Economist* 1963, p. 689; Dobson, pp. 241-4).

In general the secular change which took place with the postwar popularization of air travel was absorbed into the system by the judicious introduction of scheduled fare reductions in 1952/3 (Tourist Class) and again in 1958/9 (Economy Class). It was this process of popularization which fed the phenomenal growth in passenger air traffic, exceeding even that of other industries of the postwar consumer boom. It was also responsible for international air transport making money for the first time.

178

Profits were now possible as piston-engined technology reached its highest expression in aircraft like the Lockheed Super Constellation and the Douglas DC7C. And as airlines became profitable, or at least had the potential to be so, there was an increasing expectation that the *chosen instruments*, state-owned and hitherto subsidised, would now pay their own way.

This process of commercialisation was accompanied by a retreat from the heavy emphasis on colonial links in route structure; for the British carrier BOAC, for example, it meant a transfer of capacity from the Empire to the North Atlantic. As air travel replaced the sea voyage on the Atlantic, it became the leading profit-maker for all European flag carriers. In 1948 only 28 per cent of passengers crossing the Atlantic went by air, in 1963 it was 78 per cent (Sealy 1966, p. 68). By 1961 AC's concentration on the route had advanced to the point where the services there had 'become the pivot upon which the Corporation's fortunes must to a very large degree turn' (BOAC Annual Reports & Accounts, 1962, p. 56). With colonial disengagement came a loss of territorial bargaining power. This was accentuated by technology as the increased range of aircraft diminished the significance of previously vital staging posts, e.g. Iceland and Ireland on transatlantic services. However technological progress was incremental and the institutional framework adapted itself 'painlessly'(Naveau 1989, p. 110). The sovereignty claims of the colonial power were simply replaced by those of newly independent states.

It was not to be route networks or aircraft technology or even the sabre-rattling of a disenchanted CAB which threatened civil aviation's postwar institutional arrangements, rather the market forces released by air travel's popularization and democratization. In the late 1950s, for the first time, average levels of demand began to match and outstrip supply, which in any case, as we have seen, reflected political considerations rather than the true size of market. Further capacity was needed and was created, firstly with the introduction of big jets (Boeing 707/Douglas DC8) after 1959, and secondly with the appearance of new non-scheduled airlines.

Up until 1960 most passengers went on IATA-controlled scheduled services, but thereafter there was a vast growth of non-scheduled charter flights, where seats were sold either to members of an affinity group, or put together with hotel accomodation and sold as a holiday package known as an Inclusive Tour (IT). Such non-scheduled services quickly became a distinguishing feature of European air transport and by the 1980s composed around 60 per cent of its total passenger market. Most of this was IT charter flights carrying leisure traffic to the Mediterranean and other holiday resorts. What was happening therefore was that the growth area of air transport in Europe was being catered for by charter operators, leaving the IATA-bound scheduled carriers to make their revenue predominantly from business travellers (Wheatcroft and Lipman 1986, pp. 23-5; Barrett 1987).

Before long the industry in Europe was polarised between scheduled flag-carriers like British Airways, Air France and Lufthansa which operated to a full and specified timetable, and non-scheduled airlines like Britannia Airways, Dan-Air and Condor Flugdienst (a Lufthansa subsidiary) which concentrated on IT in the peak season. The flag-carriers served routes in what might be described as a hierarchical spoke network: based on a capital hub, reflecting national sovereignty and determined by bilateral agreements between governments rather than in direct reponse to traffic demand. Their costs were high and average load factors rarely better than 65 per cent – a problem which they traditionally tackled with so-called *pooling agreements* between themselves. The non-scheduled airlines, by contrast, developed specific routes on a linear structure, often originating and terminating at provincial airports, eg. Luton to Malaga. These secondary airports served localised catchment areas, thus raising mobility between traffic-generating and traffic-receiving points, and broadening the market base of the European industry. Because they had fundamentally lower operating costs they could offer much lower fares than the scheduled carriers and the latter's attempts to match their prices with promotional or off-peak fares within the IATA mechanism were generally futile (Ellison and Stafford 1974, p. 8; Lyth and Dierikx 1994, pp. 97-116).

Non-scheduled airlines had been hardly considered at Chicago in 1944 and no regulatory institutions had been created for their control. Whatever non-scheduled activity had been envisaged then, e.g. individual charters, it certainly did not encompass the dimensions which IT activity had reached in Europe by the 1970s. A whole new industry had sprung up *outside* the institutional framework constructed so painstakingly at Chicago and Bermuda, operating under loose national licensing regimes based on quotas and product definition. It was an industry driven by market forces and indifferent to political constraints and consequently an industry viewed with fear and suspicion by the beneficiaries of the IATA-system, much as the defenders of an impregnable fortress would view a plundering horde of bandits laying waste to the countryside around its walls. The 1970s were a momentous decade for international air transport: besides the oil shock and economic recession which slowed its almost unbroken growth record since the early 1950s, the industry was thrown into confusion by overcapacity resulting from the introduction of wide-bodied aircraft like the Boeing 747 and the outbreak of fare discounting which the scheduled carriers launched in an attempt to meet the competition from charters. The *grey market* which this practice created had the effect of blurring the distinction between scheduled and non-scheduled carriers, a process which was accelerated as the latter began to operate regular services like Freddie Laker's *Skytrain* in 1977 (Joensson 1987, p. 43).

Under these strains one might have expected the institutional structure of international civil aviation to crack or at least show signs of fatigue. Either the destabilising effect of marauding European charter carriers on the Chicago citadel, or consumer-driven pressure from the Americans to abandon the high-fare IATA system, or new bilateral friction between the flag-carriers themselves; any of these developments had the potential to weaken the Chicago/Bermuda regime and the central principle of air sovereignty. In fact it survived all three.

III

Many of the challenges to civil aviation's institutional arrangements in the late 1970s came either directly or indirectly from the United States, the one country whose air transport sector had stood head and shoulders above that of the rest of the world since the end of the Second World War. Because the American domestic industry was so big, it was bound to have an impact on international aviation. Moreover America was the largest and richest source of passenger traffic and, since the advent of regular non-stop transatlantic flights in the 1950s, the market with the greatest commercial potential for European flag-carriers. As the European airlines had grown in size and efficiency the importance of access to the American market had increased; indeed it had become vital to the profitability which was now expected of them.

Whereas in 1945 the issue of sovereignty was political and focused on territory, by 1975 it had become more commercial and concerned with the generation of traffic. The American authorities in particular now took a more proprietory attitude towards American passengers, as European airlines were carrying a larger proportion of them across the Atlantic. On the one hand there was a conviction in the CAB, shared by the main US international carriers, that as a *quid pro quo* for greater European access to American gateways there should be more 5th Freedom rights granted in Europe to the Americans. On the other hand there was a desire to see a relaxation, if not removal, of the regulatory regime which the United States had tolerated since 1946, in order that the US carriers could more effectively exploit their greater efficiency in the international air transport market. Even as late as 1978 American airlines were still far more efficient than their European counterparts: in terms of comparative manpower useage, for example, carriers such as Delta, Eastern, Continental, American and TWA were between 50 and 100 per cent more efficient than SAS, Lufthansa, Swissair, Air France or British Airways (measured by passengers per employee) (Airline Users Committee of the Civil Aviation Authority, *European Air Fares*, CAA 1979).

The Americans tried to approach the problem at both the bilateral and multilateral levels. Bilaterally they sought critical revisions in their agreements with important European partners with the aim of encouraging greater competition through the relaxation of controls on capacity and the designated number of carriers. Multilaterally they attacked IATA with the hope of widening the market through scheduled fare reductions. Both initiatives were inspired by a growing ideological desire for market liberalisation and greater competition, which was particularly strong in the CAB under Alfred Kahn's chairmanship and which had led to the landmark deregulation of American domestic airlines in 1978.

The United States' most important bilateral agreement was of course the one signed at Bermuda with Britain in 1946. It was now under increasing attack from American supporters of regime liberalisation and deregulation. Like all bilateral deals, Bermuda had been based on opposing national interests tempered by a mutual willingness to compromise, and like all bilateral deals it remained subject to revision at some point in the future with the ebb and flow of national assertiveness – on either side (Naveau 1989, pp. 107-8). Nonetheless it was probably a surprise to the Americans that before they could set in motion the process of revision in 1976, the British themselves had denounced Bermuda on the basis of an entirely opposite conviction, namely that the American carriers Pan American and TWA enjoyed too many 5th Freedom rights from London into European gateways like Paris, Amsterdam and Frankfurt. The British were in a better position than they had been in 1946, but they still had a strong interest in maintaining a high level of control, particularly on capacity. In the the so-called *Bermuda 2* agreement that was eventually signed between the two countries in 1977, they achieved a lot of what they wanted and the Americans came away feeling they had been forced into retreat at the international level at exactly the moment when the forces of deregulation were in the ascendancy at home (Shovelton 1979, pp. 289-293; Dobson 1995, pp. 119-40).

Bermuda 2 was not repeated by the Americans with any other European state and certainly did not serve as a model in the way that its predecessor had done. It served instead as a reminder, if one was needed, that the institutional arrangements at the international level were deeply rooted and the Europeans would protect their national interests as tenaciously in the 1970s as they had in the 1930s. The multilateral attempt at reform which the CAB now launched, seemed if anything to confirm the fact. In 1978 the CAB withdrew its anti-trust immunity from IATA fare resolutions and called upon the organisation and its airline members to *show cause* why it should not be prosecuted for fixing prices to the detriment of the consumer. The *Show Cause Order* (SCO) was a direct assault on Chicago/Bermuda because IATA was the main operational mechanism within the system. It was so intimidatory in its nature that not only did it cause the world's scheduled airlines to close ranks behind the IATA secretariat but it also produced dissension between the CAB and the other responsible Washington departments. Eventually the CAB was forced to back down on the SCO, the ideological crusade which it represented blunted on a wall of European pragmatism (Dobson 1995, pp. 154-72, Joensson 1987, pp. 124-48).

More important, the failure of the SCO showed the remarkable resilience of IATA. As a constraining institution it had its enemies and undoubtedly sheltered the inefficient, but it retained widespread support both in government and airline management, so that even the most powerful actor in the industry could not alter its nature or weaken its power. '110 IATA members received over $1 billion in tax concessions, subsidies etc. between them in 1975' noted *The Economist* (1976, pp. 72-3), 'and with all that they still lost money'. The sweeping deregulation of the US domestic air transport industry in 1978 led to expectation on the part of American liberalisers, as well as some advocates in the new Conservative government in Britain, that the doctrine of *open skies* and greater competition could be successfully transferred to Europe. This expectation was largely disappointed and, as we have seen, American attempts to export regime change were abortive. The US challenge to Chicago/Bermuda was motivated by the gradual loss in market share of American carriers, especially on the North Atlantic, and the belief that only a more competitive environment where they could outperform the IATA-controlled airlines would allow them to regain their earlier predominance. The challenge was couched in terms of benefits to consumer, but few European airlines accepted the argument. Even in the case of the British and Dutch, who initiated new scheduled competition in the early 1980s, it was liberalisation in *Europe* that they were pursuing, not on the North Atlantic.

The consumerist argument, which had always had a more receptive audience in the United States than in Europe, was hard to resist for politicians with an eye on the long-suffering European air passenger. Lower European air fares would obviously be popular, but the greater competition championed by Britain and Holland was generally opposed by other European Union states which took a more traditional and protectionist approach. Moreover the consumer still came second when the interests of a *chosen instrument* were at stake, as the inconsistent approach of the British to fare reductions in the early 1980s shows; before the privatisation of the formerly state-owned British Airways was completed there was a reluctance to do anything that might tarnish the prospects for future investors in the airline (Dobson pp. 180-183).

The increasing consumer orientation of the world economy in the 1980s was bound to have an impact on air transport and the vociferous air transport consumers lobby was making it more difficult to ignore the significant difference in fares between Europe and America. How did the old regulatory institutions, created with a strong production-orientation, cope with this global shift? The answer is that European resistance to American-style deregulation and what was seen as a rampant consumer ethic, remained strong. In 1985 a contributor to the annual *Lufthansa Yearbook* encapsulated the essential difference between the two continents when he complained that the United States was destroying the co-operative basis of the international airline industry by treating people exclusively as consumers, instead of consumers *and* producers. The previously harmonious relations between international flag-carriers were being replaced with comfrontation, in the name of cheaper services for the consumer (Cesarz 1985, p. 74).

By the mid-1980s it was clear that deregulation in the name of consumer freedom was not going to be adopted in Europe with the same alacrity that it had been in America. Older, more deeply rooted traditions and the institutions which represented them, would prevail, or at least absorb and blunt the driving force of the new consumerism. The founding principle of international civil aviation and the institutions built up around it, would survive. For many IATA members deregulation, and American attempts to export it, were disguised forms of economic imperialism to be resisted at all costs; to put it in Machiavellian terms, they had a strong interest in preserving the exisiting arrangements.

'The truth', noted *The Economist* (1984, p. 69) forty years after the Chicago conference, 'is that no government has an aviation policy based on altruistic concerns for the consumer; the dream of open skies died ... when the Chicago convention confirmed the soverignty of national air space'. And that principle was already nearly thirty years old when it was confirmed. The success in the implementation of deregulation in the United States lay precisely in the fact that it was limited to the domestic air transport industry which unlike that of any other nation was huge and self-sufficient. As soon as the idea was attempted at an international level it ran headlong into the obstacle of sovereignty rights: in Europe it had to resolve the interests of twenty countries instead of one.

It seems increasingly likely, after 75 years of practical experience, that the liberalisation of air transport's constraining institutions is incompatible with the maintenance of national sovereignty over air space. The question is why should this hallowed principle be maintained, or rather why does it survive?

It is tempting to conclude that air sovereignty, while not necessarily the most efficient institutional approach, is nonetheless the most durable institutional concept because it provides equality between the largest and most efficient airlines, and the smallest and least inefficient – between the profit-makers and the losers. Of course it is an equality of the lowest common denominator and this has been the source of most American complaints against it since the end of the Second World War. That the long-term American challenge to Chicago/Bermuda has resulted in changes *within* the institutional regime rather than the creation of a new regime, that the rules of IATA have simply been modified and made more flexible rather than totally abolished, seems to support the theory that institutions are indestructible. Certainly in the case of air transport institutions are never destroyed but simply given new sources of power or subjected to timely bypass surgery. They are maintained rather than exchanged. They evolve, but their evolution is conditioned by path dependency. For air transport that path was decided by the historical reference point of 1919, when the dogma of air sovereignty was unanimously adopted. Thereafter the industry became inevitably politicised and the institutional structure reflected the fact. As the Americans have discovered through long experience of dealing with the Europeans, market forces, and their potential for liberalisation, were counterposed to the institutions because those institutions had been created to provide a stable, not necessarily an efficient, supply of air transport.

11. Path Dependence and Institutional Evolution – The Case of the Nationalisation of Private Railroads in Interwar Sweden

Jan Ottosson

INTRODUCTION*

The process of regulation and deregulation of the economy is one important strand, where politics and economics meets. However, the interaction between policy action and economy and the important question *why, for what causes*, does the state and its orders intervene in the economic process, has been far too neglected in the new institutional economics (NIE), as represented by Williamson (1985; 1991, for critical approaches, see Dugger 1993 and North 1990). With regard to this question there is a problematic gap in the theoretical literature. Most certainly, within mainstream neo-classical theorising, a peculiar dichotomy prevails. On the one hand in many models, it is proposed – ceteris paribus – that the state and its orders is always ready and ripe to support the most 'efficient' organisational solution, as argued in earlier works of North and Thomas (1973), with the historical example of England as a success story in this respect. This is of course as flawed as the opposite standpoint emphasised in other institutional theorising, where the state intervenes and disturbs the market process in order to increase its own power (Dugger 1993, p. 189). Especially within the public choice tradition there is a sceptical view of government, particularly of regulatory matters. On the other hand, the old institutionalists generally held a more positive, sometimes overoptimistic, view of the possibilities of an intervening state (Rutherford 1994, pp. 159, 162). This flawed dichotomy is of course unsatisfactory and not particularly fruitful. To acquire a better understanding of the role of the state in economic development, we must begin to acknowledge that states act and intervene in the economic sphere in an historical context. We cannot take for granted that the state intervenes either to support the most efficient solution, or seeking to increase its powers for its own purposes. In order to understand the motives of acting on behalf of the state and its orders, we must acknowledge the possible existence of 'national styles', paradigms and specific regulative orders thriving upon the existence of path dependency and enforcing further path dependency (Rutherford 1994, p. 168, Dunlavy 1994, Dobbin 1994). Indeed, if this is what Rutherford (1994, p. 172) means by asking for less dogmatism and more pragmatism regarding policy matters in NIE and OIE, there is reason to agree. In line with this argument, a more sophisticated view of the need for studying the interaction between economics and politics has been presented by historical institutionalism. Recent research concerning industrial politics within this tradition suggests that a comparative approach with historical perspective gives deeper understanding of the different shaping of industrial policies, that is, how do political structure and industrial change interact (Dunlavy 1994; Thelen and Steinmo 1992).

The aim of this article is to examine the motives behind state intervention in the modern transport sector as one of the most interesting fields where the interaction between the state and the private sector has been of immense importance since the 19th century.

I try to show that such interaction between the state and market economy must be understood from the background of a specific historical occurrence and will not easily be understood either as a consequence of the state finding the most efficient solutions or seeking to increase its own omnipotence. The railways highlight the issues of regulation and deregulation, since public and private interests interact and sometimes counteract. The reasons for this interdependence and the close relation between politics and markets are the large sums invested, as well as the importance and interaction of transport systems in the economy and society as a whole. Of special interest here is one element of state intervention, the case of nationalisation of railroads. The nationalisation issue brings the question of public versus private ownership as well as different views upon state action in market economies into focus. The traditional argument of market failures, being the *raison d'être* of public ownership and nationalisation, gives little guidance of exactly why the public enterprise is preferred, instead of other regulatory regimes. Increasing returns of scale and positive externalities can, broadly speaking, produce two policy options; regulations or public ownership, but, apparently, this explanation does not explain why the first has been favoured in the US, and the latter in some European countries (Domberger and Piggot 1994, p. 34). Also, this argument does not explain why different public and private ownership structures are chosen in different sectors of the economy, despite these sectors experiences of market failure characteristics. In the English case, some network industries were nationalised, while others, facing even worse economic or organisational problems, apparently faced a more mixed ownership structure. Therefore, the market failure type of argument needs to be complemented with explanations as to why and how this process differed and changed in various countries. Thus, it is of special interest here to look closer at the railways and the ownership question. The various experiences in the European countries will be discussed from the viewpoint that different factors constituted various ownership structures and institutions and that various processes could be found in the railway nationalisation case. I argue that the way nationalisation occurs and what it means differ depending on historical patterns of development. Four different paths will be recognised in the following; the English liberal way, the pronounced role of state ownership in Prussia before the interwar period, France having a dominant state and strictly regulated private companies, and Sweden, representing a middle way, permitting both private and state ownership of the railway. But, as I am aiming to show, the regulation of private railroads together with an ideologically coloured recognition of economic planning, had turned all countries towards state ownership of the railroads in the late 1940s. However, the process differed depending on path dependent institutional settings and different policy regimes.

The railways experienced fierce competition from road transport in several countries after the First World War. With Svennilson's word, few sectors of the European Economy were so thoroughly transformed as the transport industry. The road transport competed with rail all over Europe. The railway industry gave an overall impression of a depressed industry with financial weakness, with a relatively slow rate of modernisation (Svennilson 1954, p. 144). The important function and place in the economic and military structure – as shown in the First World War – made the railways central in the national interest. Due to the large interest at stake either through state ownership or state subsidies, generally different protective measures were taken against competition from road transport (Svennilson 1954, partly quotations, p. 145). However, the role of the state, and the attitude of the state towards the transport system, did differ in interwar Europe.

ENGLAND

The pre-First World War railway policy was more economically liberal, compared with the continental experiences. The Railway Act of 1921 marked however the entrance of a new period in the railway sector, abandoning the free competition policy (Crompton 1995, pp. 116–17). It was argued that state action was needed since natural amalgamations were slow and public control was required in fields where large producers and tariff policies were needed. Central was the gain of large-scale enterprises. The new amalgamation with four large collaborating companies was the result of the Railway Act. The action of these companies was however limited by strict regulation, and their adaptation to the new competition from lorries was small. However, they were not publicly owned, and no central planning existed. Instead the government restricted road transport in favour of both large railroads, as well as larger companies operating in road freight and road passenger traffic. Thus, contrary to the continental experience, the role of state ownership was never actually any question on the political agenda in interwar Britain, despite the stronger political influence of Labour, which officially promoted a nationalisation of industries. After the Second World War, the new Labour government started the new economic programme. One of the major economic sectors which was planned to be nationalised was the transport sector and in 1948 the English rail roads was nationalised.

There are several explanations behind the development of the nationalisation process. Several prominent scholars (Gourvish 1986) analyses the nationalisation process in Britain between 1945 and 1951 as a response and the only outcome of industries with long-standing problems, while on the other hand also acknowledging that contemporary actors described the Labour socialist vision after the war. However, Foreman-Peck and Millward suggests that not only Labour, but also other parliamentary parties and experts all supported, one way or the other, the nationalisation process (Foreman-Peck and Millward 1994). Also, the experience of the war, with its central planning was put forward by Crompton (1995, p. 141). Foreman-Peck and Millward explain the performance with factors emphasising different institutional settings, for example, different industries were organised in several different ways; railways had quite another structure compared with gas or electricity, in steel the ownership structure was mixed, while cotton remained private (Foreman-Peck and Millward 1994, p. 271). For transport, factors such as safety, externalities, economies of scale and rights of way were important. Another important force in this respect were collective action (e.g. unions and employers), and political pressures of the members of parliament. Further, between 1914 and 1940 another three factors were at hand. First a tendency towards increasing government action in high-tech industries (capital-intensive, new technologies) could be noted. Secondly, the stagnating interwar economy made governments become involved more directly in economic performance. Thirdly, technological and administrative changes were made in order to undertake large industrial companies settings. The English government was influenced by the US and Germany, and the development of new industries. The generally protective and anti-competitive policies were evidnet not only in manufacturing but also in the transport field in England. The process of nationalisation thus had many components, but the idea of a 'national unified framework with a public purpose' with the purpose of redistributing income seems to be central (Millward and Foreman-Peck 1994, quote, p. 299). The English case gives an interesting example of a shift from a liberal market-oriented policy in the railway case, towards a state-owned solution during the period studied. As argued above, several explanations of this changing attitude might be at hand, both long-term structural economic changes, and a more positive attitude towards large companies and economic planning as well as the experiences of war economy planning. However, also the change in politics and the Attlee-government post-war plan for nationalisation were decisive in forming this particular process.

THE CONTINENTAL EXAMPLES

The most well-known example of a state-dominated railway system is perhaps Prussia. However, as Dunlavy (1994) shows, the early Prussian rail road policy was more liberal than earlier believed. Also, before the French-German war in 1870-71, the railroad system was regionalised, and different solutions were chosen in different German states. Bismarck tried to unify the whole railway system in 1873, but failed, due to the resistance of the southern states. In Prussia, the nationalisation was made in 1879. The successful nationalisation of the Prussian private rail roads was made voluntarily, the economic crises of the 1870s making the discussions more favourable towards a state intervention. The official motives for the nationalisation was the speculative character and low financial stability of some private rail roads, together with a waste of capital. Another important motive was the military aspect of having a unified rail system. The Prussian initiative started a wave of nationalisations through Germany. However, first until after the First World War the different state rail companies were unified into the Reichseisenbahn in 1920. (SOU 1923:7, pp. 107–52; Dunlavy 1992, 1994).

In France, with its long political tradition of central planning and co-ordination, the organisation of private rail roads was a compromise between the state and the private companies. The organisation of the six large private regional companies together with a state railway and massive state regulation was originally designed in the mid-19th century (Dobbin 1994, p. 144–5). Also, the French system was designed with military purposes. The reorganisation in 1921 resulted in a reform among the five large monopolies – one of regional companies was nationalised in the late 19th century – which made the system more centralised. According to Foreman-Peck and Millward (1994), the French railroads experienced a deficit until three years at the end of the 1920s. In interwar France the competition from lorries – as in several other countries – together with the effects of the Great Depression in the early 1930s made the financial situation burdensome for the private railroads. This has been considered the direct motive of nationalisation in 1937. The arguments for total railway nationalisation were of course not new. Already from the early days of the French railroad system, a strong official opinion argued for total state control. The only reason the private firms were tolerated to operate was that the state finances obviously could benefit from giving the companies a charter for 99 years (Dobbin 1994). This dual system operated in the first phase with a large number of railway companies, and in the second phase, merging into the six regional companies. The official view was that the state could better see the interest of the whole nation, in contrast to private owners, with only a profit motive. Also, the rationality and superior experience of the French state engineers was given as a strong argument for the state control (Dobbin 1994).

THE NATIONALISATION PROCESS IN SWEDEN

Sweden chose a dual system in the 1850s, giving the state railroad the right to traffic the main lines. The secondary lines were chartered to private companies. The dual system eventually had an embedded conflict between the private and the public. Proposals for nationalisation of smaller private railways were at hand from the 1870s onwards. During the interwar period several private owned companies faced severe economic problems. Through a process of several small steps, where the state emerged as rescuing the worst hit private rail roads, the Swedish parliament voted for a nationalisation of all private railroads in 1939 (Andersson-Skog 1993; Andersson-Skog and Ottosson 1994).

The Swedish debate concerning the nationalisation of the railroad system was characterised by three different phases. The first debate started in parliament in the 1870s. One of the major themes was the fear of a merger movement among the private railroads (Malmqvist 1956). The general idea of a total nationalisation of the railroad system dominated. After 1922 and a decade onwards, the merger solution was central. The debate concerned whether this merger movement should be promoted through legislation or by initiatives from the private actors themselves. Here, the Swedish debate seems to have been influenced by the English and American development. However, contrary to the development in e.g. England, the Swedish discussion concerning the merger movement did not give any substantial results. In the third phase, the debate took quite another turn, due to the depression, with substantial financial difficulties for the private railroads, ending with nationalisation in 1939 (Alvfors 1977, p. 22). Another important factor was the changed political situation. In 1932 the social democrats won the election. The political initiative in the early 1930s arguing for a nationalisation originated from prominent railway labour union persons. A few years later, representatives from the labour union, especially the railroad union, held important government positions during a formative period in the nationalisation process. The motions in the Swedish parliament also gave other motives for the nationalisation of the private railroads: the planned economy was preferred instead of private solutions. The arguments were oriented towards solving the financial problems of the private railroads, giving more emphasis on a planned economy, and the benefit of the society as a whole. The railroads were more seen as a part of the public good/utility. Especially the economist Gunnar Myrdal's argument concerning public enterprises seems to have been important in this respect, according to Alvfors (1977, p. 40). Ironically, as Malmkvist (1956) commented; the weakness of the merger movement proved to be one important argument in the 1939 nationalisation, while the fear of a strong merger movement was one argument put forward during the first nationalisation debate in 19th century Sweden. Between 1933 and 1936, the opinion was divided, several smaller private railroads as well as local opinions were positive towards nationalisation, especially the municipally owned rail road companies with troubled finances, hoping for financial salvation (Alvfors 1977, p. 60). On the other hand, the state owned Statens Järnvägar were first against these ideas. However, in 1936 Statens

Järnvägar, the opinion changed towards a more positive attitude towards nationalisation (Andersson-Skog 1993, 1995; Alvfors 1977). In the parliament, the earlier somewhat hesitant attitude changed towards a marked debate position between the conservative party and the social democrats, the former arguing for a merger solution, the latter proposing a nationalisation solution. On the other hand, the large railroad companies, which experienced dramatically improved profits from 1933 onwards, together with the Swedish private railroad association (Svenska Järnvägsföreningen) strongly opposed the idea of nationalisation.

The largest - and most successful rail road companies - were majority owned by two cities, Gothenburg and Västerås. These companies are interesting examples of municipally owned companies, and the strong local opposition against state ownership in these two cities. The town of Gothenburg owned the majority of shares in Bergslagernas Järnvägsaktiebolag (BJ), as well as Gävle-Dala Järnvägsaktiebolag. BJ had large hidden reserves, and also held large ownership interests in the expanding bus market (*Affärsvärlden* February 3, 1944, p. 88 and 90). Together these companies controlled GDG, a network of closely connected and co-operating rail road and bus companies. Also, the town of Gothenburg owned substantial parts of the shares in Göteborg-Borås, Borås-Alvesta and Västergötland-Göteborgs järnvägsaktiebolag. These companies were important links between industries and mines to the harbour of Gothenburg (Attman, 1963, Alvfors, 1977, p. 95). The town of Västerås, situated at lake Mälaren, held majority interests in another one of the largest private rail road companies, Stockholm-Wästerås-Bergslagernas Järnvägsaktiebolag, SWB. The purpose of owning this rail road company was, according to Alvfors (1977, p. 95), that the town wanted to promote the harbour as well as the major industries in the area, especially ASEA. Together with the financial family Wallenberg owned Halmstad-Nässjö Järnvägsaktiebolag, they operated over one third of total private normal gauge (*Statistisk Årsbok för Sverige 1935*, p. 176 and 180).

The 1936 public investigation concerning the nationalisation issue (SOU 1938:28) found that the merger alternative probably would give better economic results, compared with nationalisation. The committee, however, preferred the nationalisation solution arguing that the merger solution failed before (SOU 1938:28, p. 103; Alvfors 1977). The reactions from different organisations, state agencies, industrial and trade associations were primarily positive to some kind of nationalisation solution. The opinions were divided between representatives from e.g. the private railroad association, the chambers of commerce and Industriförbundet (the Swedish

Industry Association), arguing for part nationalisation, leaving the largest private railroads in private ownership. On the other hand, the labour union as well as several of the state agencies favoured a total nationalisation.

The Minister of Transport, Mr Albert Forslund, eventually became Minister of Social Affairs and was replaced by Mr Gerhard Strindlund (Peasant party). This did not change the attitude towards the nationalisation issue. On 3rd March 1939 Mr Strindlund made a proposition in the parliament which voted for the nationalisation in May the same year. In the final parliamentary debate the social democrats emphasised the rationalisation argument, while the conservatives pointed at the socialistic implications. The rationalisation argument was mainly based upon the belief that a unified railroad system would serve the public better, thus better providing the interest of the nation.

The schedule for the nationalisation was set to five years. Due to the war, this process was slowed down. Also other factors, such as complex negotiations between the city of Gothenburg and Västerås and the state contributed. However, the slow pace seems to have been a matter of some dispute. Some business press commentators viewed the state authorities as being main responsible for the late schedule (*Affärsvärlden*, June 15, 1944, p. 500). A special commission was appointed to deal with unsolved questions regarding the nationalisation issues. Not in any case enforcement was taken as a measure. A special negotiation committee - the so called Leo-nämnden - was used twice (Kjellvard, 1949). SWB was nationalised in 1944 and the first of July 1947 the trafikförvaltningen Göteborg-Dalarna-Gävle was nationalised (the first year it existed as a stateowned company, after this year the company was incorporated in Statens Järnvägar. GDG had seven companies and (Attman, 1963, pp).

Contrary to these complicated negotiations, the Wallenberg-owned Halmstad-Nässjö Järnvägar was nationalised in 1945 (Lindgren, 1994, p. 70). The Wallenberg Family, one of the most prominent financial groups in Sweden, was one of the founders of the private owned Halmstad-Nässjö Järnvägsaktiebolag. In 1929 the group owned 57,6 of the shares in the company (Lindgren, 1994, p. 63). After the decision in the Swedish parliament to nationalise the private railroads, the first iniative to negotiate originated from the committee in Svenska Järnvägsstyrelsen in spring 1944. The bank manager Marcus Wallenberg J:r, member of the board of HNH, was appointed by the largest stockholder Investor, an investment company closely affiliated to the Wallenberg Family and Stockholms Enskilda Bank, to negotiate. In the beginning of 1945 a final proposal was reached and both the Swedish parliament as well as the board meeting accepted this proposal.

Marcus Wallenberg seems to have been enthusiastic to sell the rail road company, and instead take interest in civil aviation (Lindgren 1988; 1994, p. 70 and 72; SJ, archive, Kungliga Järnvägsstyrelsen, Järnvägsförstatliganden, E IIa, Handlingar Enskilda järnvägsföretag, vol. 13-17, Halmstad-Nässjö Järnvägsaktiebolag).

To sum up, Alvfors gives the geographical division between those in favour of a total nationalisation an important role in explaining the bridge in the debate, while Malmkvist (1956) puts forward the failed merger movement. Andersson-Skog (1993) also concludes that the failure of the voluntary merger movement was important in this respect and depended to some extent on the large companies' reluctance to buy smaller companies. These arguments are supplemented by conflicting interests between municipal owners of the private railroads, as well as the changed political situation in Sweden. Thus, path dependent institutional factors, the role of politics and purposeful actors did play significant roles in turning this process towards the 1939 nationalisation decision.

CONCLUSION

Comparing the development of nationalisation in the countries studied, the main difference is the marked policy patterns as well as the policy shifts. The paths chosen towards public ownership included several steps, as well as various mixes of regulatory regimes. The view upon the state shifted among the countries, from a positive attitude towards the state in France and Germany, emphasising the superior planning and allocative potential of the state, compared to the narrow profit-maximising firm. This positive role of the state was also at hand in Sweden, also emphasising the different roles of the state and the private companies. In England, the sceptical liberal view of the state changed dramatically towards a more positive attitude of various types of state intervention. Thus, the earlier experiences of state intervention and the view of the state did play a role in the various paths towards state intervention. The three phases of the Swedish debate concerning railway nationalisation had indeed different connotations, due to the shifting political circumstances. The merger alternative to nationalisation in Sweden was seen either as a threat or the rescue for private railroads. However, the merger movement failed in Sweden, due to local resistance among private and municipal owners. The Swedish policy discussion shift towards nationalisation in the beginning of the 1930s was introduced by social democrats with a background in the railway union. Also in Britain, the policy shift towards nationalisation was marked by the stronger position of the labour government after the war. The dual systems in France and Sweden were different compared with Germany, thus showing that continental railway policies also allowed private railroads. Despite the strong role of the state in both Germany and France, the railway nationalisation policy differed. Without taking notice of the countries' marked different policy styles, the shift of nationalisation policy can not be explained.

The main conclusions to be drawn from these stylised historical examples are the various policy solutions chosen in the countries studied, at different times, with marked policy styles, to paraphrase Thomas Hughes. Also, the national policy measures chosen were dependent on earlier historical experiences. The making of railway systems and nationalisation processes in different countries offers new insights into the various interaction patterns between political actors, structures and the economic sphere of society. It also provides us with new knowledge of the dynamic aspects of changing state policy and the forming of policy patterns (Dunlavy 1992, 1994). Thus, applying the dichotomy of seeing the state either as a promoter of optimal policy solution or rent seeker, as discussed in the introduction, seems rather vain. Instead, analysing state interventionism and the role of the state in a historical, comparative perspective enables us to make more complex distinctions of the action and the order of the state.

NOTES

* Earlier draft versions of this paper has benefitted from conference comments received in Stockholm, May, 1995, Rethymno, Creete, October 1995. I am very grateful to Lars Magnusson, who permitted me to use arguments from a joint conference paper (Magnusson and Ottosson 1996), regarding this issue.

References

Akerlof, G. (1970), 'The Market for Lemons: Quality Uncertainty and the Market', *Quarterly Journal of Economics,* 84, pp. 487–500.

Alchian, A.A. (1950), 'Uncertainty, evolution and economic theory', *Journal of Political Economy*, 58, pp. 211–22.

Alchian, A.A. and Demsetz, H. (1972), 'Production, Information Costs, and Economic Organisation', *American Economic Review*, 62, pp. 777–95.

Allen, P. (1994), 'Evolutionary Complex Systems: Models of Technology Change', in: Loet Lydesdorff and Peter Van den Besselaar, (eds), *Evolutionary Economics and Chaos Theory*, St. Martin's Press, New York.

Alvfors, K.-G. (1977), *Järnvägsförstatligandet. Svensk järnvägspolitik under 1930-talet*, Svenska Järnvägsklubbens skriftserie nr 21, Eksjö.

Amin, A. and Dietrich, M. (1991), 'From Hierarchy to "Hierarchy": The Dynamics of Contemporary Corporate Restructuring in Europe', in: A. Amin and M. Dietrich (eds), *Towards a New Europe? Structural Change in the European Economy*, Edward Elgar, Aldershot.

Andersen, E.S. (1994), *Evolutionary Economics. Post-Schumpeterian Contributions*, Pinter Publishers, London and New York.

Andersson-Skog, L. (1993), 'Såsom affärsföretag till namnet, men allmänna inrättningar till gagnet'. SJ, järnvägspolitiken och den ekonomiska omvandlingen efter 1920 (Diss), *Umeå Studies in Economic History,* No. 17, Umeå.

Andersson-Skog, L. (1994) 'Some aspects on investments in infrastructure in the Nordic countries 1870–1930. The case of Railways and Telecommunications', in: Krantz, Olle (ed.), *Cross-Country Comparisons of Industrialisation in Small Countries 1870–1940,* Occasional Papers in Economic History – Umeå University, no. 2, Umeå.

Andersson-Skog, L. and Ottosson, J. (1994), 'Institutionell teori och den svenska kommunikationspolitikens utformning – betydelsen av ett historiskt perspektiv', *Working Paper in Transport and Communication History*, No. 1, The Research Group 'Transports and Communications in Perspective', Departments of Economic History, Umeå University and Uppsala University, Uppsala, Sweden.

Antonelli, C. (ed.) (1988), *New Information Technology and Industrial Change: the Italian Case*, Kluwer Academic Press, Boston, Dordrecht, London.

Antonelli, C. (1995), *The Economics of Localized Technological Change and Industrial Dynamics*, Kluwer Academic Press, Boston, Dordrecht, London.

Appel, B-M. (1993), *Entwicklungsbedingungen für Luftverkehrsunternehmen in Deutschland, 1919-1926*, Peter Lang, Frankfurt a.M.

Argyris, C. and Schön, D. (1978), *Organisational Learning*, Addison-Wesley, Reading, Mass.

Armstrong, P. (1985), 'Changing management control strategies: the role of competition between accounting and other organisation professions', *Accounting, Organisations and Society*, vol. 10, pp. 129-48.

Armstrong, P. (1987), 'Engineers, management and trust', *Work, Employment and Society*, vol. 1, pp. 421-40.

Armstrong, P. (1991), 'Contradictions and social dynamics in the capitalist agency relationship', *Accounting, Organisations and Society*, vol. 18, pp. 1-25.

Arrow, K. (1962), 'Economic Welfare and the Allocation of Resources for Invention', *NBER The Rate and Direction of Incentive Activity: Economic and Social Factors*, Princeton University Press, Princeton.

Arrow, K. (1994a), 'Methodological Individualism and Social Knowledge', *American Economic Review*, May.

Arrow, K. (1994b), 'Information and the Organisation of Industry', *Rivista Internazionale di Scienze Sociali*, Occasional Paper, April.

Arthur, W.B. (1986), 'Industry Location and the Importance of History', *Center for Economic Policy Research*, 84, Stanford University.

Arthur, W.B. (1988a), 'Self-reinforcing mechanisms in economics', in: P. W. Anderson, K.J. Arrow and D. Pines (eds), *The Economy as an Evolving Complex System*, Addison-Wesley, Redwood City, Cal.

Arthur, W.B. (1988b), 'Competing technologies: an overview', in: G. Dosi, C. Freeman, R. Nelson, G. Silverberg and L. Soete (eds), *Technical Change and Economic Theory*, Pinters Publishers, London pp. 590–607.

Arthur, W.B. (1989), 'Competing technologies, increasing returns, and lock-in by historical events', *Economic Journal*, 99, pp. 116-31.

Arthur, W.B. (1991), 'Path dependence, self-reinforcement, and human learning', *American Economic Review* 81, reprinted in Arthur (1994), pp. 133–58.

References

Arthur, W.B. (1994), *Increasing Returns and Path Dependence in the Economy*, University of Michigan Press, Ann Arbor.

Attman, A. (1963), *Göteborgs Stadsfullmäktige 1863–1962, I:2, Göteborg 1913–1962*, Elanders, Göteborg.

Attman, A. *et al.* (1976), *L.M. Ericsson 100 år*, Vol. I, Bonniers, Stockholm.

Auster, P. (1995), *The Red Notebook*, Faber and Faber, London.

Axelsson, B. and Easton, G. (eds) (1992), *Industrial Networks – A New View of Reality*, Routledge, London.

Barrett, S.D. (1987), *Flying High: Airline Prices and European Regulation*, Adam Smith Institute.

Baumol, W.J. (1982), 'Contestable Markets: an uprising in the theory of industrial structure', *American Economic Review*, 72, pp. 1–15.

Baumol, W.J. and Stewart M. (1971), 'On the behavioural theory of the firm', in: R. Marris and A. Wood (eds), *The Corporate Economy*, Macmillan, London.

Bellah, R.N., Madsen, R., Sullivan, W.M., Swidler, A. and Tipton, S.M. (1985), *Habits of the Heart*, University of California Press, Berkeley.

Best, M.H. (1990), *The New Competition: Institutions of Industrial Restructuring, Harvard University Press*, Cambridge, Mass.

Bianchi, M. (1990), 'The unsatisfactoriness of satisficing: from bounded rationality to innovative rationality', *Review of Political Economy*, 2, pp. 149–67.

Binmore, K. (1994), 'De-Bayesing game theory', in: K. Binmore, A. Kirman and P. Tani (eds), *Frontiers of Game Theory*, MIT Press, Cambridge, Mass.

Birkhead, E. (1960), 'The Financial Failure of British Air Transport Companies, 1919–1924', *Journal of Transport History*, IV (3), May, pp. 133–45.

Birnbaum, J.H. and Murray. A.S. (1987), *Showdown at Gucci Gulch*, Vintage, New York.

Blauwhof, G. (1994), 'Non-Equilibria Dynamics and the Sociology of Technology', in: L. Lydesdorff and P. Van den Besselaar (eds), *Evolutionary Economics and Chaos Theory*, St. Martin's Press, New York.

Block, F. (1990), *Postindustrial Possibilities: A Critique of Economic Discourse*, University of California Press, Berkeley.

Bond, B. (1984), *War and Society in Europe, 1870–1970*, Oxford University Press, Oxford.

Brancker, J.W.S. (1977), *IATA and What it Does*, Leyden.

Brennan, G. and Buchanan, J.M. (1985), *The Reason of Rules: Constitutional Political Economy*, New York.

Bridgeman, P. (1955), *Reflections of a Physicist*, Philosophical Library, New York.

Broadbent, J., Dietrich M. and Laughlin, R. (1995), 'The development of principal-agent, contracting and accountability relationships in the public sector: conceptual and cultural problems', *Critical Perspectives on Accounting*, forthcoming.

Bruetting, G. (1979), *Das Buch der deutschen Fluggeschichte*, Bd.3, Stuttgart.

Brunner, H.-P. (1994). 'Technological Diversity, Random Selection in a Population of Firms and Technological Institutions in Government', in: L. Lydesdorff and P. Van den Besselaar (eds), *Evolutionary Economics and Chaos Theory*, St. Martin's Press, New York.

Burden, W. (1943), *The Struggle for Airways in Latin America*, Council on Foreign Relations, New York.

Calissano, P. (1992), *Neuroni, mente ed evoluzione*, Garzanti, Milano.

Campbell, J.L. (1993), 'Institutional Theory and the Influence of Foreign Actors on Reform in Capitalist and Post-Socialist Societies',in: J. Hausner, B. Jessop and K. Nielsen (eds), *Institutional Frameworks of Market Economies: Scandinavian and East European Perspectives*, Avebury Press, Aldershot.

Campbell, J.L. (1995), 'Institutional Analysis and the Role of Ideas in Political Economy', Unpublished manuscript, Department of Sociology, Harvard University.

Campbell, J.L. and Allen, M.P. (1994), 'The Political Economy of Revenue Extraction in the Modern State: A Time-Series Analysis of U.S. Income Taxes, 1916–1986', *Social Forces,* 72 (3), pp. 643–69.

Campbell, J.L. and Lindberg, L.N. (1990), 'Property Rights and the Organisation of Economic Activity by the State', *American Sociological Review*, 55, pp. 634–47.

Campbell, J.L. and Lindberg L.N.(1991), 'The Evolution of Governance Regimes', in: J.L. Campbell, L.N. Lindbergh, and R. Hollingsworth, (eds), *Economic governance and the analysis of structural change in the American economy*, Cambridge University Press. Cambridge.

Campbell, J.L. and Pedersen, O.K. (1995), 'The Evolutionary Nature of Revolutionary Change in Postcommunist Europe', Unpublished manuscript, Department of Sociology, Harvard University.

Campbell, J.L., Lindbergh, L.N. and Hollingsworth, R. (eds), (1991), *Economic governance and the analysis of structural change in the American economy*, Cambridge University Press, Cambridge.

Casson, M. (1991), *The Economics of Business Culture*, Clarendon Press, Oxford.

Casson, M. (1994), 'Information Costs: Their Influence on Organisational Structure and the Boundaries of the Firm', EMOT Workshop on 'The Changing Boundaries of the Firm', Como, 21–23 October.

Cesarz, F. (1985), 'Die Deutsche Lufthansa: Nationale Rolle und Unabhaengigkeit', *Lufthansa Jahrbuch*.

Chandler, A.D. (1977), *The Visible Hand*, Harvard University Press, Cambridge, Mass.

Chandler, A.D. (1990), *Scale and Scope: the dynamics of industrial capitalism*, Harvard University Press, Cambridge, Mass.

Coase, R. (1937), 'The Nature of the Firm', *Economica*, pp. 386–405.

Cognitive Science (1993), Special issue: Situated Action, 17/1.

Commission of the European Communities (1985), *Completing the internal market: White paper from the Commission to the European Council*, Luxembourg.

Commission of the European Communities (1988), 'Commission Regulation (EEC) no 2671/88 of 26 July 1988 on the application of article 85 (3) of the treaty to certain categories of agreements between undertakings, decisions of associations of undertakings and concerted practices concerning joint planning and coordination of capacity, sharing of revenue and consultations on tariffs on scheduled air services and slot allocation at airports', *Official Journal*, No. L 239.

Commission of the European Communities (1988), 'Commission Regulation (EEC) no 2672/88 of 26 July 1988 on the application of article 85 (3) of the treaty to certain categories of agreements between undertakings relating to computer reservation systems for air transport services', *Official Journal*, No. L 239.

Commission of the European Communities (1991), 'Commission Regulation (EEC) no 84/91 of 5 December 1990 on the application of article 85 (3) of the treaty to certain categories of agreements, decisions and concerted practices concerning joint planning and coordination of capacity, consultations on passenger and cargo tariffs rates on scheduled air services and slot allocation at airports', *Official Journal*, No. L 10.

Commission of the European Communities (1992), 'Commission Regulation (EEC) no 3618/92 of 15 December 1992 on the application of article 85 (3) of the treaty to certain categories of agreements, decisions and concerted practices in the air transport sector', *Official Journal,* No. L 367.

Council of the European Communities (1987), 'Council Regulation (EEC) no 3975/87 of 14 December 1987 laying down the procedure for the application of the rules on competition to undertakings in the air transport sector', *Official Journal,* No. L 374.

Council of the European Communities (1989), 'Council Regulation (EEC) no 4059/89 of 21 December 1989 laying down the conditions under which non-resident carriers may operate national road haulage services within a member state', *Official Journal,* No.L 390.

Council of the European Communities (1990), 'Council Regulation (EEC) no 2344/90 of 24 July 1990 amending regulation (EEC) no 3976/87 on the application of article 85 (3) of the treaty to certain categories of agreements and concerted practices in the air transport sector', *Official Journal,* No. L 217.

Council of the European Communities (1991), 'Council Regulation (EEC) no 296/91 of 4 February 1991 amending regulation (EEC) no 4059/89 laying down the conditions under which non-resident carriers may operate national road haulage services within a member state', *Official Journal,* No. L 36.

Council of the European Communities (1991), 'Council Regulation (EEC) no 1284/91 of 14 May 1991 amending regulation (EEC) no 3975/87 laying down the procedure for the application of the rules on competition to undertakings in the air transport sector', *Official Journal,* No. L 122.

Council of the European Communities (1992), 'Council Regulation (EEC) no 2410/92 of 23 July 1992 amending regulation (EEC) no 3975/87 laying down the procedure for the application of the rules on competition to undertakings in the air transport sector', *Official Journal* no. L 240.

Council of the European Communities (1992), 'Council Regulation (EEC) no 2411/92 of 23 July 1992 amending regulation (EEC) no 3976/87 on the application of article 85 (3) of the treaty to certain categories of agreements and concerted practices in the air transport sector'. *Official Journal* no. L 240.

Council of the European Communities (1993), 'Council Regulation (EEC) no 3118/93 of 25 October 1993 laying down the conditions under which non-resident carriers may operate national road haulage services within a member state', *Official Journal,* No. L 279.

Court of Justice of the European Community (1974), 'Judgement of the Court of 4 April 1974: Commission of the European Communities v.

French Republic, Case 167/73', *Reports of cases before the Court 1974*, Luxembourg.

Court of Justice of the European Community (1985), 'Judgement of the Court of 22 May 1985, Case 13/83', *Reports of cases before the Court 1985*, Luxembourg.

Conlan, T.J, Wrightson, M.T. and Beam, D.R. (1990), 'Taxing Choices', *Congressional Quarterly Press*, Washington.

Cooper, J.C. (1947), *The Right to Fly*, New York.

Corbett, D. (1965), *Politics and the Airlines*, London.

Crompton, G. (1995), 'The Railway Companies and the Nationalisation Issue 1920–1950', in: R. Millward and J. Singleton (eds), *The Political Economy of Nationalisation in Britain 1920–50*, Cambridge University Press, Cambridge.

Cyert, R.M. and March, J.G. (1963), *A Behavioural Theory of the Firm*, Englewood Cliffs, Prentice Hall, New Jersey.

Dasgupta, P. and Maskin, E. (1987), 'The Simple Economics of Research Portfolios', *Economic Journal*, 97, pp. 581–95.

David, P.A. (1975), 'Learning by Doing and Tariff Protection: A Reconsideration of the Case of the Ante-bellum United States Cotton Textile Industry', in: P. David (ed.), *Technical Choice, Innovation, and Economic Growth*, Cambridge University Press, Cambridge, pp. 95–168.

David, P.A. (1985), 'Clio and the Economics of QWERTY', *American Economic Review*, 75, pp. 332–7.

David, P.A. (1988), 'Path-Dependence: Putting the Past into the Future of Economics', *Technical Report No. 533, November 1988, The Economics Series*, Institute for Mathematical Studies in the Social Sciences, Stanford University, Stanford.

David, P.A. (1994), 'Why are Institutions the "Carriers of History"?: Path Dependence and the Evolution of Conventions, Organisations and Institutions', *Structural Change and Economic Dynamics*, Vol. 5, No. 2.

David, P.A. and Foray, D. (1994), 'Dynamics of Competitive Technology Diffusion Through Local Network Structures: The Case of EDI Document Standards', in: L. Lydesdorff and P. Van den Besselaar (eds), *Evolutionary Economics and Chaos Theory*, St. Martin's Press. New York.

Davidson, D. and Harman, G. (1972), *Semantics of Natural Language*, Reidel, Dordrecht.

degli Abbati, C. (1986), *Transport and European Integration*, Luxembourg.

Denzau, A.T. and North, D.C. (1994), 'Shared mental models: ideologies and institutions', *Kyklos*, vol. 47, pp. 3–31.

References

Despicht, N. (1969), *The Transport Policy of the European Communities*, London.

Devine, P.J. (1985), 'The Firm', in: P.J. Devine, N. Lee, R.M. Jones and W.J. Tyson, *An Introduction To Industrial Economics*, George Allen & Unwin, 4th ed London.

Dierikx, M.L.J. (1988), *Begrensde Horizonten. De internationale burger-luchtvaartpolitiek van Nederland in het interbellum*, Zwolle, pp. 85–99.

Dietrich, M. (1993), 'Total Quality Control, Just-in-Time Management and the Economics of the Firm', *Journal of Economic Studies*, vol. 20 (6), pp. 17–31.

Dietrich, M. (1994), *Transaction Cost Economics and Beyond: towards a new economics of the firm*, Routledge, London.

Dietrich, M. and Al-Awadh, M. (1995), 'Strategic coherence and competitive advantage', Sheffield University Management School Discussion Paper, 95.15.

Dietrich, M. and Roberts, J. (1995), 'Economics and the Professions: the limits of free markets', paper presented at the conference Sociology and the Limits of Economics, University of Liverpool, April 1995.

Dietrich, M. and Schenk, H. (1993), 'A Bandwagon Theory of the Firm', *Management Report Series No. 157*, Erasmus Institute for Advanced Studies in Management, Erasmus University, Rotterdam.

DiMaggio, P. and Powell, W. (1991), 'Introduction', in: W. Powell and P. DiMaggio (eds), *The New Institutionalism in Organisational Analysis*, University of Chicago Press, Chicago.

Dobbin, F. (1993), 'The Social Construction of the Great Depression: Industrial Policy During the 1930s in the United States, Britain, and France', *Theory and Society,* vol. 22, pp. 1–56.

Dobbin, F. (1994a) *Forging Industrial Policy. The United States, Britain, and France in the Railway Age*, Cambridge University Press, Cambridge.

Dobbin, F. (1994b), 'Cultural Models of Organisation: The Social Construction of Rational Organizing Principles', in: D. Crane (ed.), *The Sociology of Culture: Emerging Theoretical Perspectives*, Blackwell, Cambridge, Mass.

Dobson, A.P. (1991), *Peaceful Air Warfare*, Oxford.

Dobson, A.P. (1995), *Flying in the Face of Competition*, Avebury, Aldershot.

Domberger, S. and Piggot, J. (1994), 'Privatization Policies and Public Enterprise: A Survey', in: M. Bishop, J. Kay and C. Mayer (eds), *Privatization & Economic Performance*, Oxford University Press, Oxford.

Dosi, G. (1984), *Technical Change and Industrial Transformation*, MacMillan, London.

Dosi, G (1988), 'Sources, procedures, and microeconomic effects of innovation', *Journal of Economic Literature*, 26: 1120–71.

Dosi, G. *et al.* (eds) (1988), *Technical Change and Economic Theory*, Pinter, London.

Dosi, G., Gianetti, R. and Toninelli, R. (eds), (1992), *Technology and Enterprise in a Historical Perspective*, Oxford University Press, Oxford.

Dosi, G. and Marengo, L. (1994), 'Some elements of an evolutionary theory of organisational competencies', in: R.W. England (ed.), *Evolutionary Concepts in Contemporary Economics*, University of Michigan Press, Ann Arbor.

Douglas, M. (1986), *How Institutions Think*, Syracuse University Press, Syracuse.

Dow, G.K. (1987), 'The Function of Authority in Transaction Cost Economics', *Journal of Economic Behaviour and Organisation*, vol. 8, pp. 13–38.

Dubois, A. (1994), *Organising Industrial Activities – An Analytical Framework*, Department of Industrial Marketing, Chalmers University of Technology, Gothenburg.

Dugger, W.M. (1993), 'Transaction Cost Economics and the State', in: C. Pitelis (ed.), *Transaction Costs, Market and Hierarchies*, Blackwell, Oxford, UK, and Cambridge, USA.

Dunlavy, C.A. (1992), 'Political Structure, State Policy, and Industrial change: Early Railroad Policy in the United States and Prussia', in: S. Steinmo, K. Thelen and F. Longstreth (eds), *Structuring Politics. Historical Institutionalism in Comparative Analysis*, Cambridge University Press, Cambridge.

Dunlavy, C.A. (1994), *Politics and Industrialization. Early Railroads in the United States and Prussia*, Princeton University Press, Princeton, New Jersey.

Easton, D. (1965), *A Framework for Political Analysis*, Englewood Cliffs.

Edsall, T.B. (1984), *The New Politics of Inequality,* Norton, New York.

Eggertsson, T. (1990), *Economic Behavior and Institutions*, Cambridge University Press, Cambridge.

Eggertsson, T. (1993), 'The Economics of Institutions: Avoiding the Open-Field Syndrome and the Perils of Path Dependence', *Acta Sociologica*, 36, pp. 223–37.

Egidi, M. (1991), 'Innovazione, tecnologia ed organizzazione come attività Problem solving', in: M. Egidi, M. Lombardi, R. Tamborini (eds), *Cono-*

scenza, incertezza e decisioni economiche. Problemi e ipotesi di ricerca, Milano, Franco Angeli.

Egidi, M. (1992), 'Organisational Learning and the Division of Labour', in: Egidi M. and Marris R. (eds), *Economics, Bounded Rationality and the Cognitive Revolution*, Edward Elgar Publ. Aldershot.

Ellison, A.P. and Stafford, E.M. (1974), *The Dynamics of the Civil Aviation Industry*, London.

Erdmenger, J. (1983), *The European Community Transport Policy: Towards a Common Transport Policy*, London.

Eurostat (1993), *Transport, Annual Statistics 1970–1990, Theme 7C*, Luxembourg.

Fabbri, G. and Orsini, R. (1991), 'Una rete neurale per studiare l'avversione al rischio', *Giornale degli economisti e annali di economia*, Marzo-Aprile, pp. 163–77.

Fearon, P. (1974), 'The British Airframe Industry and the State 1918–1935', *Economic History Review*, 27, May, pp. 249–51.

Flavell, J.H. (1967), *The Developmental Psychology of Jean Piaget*, Van Nostrand, Princeton, N.J.

Fligstein, N. (1987), 'Intraorganisational power struggles: the rise of finance personnel to top leadership in large corporations, 1919–1979', *American Sociology Review*, no. 52, pp. 44–58.

Fligstein, N. (1990), *The Transformation of Corporate Control*, Harvard University Press, Cambridge, Mass.

Fligstein, N. and Mara-Drita, I. (1996), 'How to Make a Market: Reflections on the Attempt to Create a Single Unitary Market in the European Community', *American Journal of Sociology*, forthcoming.

Ford, D. (1990), *Understanding Business Markets: Interaction, Relationships, Networks*, Academic Press, London.

Foreman-Peck, J. and Millward, R. (1994), *Public and Private Ownership of British Industry 1820–1990*, Clarendon Press, Oxford.

Freidman, M. (1953), 'The Methodology of Positive Economics', in: M. Freidman (ed.), *Essays in Positive Economics*, University of Chicago Press, Chicago.

Friedland, R. and Alford, R.A. (1991), 'Bringing Society Back In: Symbols, Practices and Institutional Contradictions', in: W. Powell and P. DiMaggio (eds) *The New Institutionalism in Organisational Analysis*, University of Chicago Press, Chicago.

Friedsen, E. (1983), 'The theory of the professions: the state of the art', in: R. Dingwall and P. Lewis (eds), *The Sociology of the Professions: lawyers, doctors and others*, St Martins, New York.

Fritzsche, P. (1992), *A Nation of Flyers: German Aviation and the Popular Imagination*, Harvard University Press, Harvard.

Gans, H.J. (1988), *Middle American Individualism*, Oxford University Press, New York.

Gardner, H. (1985), *The Mind's New Science*, Basic Books, New York.

Geach, P. and M. Black (1977), *Translations from the Philosophical Writings of Gottlob Frege*, Blackwell, Oxford.

Gentner, D. (1982), 'Are Scientific Analogies Metaphors?', in: D.S. Miall (ed.), *Metaphor: Problems and Perspectives*, Harvester, Brighton.

Gersick, C.J.G. (1991), 'Revolutionary Change Theories: A Multilevel Exploration of the Punctuated Equilibrium Paradigm', *The Academy of Management Review*, 16 (1), January, pp. 10–36.

Gidwitz, B. (1980), *The Politics of International Air Transport*, Lexington, Mass.

Glete, J. (1994), *Nätverk i näringslivet*, SNS Förlag, Stockholm.

Goedhuis, D. (1942), 'Civil Aviation after the War', *American Journal of International Law*, 36, pp. 596–613.

Gourvish, T.R. (1986), *British Railways 1948–73*, Cambridge University Press, Cambridge.

Granovetter, M. (1982), 'The Strength of Weak Ties', in: P. Marsden and N. Lin (eds), *Social Structure and Network Analysis*, Sage, Beverly Hills.

Granovetter, M. (1985), 'Economic Action and Social Structure: The Problem of Embeddedness', *American Journal of Sociology,* 91, pp. 481–510.

Granovetter, M. (1993), 'The Nature of Economic Relationships', in: R. Swedberg (ed.), *Explorations in Economic Sociology*, Russell Sage Foundation, New York.

Gravelle, H. and Rees, R. (1992), *Microeconomics*, London, Longman (2nd edition).

Gregory R.L. (1987), *The Oxford Companion to the Mind*, Oxford University Press, Oxford.

Groenewegen, J., Kerstholt, F. and Nagelkerke, A. (1995), 'On Integrating New and Old Institutionalism: Douglass North Building Bridges', *Journal of Economic Issues*, XXIX, no. 2, June.

Guillén, M. (1994a), *Models of Management: Work, Authority and Organisation in Comparative Perspective*. Chicago, University of Chicago Press.

Guillén, M. (1994b), 'The Age of Eclecticism: Current Organisational Trends and the Evolution of Managerial Models', *Sloan Management Review,* 36 (1), pp. 75–86.

Guindey, G. (1977), *The International Monetary Tangle: Myths and Realities*; Blackwell, Oxford.

Hall, P. (1993), 'Policy Paradigms, Social Learning, and the State: The Case of Economic Policymaking in Britain', *Comparative Politics,* 25 (3), pp. 275–96.

Hall, P. (1994), *Innovation, Economics and Evolution*, New York, Harvester Wheatsheaf.

Hamel, G. and Prahalad, C.K. (1994), *Competing for the Future*, Harvard Business School Press, Boston Mass.

Hattam, V. (1993), *Labor Visions and State Power*, Princeton University Press, Princeton, NJ.

Hayek F. (1937), 'Economics and Knowledge', *Economica*, n.s. IV, n. 13.

Hayek F. (1945), The Use of Knowledge in Society, *American Economic Review*, 35 (4), pp. 519–30.

Hayek F. (1952), *The Sensory Order. An Inquiry into the Foundations of Theoretical Psychology*, London, Routledge & Kegan Paul

Hayek F. (1963), 'Rules, Perception and Intelligibility', *Proceedings of the British Academy*, XLVIII, pp. 321–44.

Hayek F. (1967), 'Résultats de l'action des hommes mais non de leurs dessins', in: *Les fondements philosophiques des systèmes economiques. Textes de Jacques Rueff et essais rédigés en son honneur*, Paris.

Hayek F. (1973), *Law, Legislation and Liberty. A New Statement of the Liberal Principles of Justice and Political Economy, vol. I, Rules and Order*, Routledge & Kegan Paul, London.

Hayek F. (1988), *The Fatal Conceit. The Errors of Socialism*, Routledge, London.

Hayek F. (1994), *Hayek on Hayek. An Autobiographical Dialogue*, Routledge, London.

Heclo, H. (1974), *Modern Social Politics in Britain and Sweden*, Yale University Press, New Haven, Conn.

Heimburger, H. (1931), *Svenska telegrafverket, Vol. 1, Det statliga telefonväsendet 1881–1902,* Gothenburg.

Heiner, R.A. (1983), 'The Origin of Predictable Behaviour', *American Economic Review*, Vol. 73, No. 4, pp. 560–95.

Heyting, E. (1971), *Language Learning and the Use of Language Laboratories*, masters thesis, Michigan State University.

Higham, R. (1960), *Britain's Imperial Air Routes, 1918 to 1939*, London.

Hirschman, A.O. (1977), *The Passions and the Interests*, Princeton, Princeton University Press.

Hirschman, A.O. (1992), 'Against Parsimony: Three Ways of Complicating Some Categories of Economic Discourse', in: *Rival Views of Market Society And Other Recent Essays*, Harvard University Press, Cambridge, Mass.

Hirschleifer, J. (1987), *Economic Behaviour in Adversity*, Chicago.

Hodgson, G.M. (1988), *Economics and Institutions,* Philadelphia, University of Pennsylvania Press.

Hodgson, G.M. (1989), 'Institutional Rigidities and Economic growth', *Cambridge Journal of Economics*, 13.

Hodgson G.M. (1990), 'Optimization and evolution: Winter's critique of Friedman revisited', mimeo, Department of Economics and Government, Newcastle upon Tyne Polytechnic.

Hodgson. G.M. (1996), 'Corporate Culture and the Nature of the Firm', in: J. Groenewegen (ed.), *Transaction Cost Economics and Beyond*, Kluwer Academic Press, Boston, Dordrecht, London.

Hodne, F. (1984), *Stortingssalen som markedsplass. Statens grunnlagsinvesteringer 1840–1914,* Universitetsforlaget, Oslo.

Holland J.H., Holyoak J., Nisbett R.E., Thagard P.R. (1988), *Induction – Processes of Inference, Learning and Discovery*, Cambridge, Mass.: MIT Press.

Horwitz S. (1993), 'Spontaneity and Design. The Evolution of Institutions: the Similarities of Money and Law', *Journal des Economistes et des Etudes Humaines*, pp. 571–87.

Howard, M. (1976), *War in European History*, Oxford University Press, Oxford.

Hughes, Thomas P. (1983), *Networks of power. Electrification in Western Society 1880–1930,* Johns Hopkins University, University Press Baltimore.

Håkansson, H. (1989), *Corporate Technological Behaviour: Cooperation and Networks*, Routledge, London.

Håkansson, H. and Snehota, I. (eds), (1995), *Developing Relationships in Business Networks*, Routledge, London.

Jarlöv, V. (1956), *Kjöbenhamns Telefon i 75 År 1881–1956,* Copenhagen.

Jensen, M. and Meckling, M. (1976), 'Theory of the Firm: Managerial Behavior Agency Costs and Ownership Structure', *Journal of Financial Economics*, No. 3, pp. 305–60.

Jepperson, R. (1991), 'Institutions, Institutional Effects, and Institutionalism', in: W. Powell and P. DiMaggio (eds), *The New Institutionalism in Organisational Analysis*, University of Chicago Press, Chicago.

Joensson, C. (1987), *International Aviation and the Politics of Regime Change*, London.

Johansson, H. (1953), *Telefonaktiebolaget L.M. Ericsson, Del I. 1876–1918,* Stockholm.

John, G. (1984), 'An Empirical Investigation of some Antecedents of Opportunism in a Marketing Channel', *Journal of Marketing Research*, XXI, pp. 278–89.

Katz, M.L. and Shapiro, C. (1985), 'Network externalities, competition, and compatibility', *American Economic Review,* No. 75, pp. 424–40.

Katzenstein, P.J. (1978), *Between Power and Plenty*, Madison, University of Wisconsin Press.

Katzenstein, P.J. (1994), 'Coping with Terrorism: Norms and Internal Security in Germany and Japan', in: J. Goldstein and R. Keohane (eds), *Ideas and Foreign Policy*, Cornell University Press, Ithaca, NY.

Kay, J. (1993), *The Foundations of Corporate Success*, Oxford University Press, Oxford.

Kay, N.M. (1979), *The Innovating Firm: a behavioural theory of corporate R&D*, Macmillan, London.

Krasner, S.D. (1984), 'Approaches to the State: Alternative Conceptions and Historical Dynamics', *Comparative Politics*, Vol. 16, No. 2, January, pp. 223–46.

Kuhn, T.S. (1970), *The Structure of Scientific Revolutions*, Chicago.

Laage–Hellman, J. (1989), *Technological Development in Industrial Networks*, Department of Business Studies, Uppsala University, Uppsala.

Landesmann, M.A. and Pagano U. (1994), 'Institutions and Economic Change', *Structural Change and Economic Dynamics*, 2 (2), pp. 199–203.

Lane, C. (1989), *Management and Labour in Europe*, Edward Elgar, Aldershot.

Lane, C. (1991), 'Industrial Reorganisation in Europe: patterns of convergence and divergence in Germany, France and Britain', *Work Employment and Society*, 5, pp. 515–39.

Lane, D.A. (1993), 'Artificial Worlds and Economics, I & II', *Journal of Evolutionary Economics*, 3, pp. 89–107; 177–97.

Langlois, R.N. (1984), 'Internal Organisation in a Dynamic Context: Some Theoretical Considerations', in: M. Jussawalla and H. Ebenfield (ed.), *Information and Communication Economics*, North-Holland, Amsterdam.

Langlois, R.N. (1989), 'The New Institutional Economics: an Introductory Essay', in: R.N. Langlois (ed.), *Economics as a Process. Essays in the New Institutional Economics*, Cambridge University Press, Cambridge.

Langlois, R.N. and Everett, M.J. (1994), 'What is Evolutionary Economics', in: L. Magnusson (ed.), *Evolutionary and Neo-Schumpeterian Approaches to Economics*, Kluwer Academic Publishers, Boston, Dordrecht, London.

Latsis, S.J. (1976), 'A research programme in economics', in: J.S. Latsis (ed.), *Method and Appraisal in Economics*, Cambridge University Press, Cambridge.

Lazonick, W. (1991), *Business Organisation and the Myth of the Market Economy*, Cambridge University Press, New York.

Lewis, D.W.P. (1993), *The Road to Europe: History, Institutions, and Prospects of European Integration, 1945–1993*, New York.

Levitt, B. and March, J.G. (1988), 'Organisational learning', *Annual Review of Sociology*, 14, pp. 319–40.

Liebowitz, S.J. and Margolis, S.E. (1995), 'Path Dependence, Lock-In, and History', *The Journal of Law, Economics & Organisation*, 11 (1), pp. 205–26.

Lin, A. (1995), *The Social and Cultural Bases of Private Corporate Expansion in Taiwan*, Unpublished Ph.D. dissertation, Department of Sociology, Harvard University, Harvard.

Lindberg, L.N. and Campbell, J.L. (1991), 'The State and the Organisation of Economic Activity', in: J.L. Campbell, J.R. Hollingsworth and L.N. Lindberg (eds), *Governance of the American Economy*, Cambridge University Press, New York.

Lindberg, L.N., Campbell, J.L. and Hollingsworth, J.R. (1991), 'Economic Governance and the Analysis of Structural Change in the American Economy', in: J.L. Campbell, J.R. Hollingsworth and L.N. Lindberg (eds) *Governance of the American Economy*, Cambridge University Press, New York.

Lindenberg, S. (1996), 'Short-term prevalence, social approval and the governance of employment relations', in: J. Groenewegen (ed.), *Transaction Cost Economics and Beyond*, Kluwer Academic Press, Boston, Dordrecht, London.

Lindgren, H. (1988), *Bank, investmentbolag, bankirfirma. Stockholms Enskilda Bank 1924-1945*, EHF, Norstedts, Stockholm.

Lindgren, H. (1994), *Aktivt ägande. Investor under växlande konjunkturer*, EHF, Norstedts, Stockholm.

Linsky, L. (ed.) (1977), *Reference and Modality*, Oxford University Press, Oxford.

Lissitzyn, O.J. (1942), *International Air Transport and National Policy*, Council on Foreign Relations, New York.

Loasby B.J. (1976), *Choice, Complexity and Ignorance. An Inquiry into Economic Theory and the Practice of Decision–Making*, Cambridge University Press, Cambridge

Lundgren, A. (1994), *Technological Innovation and Network Evolution*, Routledge, London.

Lundqvist, L.J. (1980), *The Hare and the Tortoise*, Ann Arbor, University of Michigan.

Lyth, P.J. and Dierikx, M.L.J. (1994), 'From Privilege to Popularity: the Growth of Leisure Air Travel', *Journal of Transport History*, 15 (2), September, pp. 97–116.

MacDonald K.M. and Ritzer, G. (1988), 'The sociology of professions: dead or alive', *Work and Occupations*, 15, pp. 251–72.

Machiavelli, N. *(1972), The Prince, selections from The Discourses and other writings* (selected and edited by J. Plamenatz), Fontana/Collins, Glasgow.

Mackenzie, D. (1991), 'The Bermuda Conference and Anglo-American aviation relations at the end of the Second World War', *Journal of Transport History*, 2 (1), March, pp. 61–73.

Magoun, H.W. (1969), 'Advances in Brain Research with Implications for Learning', in: K.H. Pribram (ed.), *On the Biology of Learning*, Harcourt, Brace & World, New York.

Malmkvist, E. (1956), 'Järnvägsnätets förstatligande', in: *Sveriges Järnvägar hundra år. Minneskrift av Kungliga Järnvägsstyrelsen med anledning av Statens Järnvägars 100-årsjubileum*, Stockholm.

March, J.G. (1988), *Decisions and Organisations*, Basil Blackwell, Oxford.

March, J.G. (1990), *Exploration and Exploitation in Organisational Learning*, Stanford University (mimeo), Stanford.

March, J.G. and Olsen, J.P (1984), 'The New Institutionalism, Organisational Factors in Political Life', *American Political Science Review*, 78, pp. 734–49.

March, J.G. and Olsen, J.P. (1989), *Rediscovering Institutions*, New York, Free Press.

March, J.G. and Olsen, J.P (1993), 'Institutional Perspectives on Governance', Unpublished manuscript, Norwegian Research Center in Organisation and Management, Bergen.

March, J.G. and Simon, H.A. (1958), *Organisations*, Wiley, New York.

Martin, C.J. (1991), *Shifting the Burden*, University of Chicago Press, Chicago.

Martin, C.J. (1994), 'Basic Instincts: Sources of Firm Preference for National Health Reform', Unpublished paper, Department of Political Science, Boston University.

Matthews R.C.O. (1991), 'The economics of professional ethics: should the professions be more like business?', *Economic Journal*, 101, pp. 737–51.

Mattsson, L.-G. and Hultén, S. (eds) (1994), *Företag och marknader i förändring: Dynamik i Nätverk* (Firms and Markets in Transition: Network Dynamics), Nerenius & Santérius Förlag, Stockholm.

Maynard-Smith, J. (1982), *Evolution and the Theory of Games*, Cambridge University Press, Cambridge.

McGuire, P., Granovetter, M. and Schwartz, M. (1993), 'Thomas Edison and the Social Construction of the Early Electricity Industry in America', in: R. Swedberg (ed.), *Explorations in Economic Sociology*, Russell Sage Foundation, New York.

Meyer, J.W. (1994), 'Rationalized Environments', in: R. Scott and J.W. Meyer (eds) *Institutional Environments and Organisations*, Sage, Thousand Oaks, CA.

Meyer, J.W., Boli, J. and Thomas, G.M. (1987), 'Ontology and Rationalization in the Western Cultural Account', in G.M. Thomas, J.W. Meyer, F.O. Ramirez and John Boli (eds) *Institutional Structure: Constituting State, Society and the Individual*, Sage, Beverly Hills, CA.

Miles, R.E. and Snow, C.C. (1978), *Organisation Strategy, Structure and Process*, McGraw-Hill, New York.

Miller, R.and Sawers, P. (1968), *The Technical Development of Modern Aviation*.

Mitchell, B.R. (1992), *European Historical Statistics 1750–1988*, Macmillan.

Mokyr, J. (1991), 'Evolutionary biology, technical change and economic history', *Bulletin of Economic Research*, 43.

Morgan, G. (1986), *Images of Organisation*, Sage, London.

Murray, E.C. (1953), 'The Organisation and Functions of IATA and ICAO', *The Journal of the Institute of Transport*, November.

Naveau, J. (1989), *International air transport in a changing world*, Martinus Nijhoff, London & Dordrecht.

Neisser, U. (ed.) (1987), *Concepts and Conceptual Development*, Cambridge University Press, Cambridge.

Nelson, R. (1994), 'Economic Growth via the Coevolution of Technology and Institutions', in: L. Leydesdorff and P. van den Besselaar (eds), *Evolutionary Economics and Chaos Theory*, Pinter Publishers, London.

Nelson, R.R. (1995), 'Recent evolutionary theorizing about economic change', *Journal of Economic Literature*, XXXIII, pp. 48–90.

Nelson, R.R. and Winter, S.G. (1982), *An Evolutionary Theory of Economic Change*, Harvard University Press, Cambridge, Mass.

Nielsen, K. and Pedersen, O.K. (1991), 'From the Mixed Economy to the Negotiated Economy: The Scandinavian Countries', in: R. Coughlin (ed.), *Morality, Rationality, and Efficiency*, M.E. Sharpe, New York.

Nohria, N. and Eccles, R.G. (eds), (1992), *Networks and Organisations: Structure, Form and Action*, Harvard Business School Press, Boston, Mass.

Noorderhaven, N.G. (1995), 'Opportunism and Trust in Transaction Cost', in: J. Groenewegen (ed.), *Transaction Cost Economics and Beyond*, Kluwer Academic Press, Boston, Dordrecht, London.

Nooteboom, B. (1986), 'Plausibility in Economics', *Economics & Philosophy*, No. 2, pp. 197–224.

Nooteboom, B. (1989), 'Paradox, Identity and Change in Management', *Human Systems Management*, No. 8, pp. 291–300.

Nooteboom, B. (1992), 'Towards a Dynamic Theory of Transactions', *Journal of Evolutionary Economics*, No. 2, pp. 281–99.

Nooteboom, B. (1993a), 'The Conservatism of Programme Continuity: Criticism of Lakatosian Methodology in Economics', *Methodus*, June, pp. 31–46.

Nooteboom, B. (1993b), 'Transactions and Networks: do they Connect?', in: J. Groenewegen (ed.), *Dynamics of the Firm: Strategies of Pricing and Organisation*, Edward Elgar, Aldershot.

Nooteboom, B. (1994), Innovation and Diffusion in Small Firms: Theory and Evidence, *Small Business Economics*, No. 6, pp. 327–47.

Nooteboom, B. (1995), 'Towards a Learning Based Model of Transactions', in: J. Groenewegen (ed.), *Transaction Cost Economics and Beyond*, Kluwer Academic Press, Boston, Dordrecht, London.

North, D.C. (1981), *Structure and Change in Economic History*, Norton, New York.

North, D.C. (1990), *Institutions, Institutional Change and Economic Performance*, Cambridge University Press, Cambridge.

North, D.C. (1991), 'Institutions', *Journal of Economic Perspectives*, vol. 5, n. 1, pp. 97–112.

North, D.C. (1992), 'Institutions and Economic Theory', *The American Economist*, pp. 3–6.

North, D.C. and Thomas, R. (1973), *The Rise of the Western World: A New Economic History*, The University Press, Cambridge.

Offe, C. (1995) 'Designing Institutions for East European Transition', in: J. Hausner, B. Jessop and K. Nielsen (eds), *Strategic Choice and Path-Dependency in Post-Socialism*, Edward Elgar, Brookfield, Vt.

Offe, C. and Wiesenthal, H. (1980), 'Two Logics of Collective Action', *Political Power and Social Theory,* 1, pp. 67–115.

Olson, M. (1982), *The Rise and Decline of Nations: Economic Growth, Stagflation, and Social Rigidities*, New Haven.

Ostrom, E. (1990), *Governing the Commons: The Evolution of Institutions for Collective Action*, Cambridge University Press, New York.

Ostrom, E. (1991), 'Rational Choice Theory and Institutional Analysis: Toward Complementarity', *American Political Science Review,* 85(1), pp. 237–43.

Ouchi, W. (1977), 'The relationship between organisational structure and organisational control', *Administrative Science Quarterly*, 22, pp. 95–113.

Ouchi, W. (1980), 'Markets, bureaucracies and clans', *Administrative Science Quarterly*, 25, pp. 120–42.

Patterson P. and Nawa H. (1993), 'Neuronal Differentiation Factors/Cytokines and Synaptic Plasticity', in: *Cell*, vol. 72/Neuron, 10 (suppl.), January 1993, pp. 123–37.

Pedersen, O.K. (1990). 'Learning Processes and the Game of Negotiation: Wage Formation and Negotiated Economy in Denmark', paper presented at the annual conference of the Society for the Advancement of Socio-economics, Washington D.C.

Péli, G. and Nooteboom, B. (1995), 'Learning to Cooperate: The Simulation of Transaction Costs in Supplier-User Relations', paper for CMOT workshop, Los Angeles, 22–23 April.

Penrose, E.T. (1980), *The Theory of the Growth of the Firm*, Basil Blackwell, 2nd edition, Oxford.

Perrow, C. (1986), *Complex Organisations: a Critical Essay*, McGraw-Hill, London 3rd edition.

Pettigrew, A. and Whipp, R. (1991), *Managing Change for Competitive Success*, Blackwell Publishers, Oxford.

Pfeffer, J. and Salancik, G.R. (1978), *The External Control of Organisations: a Resource Dependence Perspective*, Harper & Row, New York.

Piaget, J. (1970), *Psychologie et Epistémologie*, Denoël, Paris.

Piaget, J. (1974), *Introduction a L'épistémologie Génétique*, Presses Universitaires de France, Paris.

Pierson, P. (1993), 'When Effect Becomes Cause: Policy Feedback and Political Change', *World Politics,* 45, pp. 595–628.

Piore, M.J. (1995), *Beyond Individualism,* Harvard University Press, Cambridge, Mass.

Piore, M.J. and Sabel, C.F. (1984), *The Second Industrial Divide,* Basic Books, New York.

Polanyi, K. (1944), *The Great Transformation*, Beacon Press, Boston.

Polanyi, M. (1962), *Personal Knowledge*, Harper & Row, New York.

Polanyi, M. (1967), *The Tacit Dimension*, Routledge and Kegan Paul, London.

Polanyi, M. (1969), *Knowing and Being*, Routledge, London.

Porter, M.E. (1990), *The Competitive Advantage of Nations*, MacMillan, London.

Powell, W.W. and DiMaggio, P.J. (eds) (1991), *The New Institutionalism in Organisational Analysis*, University of Chicago Press, Chicago.

Prahalad, C.K. and Hamel, G. (1990), 'The Core Competence of the Corporation', *Harvard Business Review*, May–June, pp. 79–91.

Pribram, K.H. (1969), 'The Four R's of Learning', in: K.H. Pribram (ed.), *On the Biology of Learning*, Harcourt, Brace & World, New York.

Putterman, L. (1986), 'The Economic Nature of the Firm: Overview', in: L. Putterman (ed.), *The Economic Nature of the Firm, a Reader*, Cambridge University Press, Cambridge.

Quin-Harkin, A.J. (1954), 'Imperial Airways, 1924–49', *Journal of Transport History*, 1 (4), pp. 197–215.

Rafto, T. (1955), *Telegrafverkets historie 1855–1955,* A.S. John Griegs Boktrykkeri, Bergen.

Richards, A. (1995), 'The Role of Discourse in the Management of Technology: an empirical study using case study analysis', unpublished PhD thesis, University of Sheffield, Sheffield.

Richardson, G.B. (1972), 'The Organisation of Industry', *Economic Journal*, 82, pp. 883–96.

Rizzello S. (1995a), 'Mente, organizzazioni, istituzioni. I microfondamenti del neoistituzioalismo', forthcoming *Economia Politica.*

Rizzello S. (1995b), 'The endogenous asymmetrical information', *Quaderni di ricerca*, Department of Economics, Torino.

Romanelli, E. and Tushman, M.L. (1994), 'Organisational Transformation as Punctuated Equilibrium: An Empirical Test', *The Academy of Management Journal*, 37 (5), October, pp. 1141–66.

Rosenberg, N. (1982), 'Learning by Using', in: N. Rosenberg, *Inside the Black Box: Technology and Economics*, Cambridge University Press, Cambridge, pp. 120–40.

Rosenberg, N. and Birdzell Jr, L.E. (1986), *How the West Grew Rich: The Economic Transformation of the Industrial World,* Basic Books, New York.

Rutherford, M. (1994), *Institutions in Economics. The Old and the New Institutionalism*, Cambridge University Press, Cambridge.

Sabel, C.F. (1993), 'Studied Trust: Building New Forms of Cooperation in a Volatile Economy', in: R. Swedberg (ed.), *Explorations in Economic Sociology*, Russell Sage Foundation, New York.

Sah, R.K. (1991), 'Fallibility in Human Organisations and Political Systems', *Journal of Economic Perspectives*, 5/2, pp. 67–88.

Salisbury, R.H. (1979), 'Why No Corporatism in America?', in: P. Schmitter and G. Lehmbruch (eds), *Trends Toward Corporatist Intermediation*, Sage, Beverly Hills, CA.

Samuels, R.J. (1987), *The Business of the Japanese State*, Cornell University Press, Ithaca, NY.

Schelling T. (1978), *Micromotives and Macrobehaviour*, WW Norton, New York.

Schmanlensee, R. (1992), 'Sunk Costs and Market Structure: A Review Article', *Journal of Industrial Economics*, 40 (2), pp. 125–34.

Schultz, D.P. (1974), *Storia della psicologia moderna*, Giunti Barbera, Firenze.

Schumpeter, J.A. (1934 [1983]), *The Theory of Economic Development*, Transaction Books, New Brunswick, NJ.

Schumpeter, J.A. (1983), *The Theory of Economic Development*, 1934, Transaction Books, New Brunswick.

Scott, W.R. (1994), 'Institutions and Organisations: Toward a Theoretical Synthesis', in: W.R. Scott and J.W. Meyer (eds), *Institutional Environments and Organisations: Structural Complexity and Individualism*, Sage Publications, Thousand Oaks, CA.

Seal, W.B. (1990), 'Deindustrialisation and business organisation: an institutionalist critique of the natural selection analogy', *Cambridge Journal of Economics*, 14, pp. 267–75.

Sealy, K.R. (1966), *The Geography of Air Transport*, London.

Semlinger, K. (1991), 'New Developments in Subcontracting: Mixing Market and Hierarchy', in: A. Amin and M. Dietrich (eds), *Towards a New Europe? Structural Change in the European Economy*, Edward Elgar, Aldershot.

Shackle, G. (1972), *Epistemic and Economics*, Cambridge University Press, Cambridge.

Shovelton, P. (1979), 'Bermuda 2 Et Al.', *Chartered Institute of Transport Journal*, May, pp. 289–93.

Silverberg, G., Dosi, G. and Orsenigo, L. (1988), 'Motivation, diversity and diffusion: a self-organisation model', *Economic Journal*, 98, pp. 1032–54.

Simon, H. (1947), *Administrative Behavior*, MacMillan, New York.

Simon H. (1955), 'A behavioural model of rational choice', *Quarterly Journal of Economics*, 69, pp. 99–118.

Simon, H. (1956), 'Rational Choice and the Structure of the Environment', *Psychological Review*, 63, pp. 129–38.

Simon, H. (1959), 'Theories of decision-making in economics and behavioral science', *American Economic Review*, 49, pp. 253–83.

Simon, H. (1962), 'The Architecture of Complexity', *Proceedings of the American Philosophical Society*, 106, pp. 467–82.

Simon, H. (1969), *The Science of the Artificial*, MIT Press, Cambridge, Mass.

Simon, H. (1972), 'Theories of bounded rationality', in: C.B. McGuire and R. Radner (eds), *Decision and Organisation*, Amsterdam.

Simon, H. (1976), 'From substantive to procedural rationality', in: J.S. Latsis (ed.), *Method and Appraisal in Economics*, Cambridge University Press, Cambridge.

Simon, H. (1978), 'Rationality as a process and as product of thought', *American Economic Review,* 68, pp. 1–16.

Simon H. (1979), 'Rational Decision Making in Business Organisations', *American Economic Review*, 69, pp. 493–512.

Simon H. (1982), *Models of Bounded Rationality: Behavioral Economics and Business Organisation*, vol. II, MIT Press Cambridge, Cambridge, Mass.

Simon, H. (1983), *Reason in Human Affairs*, Basil Blackwell, Oxford.

Smith Ring, P. and Van de Ven, A.H. (1994), 'Developmental Processes of Cooperative Interorganisational Relationships', *Academy of Management Review*, 19.

Smith, H.L. (1991), *Airways Abroad: The Story of American World Air Routes*, Smithsonian Institution, Washington DC (reprint).

Snow, D.E, Rochford, B., Worden, S. and Benford, R. (1986), 'Frame Alignment Processes, Micromobilization, and Movement Participation', *American Sociological Review,* 51, pp. 464–81.

Stannard, H. (1945), 'Civil Aviation: An Historical Survey', *International Affairs*, XXI (4), Oct., pp. 497–512.

Stark, D. (1996). 'Recombinant Property in East European Capitalism', *American Journal of Sociology*, forthcoming.

Statens Offentliga Utredningar, SOU 1923:7 (1923), *Statens ställning till järnvägarna i olika främmande länder*, Redogörelse utarbetad för 1918 års järnvägskommitté av A. Lilienberg, Stockholm.

Statens Offentliga Utredningar, SOU 1938:28 (1938), *Betänkande rörande åtgärder för enhetliggörandet av det svenska järnvägsnätet*, 1936 års järnvägskommitté, Stockholm.

Stiglitz, J.E. (1987), 'Technological Change, Sunk Costs, and Competition', *Brookings Papers*, 18 (3), pp. 883–937.

Storckenfeldt, E. (1893), *Statens telefonverksamhet åren 1881–1892*, Stockholm.

Strang, D. and Meyer, J.W. (1993), 'Institutional Conditions for Diffusion', *Theory and Society*, 22, pp. 487–511.

Streeck, W. (1991), 'Interest Heterogeneity and Organizing Capacity: Two Class Logics of Collective Action?', in: R. Czada and A. Windhoff-Heretier (eds) *Political Choice*, Westview Press, Boulder, CO.

Streeck, W. (1993), 'Beneficial Constraints: On the Economic Limits of Rational Voluntarism', Paper presented at the annual meeting of the Society for the Advancement of Socioeconomics, New York.

Streeck, W. and Schmitter, P.C. (eds), (1985), *Private Interest Government*, Sage, Beverly Hills, CA.

Svennilson, I. (1954), *Growth and Stagnation in the European Economy*, United Nations Economic Commission for Europe, Geneva.

Swedberg, R. and Granovetter, M. (1992), 'Introduction', in: M. Granovetter and R. Swedberg (eds) *The Sociology of Economic Life*, Westview Press, Boulder, CO.

Swidler, A. (1986), 'Culture in Action: Symbols and Strategies', *American Sociological Review*, 51, pp. 273–86.

Terna, P. (1992), 'Artificial Economic Agents', *SPIE*, vol. 1709, pp. 1003–14.

Thelen, K. and Steinmo, S. (1992), 'Historical Institutionalism in Comparative Politics', in: S. Steinmo, K. Thelen and F. Longstreth (eds), *Structuring Politics. Historical Institutionalism in Comparative Analysis*, Cambridge University Press, Cambridge.

Thiel, C. (1965), *Sinn und Bedeutung in der Logik Gottlob Freges*, Anton Hain, Meisenheim am Glan.

Tholstrup, P. (1992), *P & Ts Historie 1850–1927. Vogn og tog – prik og streg,* Copenhagen.

Thornton, R.L. (1970) *International Airlines and Politics: A study in adaptation to change,*, University of Michigan, Ann Arbor.

Tolbert, P.S. and Zucker, L.G (1983), 'Institutional Sources of Change in the Formal Structure of Organisations: The Diffusion of Civil Service Reform, 1880–1935', *Administrative Science Quarterly*, 28, pp. 22–39.

Van de Ven, A.H. and Garud R. (1987), 'A Framework for Understanding the Emergence of New Industries', *Strategic Management Research Center, University of Minnesota,* Discussion paper 66.

Vanberg, V.J. (1994), *Rules and Choice in Economics*, Routledge, London and New York.

Vromen, J.J. (1995), *Economic Evolution: An Enquiry into the Foundations of New Institutional Economics*, Routledge, London and New York.

Waluszewski, A. (1989), *Framväxten av en ny massateknik - En utvecklingshistoria* (The Emergence of a New Mechanical Pulp Technology – A Development Story), Department of Business Studies, Uppsala University, Uppsala.

Weintraub, E.R. (1988), 'The Neo-Walrasian Research Program is Empirically Progressive', in: N. de Marchi (ed.) *The Popperian Legacy in Economics*, Cambridge University Press, Cambridge.

Weir, M. and Skocpol, T. (1985), 'State Structures and the Possibilities for 'Keynesian' Responses to the Great Depression in Sweden, Britain and the United States', in: P. Evans, D. Rueschemeyer and T. Skocpol (eds), *Bringing the State Back In*, Cambridge University Press, New York

Wheatcroft, S. (1964), *Air Transport Policy*, London.

Wheatcroft, S. and Lipman, G. (1986), *Air Transport in a Competitive European market*, EIU.

Whittington, R (1993), *What is Strategy and Does It Matter?,* Routledge, London and New York.

Wiener, N. (1948), *Cybernetics or Control and Communication in the Animal and the Machine*, MIT, Cambridge, Mass.

Wilber, C.K. and Harrison, R.S. (1978), 'The Methodological Basis of Institutional Economics: Pattern Model, Storytelling, and Holism', *Journal of Economic Issues,* 12 (1), March, pp. 61–89.

Williamson, O.E. (1975), *Market and Hierarchies: Analysis and Antitrust Implications*, The Free Press, New York.

Williamson, O.E. (1985), *The Economic Institutions of Capitalism; Firms Markets, Relational Contracting*, The Free Press, New York.

Williamson, O.E (1987a), *Critical Perspectives on Organisation Theories, Economics and Sociology: Promoting a Dialog*, Paper, ISA-RC17 Conference, July.

Williamson, O.E (1987b), 'Transaction cost economics', *Journal of Economic Behavior and Organisation*, 8, pp. 617–25.

Williamson, O.E (1988), 'Economics and sociology: promoting a dialog', in: G. Farkas and P. England (eds) *Industries, Firms and Jobs*, Plenum, New York.

Williamson, O.E. (1989), 'Transaction Cost Economics', in: R. Schmalensee and R.D. Willig, *Handbook of Industrial Organisation*, Amsterdam, North Holland.

Williamson, O.E. (1991), 'Comparative Economic Organisation: The Analysis of Discrete Structural Alternatives', *Administrative Science Quarterly*, 36, pp. 269–96.

Williamson, O.E. (1996), 'Efficiency, Power, Authority and Economic Organisation', in: J. Groenewegen (ed.), *Transaction Cost Economics and Beyond*, Kluwer Academic Press, Boston, Dordrecht, London.

Wilson, G. (1982), 'Why is There No Corporatism in the United States?', in: G. Lehmbruch and P.C. Schmitter (eds), *Patterns of Corporatist Policy Making*, Sage, Beverly Hills, CA,

Winter, S.G. (1964), 'Economic Natural Selection and the Theory of the Firm', *Yale Economic Essay*, 4, pp. 225–72.

Winter, S.G. (1986), 'The research program of the behavioral theory of the firm', in B. Gilad and S. Kaish (eds) *Handbook of Behavioral Economics*, JAI Press, Greenwich, Conn.

Winter, S.G. (1987), 'Knowledge and Competence as Strategic Assets', in D.J. Teece (ed.), *The Competitive Challenge: strategies for industrial innovation and renewal*, Harper & Row, London.

Witt, U. (1992), 'Evolutionary Concepts in Economics', *Eastern Economic Journal*, 18 (4), pp. 405–19.

Witte, J. (1985), *The Politics and Development of the Federal Income Tax*, University of Wisconsin Press, Madison.

Wittgenstein, L. (1958), *The Blue and Brown Books, (lectures 1933–35)*, Blackwell, Oxford.

Wittgenstein, L. (1976), *Philosophical Investigations*, (first ed. 1953), Blackwell, Oxford.

Zuscovitch, E. (1994), 'Sustainable Differentiation: Economic Dynamism and Social Norms', Paper presented at Joseph A. Schumpeter Society Conference, Münster, 19–21 August.

References

Zysman, J. (1993), 'How Institutions Create Historically Rooted Trajectories of Growth', Unpublished paper, Berkeley Roundtable on International Political Economy, University of California, Berkeley.

Index

accidental historical events 50
action 11, 12, 19, 28, 31, 34, 36, 48–54, 62, 64, 65–7, 69, 71–4, 78, 83, 104, 107–111, 151, 160–61, 164, 168, 187, 188, 190–91, 196
actor 10–17, 19, 21, 22–3, 25–6, 28–32, 34, 36–9, 41–2, 55, 82, 87–8, 91–2, 95, 97, 111, 153, 170, 184, 190, 193–5
adaptive learning 5, 7, 44–5, 47, 49, 54
agency 13, 22, 31, 40, 46, 97, 144–54, 198
agent 23, 35, 45, 48, 52, 83, 85, 88–93, 97, 140, 143, 147, 154, 200
Alford, R.A. 10, 13, 18, 22, 28, 206
Allen, P. 17, 18, 197, 200, 203
Arthur, W.B. 32, 49, 50, 51, 52, 53, 80, 82, 93, 95, 103, 117, 155, 198
asset specificity 36, 39
assumptions 13, 17, 18, 28–31, 103, 106, 113
Austrian school 59

backwardness 14
bargaining 12, 41, 86, 91, 177, 180
Bayesian learning 51, 52, 54
behaviour 1, 13, 30, 34, 35, 37, 38, 40-41, 44–5, 47-8, 51, 56, 61, 72, 75, 81, 86-7, 90, 93, 97, 103-04, 106–7, 109, 110, 112, 115, 118, 139, 141, 199, 210, 218
benefits 10, 13, 16, 20, 28, 42, 46, 48, 53, 82, 86, 88, 95, 184
Birnbaum, J.H. 18, 199
black box: black boxes 13, 14
bounded rationality 1, 6, 36, 37, 38, 43, 45, 47, 48, 51, 53, 61, 76, 87, 92, 111, 199, 218
bricolage 22–8, 28, 30, 32
Brunner, H.-P. 21, 200
Bush 36
business associations 19, 31

Campbell, J.L. 10, 11, 18, 20, 23, 25, 30, 31–2, 200, 211
Casson, M. 60, 88, 200, 201

change 10–13, 15, 17, 18, 20–3, 25, 26, 28, 30–33, 36, 39, 41–2, 48, 49, 60, 64, 66, 82, 87, 88, 90–91, 93, 95, 100–105, 113–19, 139–43, 147, 154–8, 164, 167–75, 179, 184, 188, 191, 194, 200, 205, 213–14, 219
choice 10–11, 13, 22, 28, 31-2, 35, 47, 59, 60, 79, 80, 83, 86, 93, 95, 100, 102, 104, 106, 111, 116, 118, 150, 170, 187, 218
Coase, R. 100, 118, 201
cognition 58, 60–61, 75–8
cognitive 7, 43, 46, 62, 66, 68–72, 75–9, 106–8, 111–12
coherence 15, 62, 81, 82, 85, 86, 89, 108, 115, 204
collective 16, 17, 19–20, 29, 30, 34, 36, 110, 191
Commons, J.R. 34, 36, 173, 215
communication 2, 60, 67, 71, 72, 74, 141, 142, 143, 146
community 15, 17, 19, 20, 29, 31
competition 13, 15–16, 21, 26, 37, 39, 50, 55, 75, 77, 104–6, 110, 146–50, 152, 159–65, 173, 175–6, 178, 181, 183–4, 189, 190, 192, 198, 209
complex 12, 19, 30, 36, 38, 68, 72, 75, 84, 85, 91, 92, 103, 108, 110, 111, 140, 177, 196
conflict 17, 36, 63, 75, 92–3, 95, 96, 104, 177, 192
Conlan, T.J. 18, 203
constraint 10–12, 13, 15, 21, 25–6, 29–30, 32, 34 –5, 43, 61, 115, 156, 169, 171, 178, 181
contract 39, 41, 49, 61
cooperation 13, 17, 24, 27, 30, 60, 83, 88–9, 142, 147, 177
co–ordination 66, 67, 72, 74, 82, 86, 88, 89, 94, 96, 110, 165, 192
corporations 17, 18, 23, 206
costs 10, 13, 22, 28, 32, 37– 40, 42, 48, 53, 80, 82, 84, 85, 87, 102, 103, 105, 114, 118, 170, 178, 181, 185

Culture 11, 13–14, 23–4, 42, 72–3, 78–79, 88, 113, 140, 158, 166, 204, 211, 213
Cyert, R.M. 40, 41, 44, 97, 203

David P.A. 26, 32, 49, 50, 58, 79, 80, 100, 155, 203, 212, 218, 219
decision 3, 8, 21, 25, 27, 30, 35, 42–4, 48, 60, 82–5, 87, 93, 94, 140, 144, 148, 150, 151, 156, 158, 164, 166, 167, 168, 171, 175, 179, 194, 218
Denzau, A.T. 39, 54, 55, 203
determinism 40, 55, 101
DiMaggio, P. 10, 11, 204, 206, 209, 216
discourse 19, 139
Dobbin, F. 14, 15, 17, 18, 25, 31, 142, 155, 192, 204
Douglas, M. 22, 23, 24, 170, 175, 179, 180, 205
dynamic 22, 27, 33, 41–3, 49, 53, 58, 78, 81, 87, 90–92, 95, 102–5, 113, 119, 157, 167, 168, 195, 198, 201

economic 10–12, 14–15, 17–22, 24–34, 39, 43, 46, 48, 49, 50, 53–56, 58–60, 77, 79, 80, 83, 85, 100–103, 105, 106, 108, 112, 113, 117–19, 139, 140–42, 151, 153, 157, 158, 172, 181, 185, 187, 189, 190–92, 194, 195, 197, 213
EEC 156, 161, 164
efficiency 14, 15, 24, 27, 33, 36, 37, 41, 42, 50, 73, 74, 78, 88, 113, 115, 178, 182
Eggertsson, T. 34, 55, 205
endogenous 40–42, 101–103, 112, 117–18, 216
equilibrium 1, 4, 49–50, 51, 54, 88, 90, 92, 94
evolution 1, 4, 5, 6, 7, 9–14, 17–18, 20–23, 25–6, 28–9, 30–33, 35, 43–5, 47, 48–53, 55–6, 61, 62, 64, 67, 70, 77–80, 89, 100–02, 104, 110, 117, 119, 153, 157, 169–71, 186, 197, 205, 209, 213
exogenous 10, 13, 59, 82, 868, 92, 101–102, 140
experimentation 12, 30, 45
externalities 1, 80, 83–4, 88, 102, 188, 190, 209

Fligstein, N. 24, 81, 82, 206
frames 11, 14, 15, 16, 19, 20, 27, 31
frequency 36, 177
Friedland, R. 10, 13, 18, 22, 28, 206

Galbraith, J.K. 34, 36

game theory 1, 32
governance 11, 12, 14, 24, 33, 34, 36–9, 41, 42, 46–8, 53, 55, 150, 200, 211
government 15, 20, 37, 141, 144, 157, 170, 171, 173, 184–5, 187, 190, 191, 193, 195
group 13, 16–19, 31, 37, 41, 74, 80–82, 88, 89, 90, 91, 146, 153, 156, 157, 170
growth 18, 21, 23, 140–43, 149, 152–4, 171, 179, 180–81, 208
Gruchy, A. 34
Guillén, M. 14, 25, 31, 32, 207
Hall, P. 18, 22, 28, 56, 203, 207
Hattam, V. 14, 31, 208
Hayek, F. 7, 59, 100, 105, 106, 108, 109, 110, 112, 115, 116, 119, 208
Heclo, H. 22, 208
heterodox 99, 100, 105, 106, 112, 139
hierarchical 66, 77, 100, 139, 181
history 18, 33, 48, 49, 55, 59, 100, 101, 112, 113, 116–17, 139, 155, 157, 166, 197, 206, 213
Hodgson, G. 24, 42, 93, 208–9

ideology 11, 24
idiosyncratic 32, 42, 80, 84, 87, 93, 94, 102, 103, 114–15
industrial districts 77, 78
inefficiency 49, 53
information 10, 37, 43, 47, 55, 59, 60, 70, 72, 75, 77, 78, 83, 84, 92, 97, 103, 107, 108, 111, 112, 117–19, 216
innovation 21–4, 27, 37, 59, 60, 64, 74–5, 77, 78, 94, 100–103, 110, 113–15, 117–19, 179, 199, 207, 214, 221
institution 1, 10–17, 19–41, 43, 55–6, 61–2, 81, 83, 93–4, 96, 100–101, 103–6, 110, 113, 115–19, 139–43, 150–52, 154–9, 166–72, 174–90, 194
interaction 11, 17–20, 26, 28–32, 58–9, 61, 62, 67, 69, 72, 78, 86, 89, 96, 104, 108, 139, 140, 154, 156, 169, 187, 188, 195
interests 8, 11, 13–17, 19, 20, 21, 24–6, 28–9, 30–32, 35, 37, 41, 70, 115, 146–8, 153, 163, 167, 179, 183–6, 188, 194
interorganizational 12, 20
interpretation 11, 13, 15, 17–20, 26, 28, 30, 32, 35, 55, 60, 61, 68, 101, 107–9, 111–13, 118, 151, 153, 167

Jevons, W. S. 59

Keynes, J.M. 99

Index

knowledge 7, 39, 43, 48, 58–61, 63, 68, 70, 75, 78, 80, 83, 87, 97, 100, 104, 105–8, 110–14, 116–19, 152, 154, 195
Krasner, S. 28, 210
Kuhn, T.S. 18, 58, 60, 64, 210

Landesmann, M.A. 210
laws 10, 12, 23, 140, 151, 162
Lazonick, W. 27, 29, 211
learning 22, 32, 38, 40, 44–5, 47, 48–9, 51–6, 58, 60, 62, 67–9, 73–4, 77–8, 79, 82, 84–8, 90, 91, 92, 96, 100, 102, 104, 105, 111, 113, 115, 116, 119, 198, 205, 207, 208, 209, 212, 214–16
learning algorithm 51–2
Liebowitz, S.J. 211
Lindberg, L.N. 11, 12, 20, 30, 31, 200, 211
lobbyists 18
lock–in 33, 48, 50, 51, 53, 55, 80, 81–3, 86–7, 91–7, 140, 198
loop 73

Mara–Drita, I. 24, 206
March, J.G. 10, 22, 27, 31, 40, 41, 44, 53, 56, 59, 69, 86, 97, 100, 106, 173, 194, 203, 211, 212
Margolis, S.E. 211
markets 23, 24, 29, 37, 42, 60, 68, 75, 77, 78, 79, 103, 115, 143, 150, 159–62, 170, 178, 188
Marshall, A. 31, 59, 79
Martin, C.J. 17, 18, 212
maximisation 41
mechanism 10, 11, 13, 19, 21, 26, 33, 43–4, 49, 50, 53–62, 70–71, 82, 87, 93, 100, 105–13, 116–18, 159, 166, 177, 181, 184, 198
Menger, C. 99
mental models 54, 203
Meyer, J.W. 28, 31, 32, 213, 217, 219
M–form 46, 47, 51
Mitchell 34, 36, 141, 152, 213
model 11–14, 54, 59, 69, 70, 86, 99, 103, 109, 111, 115, 118, 177, 183, 217–18
Munkirs 36
Murray, E.C. 18, 199, 213
Myrdal, G. 34, 36, 193

natural selection 44, 217
negative feedback 44, 50
negotiations 12, 19–20, 31, 89, 143, 149, 174, 176, 183, 204

Nelson, R. 21–2, 30, 43, 48–51, 53, 56, 84, 100, 104, 106, 111, 113, 139, 169, 213
neoclassical 1–4, 7–9, 22, 29–30, 35–7, 40–41, 43–5, 47–9, 54, 56, 59, 61, 83, 92, 187
neo–Schumpeterian 27, 29
network 1, 7, 12, 17, 25, 37, 39, 43, 51, 58, 65, 67, 69–71, 75–8, 111, 115, 139, 141–54, 164, 170, 173, 174, 180, 181, 189
new institutional economics 1, 7, 11, 36, 187, 210, 220
nexus of contracts 40
Nielsen, K. 20, 31, 200, 213, 214
nodes 64, 65, 71, 73
North D.C. 10, 11, 13, 28, 30, 32, 39, 54, 55, 61, 97, 100, 103–4, 106, 115–16, 139, 155, 156–7, 169–71, 174–75, 180, 184, 187, 203, 207, 214, 221

Olsen, M. 10, 22, 27, 31, 212
opportunism 36, 38, 76, 88
organization 11–12, 15–16, 21, 24–5, 27, 30–32, 56, 58, 69–73, 78, 102, 105, 113, 115–16, 119, 157–9, 205, 215
orthodoxy 34, 40, 55
Ostrom E. 10, 17, 25, 28, 30, 215

Pagano 210
paradigm 1, 2, 4, 7, 18, 28, 51, 56, 99, 119
Pareto 35, 41, 59, 99
path 2–10, 31–3, 38, 40, 42–43, 48–51, 53–6, 58, 60–1, 65–8, 72, 74–6, 78, 96, 99–106, 108, 112–18, 139–40, 142, 150–53, 155–7, 167, 170–1, 173, 175–6, 186, 188, 189, 194
path dependence 4, 5, 6, 8, 31–3, 38, 40, 42, 43, 48–51, 53–6, 58, 72, 76–8, 96, 99–106, 108, 112–18, 139–140, 142, 150–53, 155–7, 167, 170–1, 186, 188, 189, 194
patterns 11, 17, 19, 28–9, 31, 34, 62, 71, 78, 109, 139, 141–2, 150, 153, 154, 155, 189, 195, 210
Pedersen, N. 18, 20, 25, 31, 32, 200, 213, 215
Pierson 22, 215
Piore, M.J. 13, 17, 18, 20, 22, 28, 29, 215
policies 12, 22, 27, 31, 37, 141, 159, 173, 188, 190, 191, 195–
policy 12, 17–19, 22–3, 27–31, 34, 39, 77, 78, 95, 141–2, 144, 155, 158–61, 163, 166–7, 172–3, 177, 185, 187–8, 190, 191, 195

225

politics 10–12, 15, 17–21, 23–5, 28–9, 30–1, 34, 39, 139–42, 144, 146–53, 156–62, 164–6, 168, 172–3, 175, 179, 180–2, 187–88, 190–95
positive feedback 1, 9, 50, 51
Powell, W. 10, 11, 204, 206, 209, 216
power 12, 15, 30, 33, 36–7, 39, 42, 75, 85, 86, 91, 92, 98, 116, 119, 139–42, 146–7, 151, 156, 165, 176, 180, 186–7, 206, 209
preference, 10, 13, 19, 35, 37, 38, 59, 60, 61, 140, 146, 157
principal–agent 23, 83, 85, 88, 200
private 15, 19, 23, 24, 25, 29, 31, 36, 37, 140–54, 178, 188, 190–95
process 1, 4–9, 11–14, 17–19, 21–8, 30–33, 35, 37, 42–5, 47–50,50, 53–6, 58–9, 68, 70–72, 78–9, 82–3, 86–7, 90–91, 93–6, 100–119, 139–41, 146, 148, 150–54, 156–8, 160, 163, 166–8, 170, 175, 179–81, 183, 187, 189, 190, 192–5, 218
professional dominance 81, 87, 96
property rights 12, 24, 25, 41, 46, 140–41, 145, 153
public 15, 19, 25, 29, 31, 36, 37, 41, 102, 144, 145, 150–51, 187, 188, 190–95, 200
punctuated equilibria 28

QWERTY 58, 79, 80

rationality 10, 11,13, 22, 28, 32, 35–8, 43–8, 51, 53–4, 59, 61, 64, 66, 73, 76, 81, 87, 92, 100, 103–4, 110–11, 118, 192, 199, 218
regimes 12, 181, 188, 195
regulation 6, 9, 10, 140, 141–3, 148, 152, 154, 159, 160–62, 164, 167, 170, 188
regulatory 9, 15, 139, 140, 141, 144, 150, 152–5, 169, 170, 172, 181–2, 185, 187–8, 195
routines 4, 6, 7, 21, 25, 34, 40, 42, 43, 44, 45, 48, 49, 51, 53, 55, 64, 74, 104, 105, 111–17
rules 21, 24–5, 34, 36–7, 39, 44–5, 48–9, 53, 54, 55, 61, 80, 89, 104, 110, 115–16, 141, 144, 151, 156–9, 161, 163–6, 171, 186
Rutherford, M. 11, 21, 31, 32, 36, 56, 187, 216

Sabel, C.F. 15, 16, 20, 23, 29, 215, 217
Salisbury, R.H. 20, 217
Samuels, W. 31, 36, 217
satisficing 43, 45, 51, 52, 100, 106, 118, 199

Schumpeter, J.A. 25, 27, 59, 99, 102, 104, 197, 210, 217, 221
Scott, W.R. 11, 14, 17, 18, 22, 213, 217
Search 48
selection 12, 13, 21, 26, 33, 37, 40–44, 56, 60, 71, 76, 83, 94, 96, 217
Simon, H. 5, 7, 41, 43, 44, 45, 46, 48, 50, 51, 56, 59, 61, 62, 69, 97, 100, 103, 105, 106, 111, 118, 205, 212, 217, 218
skills 16, 42, 84, 104, 111, 113
Skocpol, T. 22, 220
Snow, D.E. 23, 81, 213, 218
social 10, 15, 22–3, 28, 34–5, 39, 42, 61, 67, 69, 70, 83, 98, 101, 103, 105, 110, 113, 119, 140, 141, 157, 170, 193, 194, 195, 198, 211
sociology 6, 10–11, 31, 60, 61, 62, 79, 220
solutions 11, 13, 16, 19, 21–7, 29, 31–2, 45, 86, 92, 152, 155, 188, 191, 193, 195
state 12, 15–17, 19, 20, 23, 24, 25, 27, 29, 30, 31, 68, 103, 105, 112, 139, 140, 141, 142, 144–54, 161–3, 170–73, 178, 180, 183, 185, 187–95, 200, 205, 206–8, 210–11, 213, 217, 220
static 1, 33, 37, 41, 42, 43, 49, 102
Steinmo, S. 11, 28, 31, 188, 205, 219
strategic lock–in 80, 83, 87, 88, 91, 92, 96, 97
strategies 16, 28, 30, 31–2, 38, 40, 42, 81, 82, 85, 88, 89, 90, 91, 92, 95, 198, 221
subsidies 30, 170, 184, 189
substitute 13, 31, 63
sunk costs 48, 84, 85, 114
Swidler, A. 23, 199, 219
symbolic 22, 23, 24, 26, 27, 62, 78
system: systems 14–16, 24, 62, 73, 79, 95, 141, 142, 149, 153, 155, 158, 159, 165, 188, 195

TCE 33, 41, 42, 43, 45, 47, 50, 51, 54, 56
technology 5, 9, 12, 21, 32, 36, 37, 38, 40, 50–1, 56, 58, 60, 70, 72, 75, 77–8, 80–81, 83, 93–6, 100–104, 113, 115, 119, 139–41, 145, 147, 150, 152, 154, 155, 170, 172, 175, 179, 180, 191
Tolbert, P.S. 27, 219
Tool, M. 34, 36
training 16, 60, 84, 94
trajectories 21, 56, 58, 142, 150, 153–4
transaction 2, 22, 36, 37, 38, 39, 40–42, 53, 58, 76, 100, 118, 170
transformation 11–12, 14, 30, 31, 70, 83, 139–40, 150, 154

transportation 14, 15
trial and error 12, 66
trust 16, 17, 23, 38, 83, 85, 179, 184
U–form 46
uncertainty 10, 34, 36, 37, 89, 92, 98, 104,
 151, 169
utility 41, 59, 83, 193

Walras, L. 99
Vanberg, V. 220
Veblen, T. 32, 34, 36

Weir 22, 220
Williamson, O.E. 1, 6, 13, 34, 36, 38–40,
 43, 45–48, 50, 51, 53–5, 61, 76, 84, 106,
 118, 187, 220–21
Wilson 20, 221
Winter, S. 21, 30, 43, 48–51, 53, 56, 84, 97,
 100, 104, 106, 111, 113, 139, 209, 221
Von Mises, L. 59
Vromen, J. 33, 56, 220
Zucker, L. 27, 219